HOW TO BE A BETTER PERSON

Seb Hunter is the author of two previous books, *Hell Bent for Leather: Confessions of a Heavy Metal Addict* (2004) and *Rock Me Amadeus: When Ignorance Meets High Art, Things Can Get Messy* (2006). He is one third of electroacoustic improvisation trio, Crater, in which he plays guitar and electronics. He lives in Winchester with his wife and young son.

Please visit his website: **www.sebhunter.com**.

D1331422

Also by Seb Hunter

HELL BENT FOR LEATHER: CONFESSIONS OF A HEAVY METAL ADDICT

ROCK ME AMADEUS: OR WHEN IGNORANCE MEETS HIGH ART, THINGS CAN GET MESSY

HOW TO BE A
BETTER PERSON

Seb Hunter

Atlantic Books
London

First published in trade paperback in Great Britain in 2009 by Atlantic Books,
an imprint of Grove Atlantic, Ltd.

Some names have been changed.

1 3 5 7 9 10 8 6 4 2

A CIP catalogue record for this book is available from the British Library.

978 1 84354 976 5

Printed and bound in Great Britain by MPG Books Group

Atlantic Books
An imprint of Grove Atlantic Ltd
Ormond House
26–27 Boswell Street
London WC1N 3JZ

www.atlantic-books.co.uk

for Roo

By three methods we may learn wisdom. First, by reflection, which is noblest; second, by imitation, which is easiest; and third, by experience, which is the bitterest.

Confucius

My house, Brentford, west London
Tuesday afternoon, during *Countdown*

The phone rang.

Unlike a lot of people, I like it when the phone rings; it might be something exciting: somebody with some money,* or good news, or a friend inviting me down the pub, or my agent with heady news of lucrative foreign rights sales.†

Usually it's none of those things; usually it's someone in a call centre, often a call centre somewhere on the Indian subcontinent. Their name is Keith, even though their name's not really Keith, it's Tajinder, but the powers that be demand they anglicize their names to make you and me feel more comfortable. I hate these cold calls as much as the next person (every time I hang up I make a promise that I'm going to go ex-directory) but I always try to be polite and hear them out, before explaining firmly that I'm not interested in a free mobile phone or anything else thank you very much, sorry, no really, goodbye now, sorry again, cheerio, goodbye! I make it cheery so as not to make them feel rejected or bad about themselves. Then I feel bad about myself for five to ten seconds before getting on with whatever I was doing before, i.e. waiting for my agent to call with news of lucrative foreign rights sales.

So the phone rang and all this went through my head again. Maybe, at last, it's someone with some money! I snatched at the receiver excitedly.

'Hello?'

---

* This has never happened.

† This has never happened either.

1

'Am I speaking with the homeowner?'

The heart sinks.

'Yeesssss.'

'My name's Sue and I'm calling from the NBCS . . .'

The Nautical . . . Bird . . . . Canoeing . . . Society?

' . . . that's the National Blind Children's Society. And we're looking for volunteers to collect money in their own neighbourhood,
delivering envelopes and then a few days later collecting them
again. Would you mind helping out?'

My mouth opened to say no thanks but then my untrustworthy
subconscious lurched into action: deliver a few envelopes on my
own street? Go and collect them afterwards? *Why the hell not?* In a
moment of sudden madness I heard myself unexpectedly pro-
nounce: 'Yes, why not. I think. Yes, OK. But hang on, erm.'

'Yes?'

'All right then.'

'Great. Just give me your address and I'll pop it all in the post.
Instructions are included. Thanks.' And she hung up.

I was immediately flooded with wave after wave of delicious,
self-righteous serotonin. Somewhat pathetically, I felt an urge to
text some of my friends, informing them what a wonderful and
selfless thing it was that I had just agreed to do. I imagine this was a
similar sensation to having just had one's bank details expertly
stripped by Tigger-esque charity muggers down on the high street:
feeling a little more buoyant in your soul but with a slight yet distinct sense of unease. Did I really want to do that? Have I been had
somehow?

Sadly, this kind of reaction to having done something even
vaguely altruistic is these days the rule rather than the exception.
Most of us lead incredibly selfish lives – straight-ahead, blinkers-on,
me, moi, ich – looking out for number one. Lifelong, short-sighted
self-interest is wholly acceptable here in the early twenty-first century, indeed often positively encouraged by our inescapable
double-barrelled godheads: consumerism and cynicism.

I am a consumer. I am a cynic. But I would like to be less so. I believe that being a 'good person', with all the responsibility and possibly hard work that might entail, is fundamental to leading a full and rewarding life. I'm not religious, so I have no spiritual dogma going down here – it's just a yin and yang thing: cause and effect, effect and cause making a unity of opposites. You get what you give. The love you make is equal to the love you take. As you can see, I have started to regurgitate pop song lyrics, probably in a consumerist and cynical way. And all this pop-cultural meaninglessness clogs up the parts of the brain that presumably used to – back in the olden days – be filled with hale and hearty doses of fraternal philanthropy. We used to be nicer. It's true, our grandparents insist; or at least they would if we ever listened to them. Nowadays we can't because they're in a care home, as this makes *our* lives easier. Is this the world we created?*

We children of the seventies and eighties certainly do less for other people than our parents' generation did and, indeed, still do. Part of this has to do with the fragmentation of the community, a process hurried along by Margaret Thatcher and her infamous line: 'There's no such thing as society – only individuals.' Licence to ill, in other words. More cynical is the less famous yet eviller still Thatcher quote: 'No one would remember the Good Samaritan if he'd only had good intentions; *he had money as well.*'

This state-sponsored selfishness was unprecedented; it branded a deep ideological fissure into the nation's consciousness. The great myopic gold rush had begun; a gold rush barely even mediated by over a decade of Labour government; indeed they positively encouraged it. And it's too late to force this particular genie back into its bottle now – the genie is a hedge fund expert and has assured his dominance by wiping out magic lanterns through relentless speculation on futures trading. Sigh.

My own parents were always active in their community and elsewhere. My mother was a teacher and Red Cross volunteer. My late

---

* This just *happens* to be a song title as well; and unfortunately it's a Queen one. Things can only get better. Oh, God, make it stop!

3

father would get involved in good deeds locally if there was a drink in there for him somewhere (anything pub-sponsored, for example). This giving of themselves to the community at large defined them and others like them, and continues to this day. It conferred a sense of innate Goodness; of wisdom and trustworthiness – proof that there was such a thing as society after all. In being fundamentally unfashionable myself, I feel it's my generational responsibility to attempt to preserve this unfashionable attitude. By taking my foot off the egocentric gas, could I possibly become a bit more (although not too much, thanks) like my parents and less like . . . well, me?

As an archetypical, work-shy writer who does nothing but sit on his arse all day,* I have quite a lot of spare time, probably more than most people. In the chaotic metaphysical and moral fallout I am experiencing post-NBCS phone call, I have come up with an idea of how to spend some of this time: a programme of self-improvement through volunteering. Because volunteer work – i.e. working for zero financial reward – is a far more structured and measurable way of leading a 'better' life than just giving beggars money or helping mothers with pushchairs up flights of stairs. By volunteering, you contribute to an organized infrastructure functioning exclusively in the direction of the Greater Good.

I want what follows to be an honest portrayal of these multitudinous, righteous labourings. I give myself two whole years – two years of part-time volunteer work; two years of getting properly stuck in. Not reportage: rather, earthy immersion, genuine participation and involvement; and cynicism (even pub-sponsorship) begone. Consider this a kind of learn-as-one-goes instruction manual: of fatigue-free compassion; of idealized citizenship; of inevitable humiliation, failure and deluded hubris. A step-by-step, live journal documenting the attempts of a charitable neophyte to better himself and perhaps even those around him too, through enlisted benevolence. I want to prove Margaret Thatcher† wrong. All over again.

---

* Please note, however, the relentless self-loathing, self-disgust and inevitable self-abuse that comes with this fiscally-challenged career choice.
† And Geoffrey Howe.

Brentford, West London

As a structure for this prolonged course in re-sensitization, I plan to utilize that traditional methodology of the vice-afflicted: the Twelve Step Programme; although having just perused the actual steps, I have decided to ignore their specific exhortations, since for example 'Admitted to God, to ourselves, and to another human being the exact nature of our wrongs' (Step 5), and 'Sought through prayer and meditation to improve our conscious contact with God as we understood Him, praying only for knowledge of His Will for us and the power to carry that out' (Step 11) seem to me somewhat long-winded and, to be frank, frightening. And it's fear – this extant paralysis of idleness – that I'm so keen to move beyond.

By the end of this tough, anti-ennui regime, I hope to be in a position where I'll be able to answer these two, crucial questions: can a thirty-something middle-class Englishman become a better person through volunteering? And might a prolonged prescription of selflessness deliver enlightenment even to a foul-mouthed commoner such as myself?*

A week after the phone call, the NBCS envelopes arrived. On the front of each was a pretty, smiling, wonky-eyed albino girl, surrounded by Harry Potter books. 'A Brighter Outlook' promised their slogan. I didn't really understand, so instead I decided to count the envelopes. There were forty-two. Isn't forty-two supposed to be the answer to the meaning of life, the universe and everything? It was a brilliant omen.

Well, I never delivered the envelopes. I couldn't be arsed.

I'm not going to patronize you, OK?

---

* I asked my mother what she reckoned and she replied, 'I doubt it very much.'

Step One

Oxfam, Kensington High Street branch
Monday morning

Number of Oxfam shops in the United Kingdom: 750
Oxfam net funds, April 2006: £73.5 million

The west London borough of Kensington and Chelsea is one of the most affluent urban zones in the world and the wealthiest area, per capita, in the whole of the UK. It also holds the dubious honour of being the safest Conservative parliamentary seat in the country. Kensington High Street is these people's 'strip': the cars are Porsche or Mercedes or, more likely, giant 4x4s manufactured by Porsche or Mercedes. Sunglasses are vast; children, Tarquins, out of control. The large Oxfam store is down at the north-west end of the street, almost opposite Waitrose. I have volunteered over the phone to work one shift a week; maybe even as many as two.

I arrive early, and try to get in through the front door except it's locked. A short and spiky elderly lady frantically waves me away, and I wave my arms around madly in response. Eventually she concedes, unlocks the door and opens it just a fraction. Her eyes are wild and her teeth are bared like a hyena.

'*What do you want?*'

'I am here to work,' I explain through the crack. 'For free!'

'Well, go around the back!'

She closes the door, retreats. I go around to the back and ring the bell impatiently. Soon the back door opens and here she is again.

'You're too early,' she snaps, leading me into the back of the shop where it's dim and yellow and doesn't smell of sweaty old clothes, but of cardboard. She disappears into a side office.

'Hello, my name is Seb,' I call after her. 'I spoke to Sally, the manager, and . . .' The job interview, a few days previously, had gone

OK. I was not a thief or a rapist or a granny rapist.

The elderly lady emerges again, smoothing down mountainous collars, and mutters: 'Gladys.'

I smile and reach to shake hands. Gladys offers an alarmed finger, which I lift up and down, twice. It's icy cold.

'You can hang up your coat over there. Not *there*. *Not* there. What's the matter with you? *There*.'

Gladys is Thora Hird possessed by Alan Sugar. She disappears into the office again, leaving me standing alone out in the back of the shop; everywhere lie clothes, books, boxes of Fairtrade objects, bulging bin-bags. There's a small kitchen area. It's one of those certainties that everyone bonds over a cup of tea, especially those a little older.

'Gladys, can I make you a cup of tea or coffee?'

'*What?* You want a cup of tea?' She emerges from the office and stares at me angrily.

'Yes, but would you like me to make *you* one?'

'I had one before I came.'

Gladys disappears again and I construct my coffee in wall-clock-ticking silence; then Sally arrives, thank God. Gladys scuttles out of the office.

'He's making himself a cup of tea!' cries Gladys. 'Already!'

Sally (managers are salaried and I think that's for the best, otherwise all might be chaos – good-willed, sure, but chaos). She's short-haired, wry and a bit boho. She ties on an apron.

'Look, I even tie on an apron,' she says.

I stand on the empty shop floor, next to some jigsaws. A customer aggressively rattles the locked front door and points hysterically at his Rolex Oyster Perpetual Yacht-Master II. He crouches down and begins to haw angrily through the letterbox.

'Sally, there's a scary man outside. I think he's going to break the door down.'

'We're not open till ten!' she shouts. 'You'll have to wait another five minutes!'

The man's eyes bulge with rage. He rattles the door some more and then storms off down the road. Sally sighs and goes off to get her keys and then we're open. I feel vulnerable.

Sally has decided to put me on the till with Gladys today, so that I can learn the ropes. I'm frightened. Gladys despises me, but I have no idea why this might be. OK, I have quite long hair, but I'm otherwise pretty well presented, and I'm smiling at her as much as I possibly effing can. She stares back through especially narrowed eyes; her eyebrows are painted dark, thin grey in high arches.

Soon I am trying to remove the security tag from our first sale of the day – a ladies' small black cardigan.

'Not like that. Not like *that*.' I'm elbowed aside; and then my attempt to bag the garment is met with an unfriendly gasp; almost a growl.

'Hey, don't worry, that was my first one. I'll pick it up – you'll see!'

'Not like that you won't.'

All I did was put a cardie into a plastic bag. I feel a little upset.

In a little while I am introduced to Judy, a smiling and open-faced septuagenarian employee who runs the shop's book section.

'That woman who does the books despises me,' says Gladys.

'Judy? She seems so nice.'

'Don't be fooled. She refuses to say a single word to me, ever.'

Gladys smiles for the very first time today. It's 11.05 a.m. Gladys's teeth are sharp, but not quite fangs.

As the morning grinds on, Gladys regales me with customer horror stories involving theft, drunkenness, drunken theft and many different sorts of bad behaviour, including several compli-cated ways to get security tags off garments. The relating of these tales turns Gladys visibly apoplectic. But then I get a good one. A few years ago, when Vanessa Feltz lost some weight, she stopped by the store to donate all her old 'fat' clothes. Good for her. According to Gladys, Vanessa's old clothes were then steadily bought up by a continual stream of overweight transvestites.

'I don't know how Ms Feltz would have felt about that. Ha!' cackles Gladys, deliberately ignoring a man waiting to pay for a thin, striped tie. Vanessa had performed this act of magnanimity with a large film crew in tow. Soon afterwards she put the weight back on, and popped in again (this time minus the film crew) to buy all her old stuff back.

'But the transvestites had bought all her clothes!' crowed Gladys. 'Ha-ha-ha-ha-ha!'

In between customers, I attempt to become Gladys's friend. There wasn't much else to do, really.

'So,' I offer, remembering the statistical breakdown Sally had given me over the telephone. 'After women's clothes at number one, and books at number two, what's the third bestselling section in the shop?'

'*What are you talking about?*'

While I ineptly serve another customer (they are forgiving – as you'd expect – all except the middle-aged foreign ladies), Gladys strides out back to fetch a list of each section's turnover this financial year compared to last year's.

'As you can see,' snarls Gladys, 'you don't know what you're talking about. After women's clothes comes bric-à-brac. Books are *third*.'

A man stands and waits patiently to buy several paperbacks, but he is made to wait a little longer while Gladys jabs an accusatory finger at the columns, all of which she had compiled and transcribed, as she does the cashing up and accounts too.

Gladys finally looks up. 'Yes?'

'I'd like to buy these, please.'

Gladys makes an unfriendly grunting sound.

A lady drops off a carrier bag of donated clothes.

'Don't put them there!' cries Gladys. She turns to me. 'People think they can bring all their rubbish in here instead of throwing it away. They just bring it all in and expect us to be thankful.'

I say thank you to the lady who'd dropped off the stuff.

'Don't say thank you like that – you don't know what's in there,' hisses Gladys after she'd gone.

'What should I say?'

'Say, "OK then".'

The morning brings a mad run on crockery, each piece of which must be carefully wrapped in tissue, even if it's only priced at 9p.

Gladys openly resents having to do this, and tells the customers this as she wraps. The customers then plead for her not to bother but Gladys doggedly concludes the wrapping out of malicious principle. I confess that I'm really not very good at wrapping things, or folding things – probably folding women's clothes in particular.

'Nor am I!' howls Gladys.

We had inexplicably bonded over our shared fabric ineptitude. Soon we are suppressing mean giggles over my attempts to fold a lime-green ladies' petticoat.

'It doesn't even matter!' hoots Gladys.

I decide not to ask why it's OK to screw up the folding but heinous to put it into the bag wrong.

I begin to enjoy asking people if they want a bag, in a mildly threatening and morally superior fashion. I've learned this off Gladys.

'Oh, just a small one.'

Gladys and I glare slightly aghast.

'Oh look, goodness, I've got one here already, never mind.'

We slide the petticoat across the countertop, folded in a kind of lopsided hexagon.

People generally behave like they're St Mother Teresa herself when they slip their small change into the charity shaker on the till. Gladys tends to raise a plucked and painted eyebrow at them but I can't see the problem with this myself – except when they just walk away and leave me to lean over and do it for them. I resent having to do that. This is the influence of Gladys. At 11.30 a.m. Sally brings us out coffee and biscuits on a tray.

'I *never* get this,' gasps Gladys, eyeing the tray with mock horror. '*Never.*'

I put down my coffee in the wrong place three times and then feel I've selected the wrong biscuit.

A plump woman comes in and buys a bar of Fairtrade chocolate and as I ring it up, stares pointedly at my T-shirt. My T-shirt says: ANIMALS: It's Their World Too.*

---

* I thought this might be apt in some way or other.

'Don't forget that humans are animals too,' she says.

'I'm sorry?'

'My daughter is at one of those schools that has animal protesters hanging around outside. You know – they shouldn't dig up human bodies! That's unacceptable.'

I pause. 'Aren't we all animals?'

'So why doesn't it say that on your T-shirt?'

She saunters out of the shop and then Gladys squints at my T-shirt and tuts.

'Should I change the CD?' I ask. The world music, which you can buy if you want, has come to an end.

'Whatever you like. I hate it all anyway.'

At 1.15 p.m. Gladys informs me that Maureen, the lady who takes over on the till during the afternoon shift, is even worse than her.

'Oh, my God,' I reply.

Gladys looks delighted; she even serves a customer politely. Soon Sally comes out on to the shop floor and asks whether or not I want to work the afternoon shift as well. I say no thanks, and she says OK, well, thanks then – see you on Thursday. I get my coat and leave. Gladys waves goodbye in slow motion.

'So how is your moral compass?' asks my wife Faye on my return home. 'Was that time well spent? Was it "worthwhile"?'

'I'd really rather not talk about it.'

'I'll bet the team spirit must be brilliant at a place like that.'

'Yes, it is quite something.'

Oxfam, Kensington High Street branch
Thursday afternoon
Average age of Oxfam volunteer: 84
Average age of Oxfam customer: 62

My second shift; afternoon shift.

I don't think Gladys is here; I can't see her on the till; she's not on the shop floor; I can't hear her Lancashire vowels bruising the air in the office either: nobody appears to be cowering or tiptoeing around, or weeping. The customers appear happy too – there's even some banter! – indeed, the atmosphere throughout the whole store is sufficiently sunny and upbeat for me to be certain that Gladys definitely has the day off. Or else she's downstairs in the toilet.

I am off the shop floor today – behind the scenes. I am sitting on a swivel chair out back, pricing CDs (usually £1.99), cassettes (mostly 99p), videos (often £1.99), DVDs (nobody really knows what DVDs are yet: £1.99) and lots and lots of books (99p, £1.99, £2.99 etc.). If they're 'something special', I'll check their worth online using the old wind-up Sinclair ZX Spectrum in Sally's office. I am learning that this is a particularly dangerous job: I already have a growing pile of books and CDs by my side for my own purchase later on. Including bus fares both ways, my net earnings are already in the red, and this hoard of stuff means I'm going to be facing a potential loss of well over £20 by the end of the day (although spiritually I will have gained in the region of £23.50). From a jumbled bag of donations, I lift out a large pink Barbra Streisand box-set.

'Barbra Streisand box-set!' I announce to the rest of the back-room staff (two ladies steaming clothes),* expecting them both to shout, me first! Instead they say nasty things about Barbra Streisand.

'She can't act,' says one.

'And she has a big nose,' says the other.

I take it out to show Vanessa One (we have two Vanessas) on the till.

'Look, Barbra Streisand box-set!'

'Ew,' she says. After some research, I decide to price the Barbra Streisand box-set at a competitive £9.99.

'Only £9.99, everybody,' I announce. 'That'll get snapped up. That's a snip – one went for £11 on eBay only a week ago. I'm completely serious.'

'You're thinking of Cher,' I hear at the steamer.

'Chair?'

'I'm OK standing.'

---

* I'm afraid your worst, aromatic charity shop suspicions are correct – there are *no washing machines out the back*.

The steamer goes *hissssss.*

My pound signs look too much like treble clefs. *Individualistic self-expression can be a vital, self-empowering part of the volunteering experience,* it says on a piece of paper tacked to the wall in the kitchenette.

Oxfam, Kensington High Street branch
Monday morning
Barbra Streisand worldwide record sales: 71 million (approx.)
Estimated dead in 1994 Rwandan genocide: 800,000–1,000,000
Incredibly, the Streisand box-set is still around.

'Do you know what I really hate?' muses Gladys.

Gladys has just had a row with a lady who wanted us to hold on to a few clothing items while she went to get some money, but Gladys wouldn't do so. The lady pleaded with me, too, but I was trying, fiercely, to signal that this decision had nothing whatsoever to do with me and everything to do with Gladys instead. I had meant to get this across without Gladys seeing but I don't think I managed it. I think the woman thought I was rather pathetic for not standing up to Gladys, but little did she know. Because of this episode, I am wary of Gladys's new question. I am worried that the answer might be: 'You being so pathetic and spineless.'

'I don't know. What do you hate?'

'The people who came in here after the tsunami,' says Gladys. 'Floods* of people coming in here and making donations – a lot of really big donations.'

'Were they trying to put banknotes into the shaker?' Gladys hates that.

'No, it's just, where were all these people at Rwanda? But for the tsunami, here they are with their money and all this . . . caring. *What about Rwanda?* I wanted to say.'

Customers quake slightly at the racks.

'I can see that; the genocide, right; but people can only react to

---

* I don't think this pun was intentional.

what they see in the media, and the tsunami was–'

'But Rwanda!'

'Were you here for Rwanda?'

'Of course!'

'Fewer people?'

'Hardly anybody, especially compared to the *tsunami*.' She uses the word tsunami like the *Daily Mail* uses the words asylum seeker.

But I've been brought up short by this sudden flash of context: that we're here for a reason – a very serious reason – which is to raise money, *directly*, for hundreds of thousands of people in all corners of the globe as and when necessary, like a charitable *Thunderbirds* only without the strings. So it's with a renewed sense of urgency that I turn to Gladys and breathlessly announce:'Gladys, we're running out of £1 coins. Shall I go to the office to get some more?'

'I told you to do that twenty minutes ago; you're completely useless.'

I keep myself useful.

'You know what? They think you're a god!' spits Gladys.

'Who thinks I'm a god?'

'*They* do. Young male volunteer? They think you're a god! Look at all this!' She is pointing at the small tray of biscuits that Sally's brought out with our coffee again. We sell a lady two Catherine Cookson novels, and not only that but she wants a bag too. Then Judy walks past and the air around us becomes decidedly chilly.

'*She'd* never bring me out anything. *She* wouldn't even speak to me. She despises me.'

'You told me. That's a shame, isn't it? What a shame.'

'Why? She doesn't speak to me – why is that a shame? I don't care.'

We drink our coffee in silence. Gladys turns back to the biscuits.

'Look at all those. They think you're a god!'

I am embarrassed; she's saying this really loudly.

'Well, I don't know about that. I don't have a sweet tooth, so it's

15

not like I'm really reaping any rewards. Do you think that makes me slightly less godly?'

'No.'

'Do you find this boring?' asks Gladys, during a brief lull.

'Boring?'

'Because I do.'

'No, actually I find this surprisingly fulfilling, despite, um, despite the rudeness of some of the . . . customers. But then, I guess after you've been working here a few years–'

'No, it's not that. I'm just bored. I'm just like that. I'm sorry if this offends you. And I wondered if you were feeling bored because I find this particularly boring, I have to say.'

'I'm not finding it boring yet, no – you keep me on my toes.'

'Well, I'm sorry if I upset you earlier, but–'

'No, no, it's OK. You were right, I shouldn't have left the till unattended, even for a split second.'

'Well, I'm sorry I had to shout at you like that, but anyone can just, you know, come along and, you know . . .'

'Really, it's fine, I won't do it again, ever.'

'Well, if you need assistance, just buzz the buzzer.'

'I was only getting a CD from over there for–'

'*You should never leave the till unattended.*'

Customers stare.

'Anyway, I'm not bored yet, no. Maybe soon, when I can relax, and–'

'There'll be no relaxing come Christmas. It's hell in here at Christmas. *Hell.*'

'I'll bet even you can't find that boring.'

'Oh, I do. I do. I get bored very easily.'

'Well, that's a shame, considering.'

'Why is it a shame? *Why* is it a shame if I find it boring?'

Judy walks past again and it all goes quiet. I get the impression Judy is being cool towards me because she considers me a part of the 'Gladys axis'. I feel frustrated by this, and also trapped.

★ ★ ★

A man comes in and drops off some leaflets.

'OK then,' I say to him, before he scuttles out again.

'No!' cries Gladys. 'Throw them away!'

I read one of the leaflets – four pages, double-sided, neatly typed in columns.

PEOPLE WHO PUT SEAT BELTS ON WHILST DRIVING ARE PROBABLY TRIGGERING RADIATION. THOSE IN THE KNOW NOTICE.

'Oh, it's mad leaflets,' I say.

'Put that in the bin!'

IT COSTS YOU NOTHING TO TAKE SOMETHING SERIOUSLY UNTIL IT MAY BE PROVEN WRONG. ONLY THE GESTAPO AND HIGHER RANKS ARE ORDERED TO DOWN PLAY ANYTHING OF IMPORTANCE THAT MAY BE OF DANGER TO YOU, BECAUSE YOU MAY SEE IT TRYING TO ATTACK.

'Throw it away!'

'In a minute. I'm just having a look and then I'll throw it away.'

'*Throw it away.*'

ANAGRAMS FROM PYRAMIDS: MARS DIP Y, Y DRAM SIP, ADI RM SPY, AID RM SPY, Y SPAM RID, YARDS MIPS, RAY IS D MP, MEN ARE FROM – ? WOMEN ARE FROM – ?

It quickly became boring.

'Are you going to throw it away or not?'

'No, it'll give me something to read on the bus home.'

Gladys smiles a lovely amused, pitying smile and I feel all warm inside. It's like *The Waltons*, or *Moonlighting*.

Our customers are split into seven distinct categories.

Category one: eccentric posh local (all on hearty and jovial speaking terms with the staff) – don't buy anything except the occasional Ian Fleming paperback, or cufflinks. After they have finished rousting around the shop saying eccentric things, they suddenly remember (or are reminded) that they have to pay for the book and the cufflinks. All they have in their pockets are £50 notes and small change, and they always manage *just* to be able to pay with the small change, though it takes five minutes to count it all out. They count it out in a loud and mocking posh voice and it's only afterwards you realize they've stolen the cufflinks.

Category two: mad local (all on reluctant speaking terms with the staff) – demand eye contact all the time. I wish they wouldn't; their eyes are often slightly destroyed. They pick up bric-à-brac and like to ask your opinion on it. They plonk it down on the counter and say: 'What do you think of that, eh?' Rarely do they actually purchase it; instead they stare at the item(s) really closely until finally pronouncing, 'I think no!' and striding out. Everyone breathes a sigh of relief and the staff begin to re-circulate that particular customer's call-sheet of odd behaviour.

Category three: defiant young posh individualists (a lot of pouting/swishing about) – aren't quite as sexy and/or attractive as they like to think they are. Their eyelids brood, duskily, over you while you are bagging their articles, then they toss their scarves over one shoulder and glam-flounce out. Often they'll come back three-quarters of an hour later and go through it all again, especially if they enjoy that whole 'big fish in a small pond' retail thing, or if it's raining.

Category four: the slightly ashamed not-so-posh locals (meek, ingratiating smiling) – like to justify their selections with you. 'These pants are brand new – who'd want to throw these out! Not bad for 49p, mmm?' Or: 'Four nearly new hardback books for under £10? Rude not to!' Or: 'These plates'll do for emergencies – especially as cheap as that!' This category *always* puts its change into the charity shaker – often it doesn't even cross the posh eccentric/mad locals' minds to do this; besides, all their small change went towards the Ian Fleming book.

Category five: the passing poor (eyes down for a full basket) – buy the men's clothes. (As do the occasional mid-thirties/forties upper-class homosexuals clad in tan corduroy, whiffy tweed, a sweeping beige pate and that Rupert Everett mouth thing. Saying goodbye is important to these guys – it involves four or five different and sequential eye movements.

Category six: the canny bric-à-brac/book bargain hunters – are a pain in the arse because they demand to look at all the jewellery under the sliding glass, or finger the more expensive items locked in the wall-mounted glass cabinets. Often these people arrive in pairs, and they crouch and murmur to themselves before a) walking out without saying thank you, or b) making a purchase with a smug smile, that implies *this is worth much more than you've priced it, ha-ha-ha!* We don't care – all we want is your 49p. OK, 19p.

Category seven: the truly mad, local or not, it doesn't matter (to be harried out using a broom). You have to keep an eye on the truly mad. You never know, they'll probably steal things, or even stab you, according to Gladys, and she's probably right. I'd certainly stab her.

CONSPIRACY? I WAS TOLD THERE WAS A TUNNEL BETWEEN NEW YORK AND LONDON SINCE THE 1930S. IT'S IN THE MOVIES AS A 1930S FICTION MOVIE. IF IT'S POSSIBLE TO GO THAT FAR THEN THINK ABOUT THIS. THE TWO PLACES ON THIS PLANET YOU CAN'T SEE THE THINGS IN EARTH'S ORBIT ABOVE THE PLANET ARE THE NORTH AND SOUTH POLES. YOU CAN'T SEE PAST THE HORIZON, THUS MANY THINGS MAY BE IN ORBIT ABOVE THE POLES AND COULD COME AND GO REGULARLY UNNOTICED. IF YOU PUT BOTH OF THE ABOVE TOGETHER YOU HAVE AN UNSEEN RAPID TRANSPORT SYSTEM.

I appreciate this guy's prose is probably more entertaining than mine; you can borrow the whole leaflet if you want to. I'll send it over via unseen rapid transport system. In fact I just have.

'What other charity or volunteer work do you do?' curls Gladys, right before home time.

I look at her wearily. 'You first,' I reply.

'I only work here. I was asking in case you might know of something better I could do, seeing as this is so boring. I'm on the look-out for something else to do, and I wondered if you knew of anything more exciting.'

'Really? Well, I don't do anything else. Maybe I should.'

'You should. A young man like you.'

'Perhaps.'

'Of course you should.'

'What could I do?'

'*Anything.* And then you wouldn't need to work here.'

'Well. Thanks.'

'I didn't mean it like that. You're very . . . *sensitive*, aren't you?'

'You think?'

'Yes, for someone who's led such an *easy* life.'

'Oh look, it's time for me to go home.'

'Already? You see, such an *easy* life.'

'I'll see you next week, Gladys.'

'*And off he goes.*'

Customers swivel.

Oxfam, Kensington High Street branch
Thursday afternoon

Today is the day I realize a number of things. The first I am quite shocked by: it is that we throw away the vast majority of our donated goods. Previously I had morally blanched at Gladys's vicious rejection of the public's endless thirst for unloading personal cast-offs at our front door, but as I've been out in the back of the shop today – seeing first-hand the abject quality of most of the black bin-liners of shit some people drop off – I'm fast swinging behind Gladys's cold, pragmatic 'OK then', as the most positive reply available. Just this afternoon we have been blessed with:

Three dirty old duvets (one damp, all with weird giraffe-like stains)
One mixed selection of small, dirty, broken baskets
One lopsided old suitcase
One broken sewing machine
One pick-'n'-mix carrier bag of odd socks (old person's)
One printer manual dated 1995

One broken tennis racket
Ditto pair of lacrosse rackets
One bin-liner of about fifteen crumpled and damp old man's
shirts (blotchy and noxious)
One 1950s typewriter (severely not working)
Etc.

A pattern is emerging. These items are faulty, broken, have outlived
their usefulness; they no longer continue to function as originally
conceived. In the eyes of those donating, it must feel like a shame
to throw these things out when they're *almost* fit to have actually
been used merely one or two decades ago. Oxfam could use this
though, I'm sure! Thus everything soiled, holed, botched, knack-
ered, falling apart, limp, passé, kaput and downright useless gets
chucked into the car boot and self-righteously thrown through our
open back door (we need the air).

'I'm not entirely sure we can really use this old, wet, threadbare
and clearly rotting duvet. I'm terribly sorry.'

They are consistently taken aback; horrified even: 'Oh! Well, I
wish I hadn't bothered if this is all the thanks I'm going to get!'

When you buy items at Oxfam shops, you see, you *see*, the whole
point is that they are not broken or mouldy or with parts missing.
All the good stuff (and there is a lot of good stuff amid this crap)
gets siphoned off, brushed down and priced up accordingly, and
then it hits the shop floor glowing – indeed it's goddamn luminescent. You want broken baskets? Go to a jumble sale, or a car boot
sale, or Help the Aged.*

Oxfam, Kensington High Street branch
Monday afternoon
Psychotic episodes in UK stores, 2005/6: 24
Murders in UK stores, 2005/6: 3

The queens of the shop floor, Gladys and Maureen (the elderly
lady Gladys claims is worse than her, though I find this increasingly

---

* Just a small rival charity shop diss there, readers.

difficult to believe, the more I see of both of these women), don't like me stepping on their toes (literally) out on the till. I'm trespassing on their manor and I'm too bloody cheery to the *volk*; a more cold-hearted pragmatic, 'OK then' approach is required out there at the harsh retail coalface. I'm too customer-friendly; my godly presence needs to be kept out of sight, out back where I can utilize my bulging muscular frame by lugging deliveries around. I'm not going to take this personally, if *all I'm good for* is unpacking the Christmas scented candles and pricing them and moving them around on a shelf. Hey, I'm just glad to be of use.*

Actually I'm beginning to see more clearly the fierce truth of our whole economic cycle – its beautiful purity; the following equation:

DONATION ➤ FILTER ➤ PRICE ➤ SHOP
FLOOR ➤ SALE ➤ MONEY GOES DIRECTLY TO
NEEDY HOTSPOTS.

We volunteers are merely sections in the pipe that makes this happen in the most streamlined and effective way possible. We help move things along; oil the wheels. Our shop takes up to £5,000 every day, the majority of which comes from selling things members of the public have given us for free. The whole concept is superb! My conscience is definitely beginning to feel a few fresh, green and delicious twinges of *clearance torque*. Somewhere in my soul, a tiny muscle flexes.

In the meantime I ask the ladies out back what are the worst things they've ever lifted out from donated bin-bags.

'My worst thing was probably a bag of poo,' says Vanessa Two.

'A bag of poo?'

'A carrier bag, yes, with poo in it.'

'Dog poo or human poo or what?'

Vanessa Two looks at me. 'You think I opened the bag?'

---

* And not on the till with Gladys.

'I'd rather not talk about my worst one,' says Vanessa One. 'It's too embarrassing to say.'

'I've also had trousers full of poo, sheets with poo on,' continues Vanessa Two. 'Pants full of poo, dirty socks – in fact, look, here's a bag of dirty socks right now – a used surgical truss, trousers and pants with urine and bloodstains and a dress covered in semen stains.'

'Is this Vanessa Feltz again?'

'Yes, exactly.'*

'You name it, we've seen it.'

'Dead animals.'

'Are you sure?'

'A rat, dead in a box.'

'Better than alive in a box.'

'Well, I don't know.'

We ponder what kind of rat would be the best.

Eighty-five per cent of all donations are thrown away. Oxfam spends £1 million every year disposing of it all; charity shops in the UK spend about £4 million in total getting rid of unwanted donations. In our shop, bin men come round every afternoon, and there's always so much stuff for them to lug out that we have to tip them with Fairtrade sweeties. Sometimes they'll have a wee rifle through and pick out a dusty old paperback.

'It's Jeffrey Archer!'

(I had thrown that one away accidentally on purpose.) Or they'll root out a Spanish/Greek dictionary from 1972.

'Can I really 'ave this?'

'Yes, please take it.'

So we're all happy. Except Gladys. As I'm merrily pricing up a selection of ethically sourced plastic toy safari animals – baby hippos, zebras etc. – Gladys steams out from the office where she's been cashing up and begins to tear a strip off me for not pressing the credit card machine button twice to get a copy of the receipt slip.

---

* This might be a small white lie, I can't remember

'Gladys, could I just stop you for a second here, please? You see, I have never actually done this thing you are so angrily accusing me of.'

'I'm not saying you have, but using you as an example of some-body who might have done it. Why do you do it? *Why* do you not press this button like you're supposed to?'

Gladys in vicious mode is not nice, not even funny. She reminds me of Davros except slightly more merciless.

'I don't know. As I have always pressed it.'

'But as an example of those people who don't, I'm wondering, *why* do you do it?'

'I don't know why *they* don't, Gladys.'

'I just can't see why anyone would keep doing this. I've showed you, you remember, quite clearly, how to do it, but you're not press-ing it and I'm just for the love of *God* asking you why.'

Maybe Gladys is mad, I don't know. What I do know, however, is that she is seriously pissing me off. I try to catch some of the other ladies' eyes, to get some sympathy, but they're all blindly loyal (or just blind) to Gladys and her rages. Eventually she retreats back into the office and silence descends upon our workspace once more. I am upset again. Even with just thirty seconds' exposure, Gladys has ruined my afternoon. A glistening BMW pulls up outside the back door and an Arabian gentleman calls through his wound-down window that he has some gifts for us. I go to the door; he pings his boot open.

'There,' he says through the window.

I look at him. He looks at me. I look into his boot. There are some bin-bags.

'Shall I get all these out of your boot then?' I ask, with as much withering sarcasm as I can muster, which isn't much, because I'm crap like that unfortunately.

'Yes, please, right away.'

'All right then. *I will.*'

He sits there watching me unload his three black bin-liners and then drives off. Vanessas One and Two then throw everything in his three black bin-liners away. This is all so noble, don't you think?

Step One

The Thursday Club, Botley, Hampshire
Thursday
Botley telephone code: 01489
Botley motto: 'Keep Your Verges Well-Trimmed'

When I informed my mother that I was working part-time at Oxfam in a belated effort to try to improve myself, she was pleased. But not that pleased.

'You should go and help Bob and Rosemary with their old ladies down in Botley at their Thursday Club.'

Bob and Rosemary are old family friends, although the thought of contacting them outside the usual context of Christmas alarmed me.

'What do they do with them?'

'They bus them to the town hall and then supply them with tea and biscuits and entertainment. Indeed, I have entertained them myself, with poetry and singing. Twice.'

'I could help out with that whole thing, sure. When do they do all this?'

'The Thursday Club? It tends to be on Thursdays. And yes, you should. You could help with the bus, but you could entertain them too – you could play the guitar and sing, for example.'

Everybody has all these *suggestions*. But anyway, I did call Bob and Rosemary; it sounded like it might be fun, plus it ought to provide me with some direct action, real-people, coalface feel-good experience. Also it would make a pleasant change to hang out with some nice old people for once. Rosemary said sure, it would be a pleasure to have me down helping for the day, and that she looked forward to seeing me next Thursday lunchtime. My mother subsequently informed me that Rosemary had told her she'd been 'alarmed' by my telephone call. Which is fair enough if you've ever heard me play the guitar. Not that I was planning to go anywhere near a guitar. Anyway, where the hell are we?

Bob and Rosemary live in a winningly higgledy-piggledy house in the village of Boorley Green, a mile or two outside the small town of Botley, which is a mile or two outside the city of

Southampton in Hampshire. All their old cars sit forlornly in their higgledy-piggledy garden alongside a forlorn boat sitting underneath a tarpaulin.

'Does the boat work?' I ask Bob, who is dry as a bone.

'Ah.'

'Does the boat *float*?'

My spontaneous witticism is not acknowledged; instead Bob goes inside.

While they prepare themselves for today's jaunt, I sit on their higgledy-piggledy sofa and listen to Rosemary telling me why volunteering in the Botley region is approaching crisis point.

'The elderly and retired, who used to be the staple of volunteer work, nowadays choose to jet off and spend their retirements enjoying themselves around the world. It's understandable, of course, that they want to enjoy themselves, but this has depleted our ranks quite considerably.'

'Young people aren't interested?'

'Young people have never been interested, but then any who might be are discouraged by the precautionary red tape that the government requires in order to volunteer nowadays. It used to be OK just to turn up and get on with it, but now you've got to check everybody out on the police register and fill in lots of stupid forms. All the paperwork – the formality* – puts people off coming forward. And we need these people in order to be able to carry on.'

Soon Rosemary heads off to Botley town hall in her car while Bob and I clamber into the cab of the yellow community minibus. There are fifteen-odd seats in the back. Bob drives around to our first elderly pick-up in first gear – if we come to a main road then he might risk second gear, but for the most part it's first only – so we lurch and leapfrog through cool, grey, autumnal Botley cul-de-sacs, halting in front of the occasional net-curtained bungalow whose nets twitch briefly before a cheery pensioner emerges, ven-

---

* i.e.: Are you or have you ever been a granny-rapist?

26

turing towards the minibus wrapped in winter coat and scarf. I offer my arm and help them up and inside.

'A young man!'

'Hello, I'm Seb and I'm helping out today.'

'Always nice to see a lovely* young† man!'

Then there's whispering in the back which I can't make out.

As we collect more ladies (the Thursday Club is exclusively for the benefit of the fairer sex), the atmosphere in the bus steadily improves until by our twelfth or so collection, it's positively rowdy back there. It's Olive's birthday today, but Bob's valiant attempt to lead a chorus of 'Happy Birthday' at the next stop splutters out after just a few lines. Bob tells me they're saving their energy for later, but personally I think they were a little embarrassed being forced into a cheesy ad hoc celebration like that; these ladies remind me of cats: they instinctively do the opposite of what you want or tell them to do out of some sort of subliminal rebellious principle. They're certainly not decrepit or senile – these honeys are hot to trot and cool as you like. Every time I make eye contact with *any* of them, they wink. A proper, saucy wink. I don't know whether this is instinctive or complicit.

Half an hour later we arrive at Botley town hall and disembark. The ladies know the drill; they file into the hall and sit themselves in plastic chairs at tables arranged in a horseshoe facing today's entertainment: retired Botley couple Ted and Jenny talking about their canal boat holidays. Rosemary introduces Ted and Jenny and the ladies applaud and the presentation begins; Ted wobbles the tip of a pointer across a mounted British Waterways map while Jenny passes around photographs. Everybody murmurs approvingly. I remain out of sight in the kitchen and help Bob fill a pair of giant industrial kettles for making tea while keeping one eye on the canal boat presentation through the serving hatch. Occasionally one of the ladies leans over and winks at me. Should I wink back or what?

* Adjectives.
† Verbatim.

It's only when I bring out the tea that my altruistic performance here today collapses like the pathetic house of cards I suspected it might have been all along. The ladies are all incredibly pernickety about the way they have their tea – and twenty pernickety pensioners simultaneously informing me why that cup's *not quite right* soon gets too much for me and I lose my grip on the proceedings and retire back to the kitchen with my tail (and tea-dripping tray) between my legs.

'Problems?' asks Bob.

'Problems.'

'I suspected there might be.'

By the time we sort out the tea, most of it's either lukewarm or pooled in saucers and I can sense the ladies' enjoyment of my presence has dipped considerably – the winking's all but stopped; all is silence when I approach a table bearing conciliatory biscuits. With old ladies, if you can't even get the tea right, don't bother showing up, man.

The canal boat presentation winds up. Outside it's dark as everybody files back on to the bus. Then Bob loudly announces: 'By the way, ladies, I hope Seb has told you that you'll all be featuring in his new book.'

There is a shocked silence. We all sit there for a few moments. Then I realize that the shocked silence might actually have something to do with deafness. Plus maybe the merest soupçon of complete and utter indifference.

Oxfam, Kensington High Street branch
Monday morning
Daily Mail circulation, 2005: 2.5 million (approx.)
Column inches of apoplectic editorial bile, *Daily Mail*, 2005:
28.4 million

'Before we get going this morning,' says Sally, 'you ought just to have a look at this nasty article from Thursday's *Daily Mail*. Unfortunately, a lot of our customers have been mentioning it.'

The article's pinned to the noticeboard in the kitchenette. The gist is Oxfam Exposed! – a whole page. In it, star reporter Simon wanted to get rid of some old clothes, so he sold all the nice ones on eBay for a handsome profit. Ha-ha – good old Simon. He bagged up his lesser items and brought them along to his local branch of Oxfam in, erm, Kensington, where he goes on to claim that instead of being received with humble thanks and gratitude, his kindly deposit was, erm, glowered at and accepted rather begrudgingly. Uh-oh. I look around – Gladys is nowhere to be seen.

'Where's Gladys?'

Sally pauses. 'Gladys isn't here. She's got the day off. It'll just be you on your own today.'

I suspect Gladys is in hiding – in a safe house somewhere. Intrepid Simon also accuses Oxfam of charging too much for its clothes; and he's right, in that our clothes are more expensive than some other charity shops', but then Oxfam has chosen to position itself as the Waitrose of the marketplace – you can buy our clothes without fear of faecal matter in the crotch zone.* Usually. And it's not like anyone's profiting from this minor mark-up – except perhaps for those in the developing world.

Out on the shop floor, in an attempt to ward off any potential *Daily Mail* readers' ire, I put a Mamas and Papas CD over the Tannoy system. Surely not even these rich bitches would stoop so low as to come and have a pop at an Oxfam volunteer while 'California Dreaming' beams through the air like a fuzzy rainbow of friendly niceness.

'Your clothes *are* rather expensive, aren't they?'

We've been open only forty-five minutes when this happens for the first time. Then it happens again at 11, 11.25, midday and once more at 1.15. Really, it's like when sharks sniff out a drop of blood in the middle of the ocean. I opt for a neutral but moderately combative: 'Oh, are they?' with hand placed provocatively on hip.

'Yes, they are a little, don't you think?' (They are purchasing a pack of charity Christmas cards, and they have only a £50 note. It's

---

* Unless you ask nicely.

either that or the platinum Amex.)

'You don't have to buy them,' I reply testily. 'You *could* go to Harvey Nicks.'

'Oxfam is not here to provide bargains for the population of Kensington and Chelsea,' inserts Sally firmly, every time.

The customer then pouts slightly, before wafting haughtily back out on to the street. I do hope they all enjoyed coming in and making their points like this, and I hope they felt better about themselves afterwards. We all feel great.

The Thursday Club, Botley, Hampshire
Thursday
William Cobbett on Botley:
'It is the most beautiful village in the world!'
Cobbett's place of residence at the time of quote above:
High Street, Botley

It's a freezing cold, bright, sunny winter's day and I am having the time of my life. My heart is suffused with joy and wellbeing and a wild, carefree delirium. There's no punchline here: Tracey (the usual minibus driver – she was off last week, she wasn't in the mood) and I are scooting through the 'burbs, picking up the ladies one by one. We stop at the top of their cul-de-sac and out they pop, wrapped up warm in winter coat and scarf and gloves, beaming, delighted, shuffling across the icy paving stones towards the bus where I'm standing in my own coat and scarf by the door, step in place, greeting them with a big smile and an arm to lean on. They're greeted by the rest of the girls; make themselves comfy; I slide the door shut behind them, hop back into the cab and on we trundle. I am at peace. I am *joyous*. The pure, positive simplicity of all this is somewhat revelatory to me; in no way had I expected bussing pensioners to a small town hall to be quite so much fun. Yet it is. It's *immense* fun. Indeed I am finding it blissful. I get so carried away that Tracey drives straight past the next pick-up stop as I am distracting her talking about, erm, actually I am lecturing her on the brilliance of the band Black Sabbath.

'You've forgotten Betty!' come cries from behind us.

Then we begin to discuss Supertramp, who unfortunately Tracey thinks are brilliant.

'And now you've forgotten Mim!'

Tracey has to perform some tricksy reversing manoeuvres.

There's no outside entertainment today, so we're playing a game instead. The game is 'Guess Who It Is?'. Everyone's brought along a photograph of themselves as a toddler – or child, or at least a little younger – and all the photos get mixed up on tables and we all have to guess who's who. No offence to Ted and Jenny, but this is much more exciting than the canal boats. It gets pretty competitive; elbows fly about as we mingle at the tables, bluffing, double bluffing and simply forgetting which one is me. That one. Or could be that one. Fortunately we've all written our names on the back in pencil. Or we were supposed to. My own photograph is less sepia than the others, although this doesn't stop everyone from getting me just as wrong as everybody else. Before anybody topples over, we break for timely refreshments. Today is going so brilliantly that even the tea-distributing goes well: I'm firm; resolute; bold.

'Strong ones. Weaker ones. Biscuits!'

They drink it without a peep. I collect the cups; even wash up. My good fortune continues into the raffle, where I win an economy tin of meatballs.

'Well done,' mutters Gladys (a different Gladys) bitterly. My luck runs out, however, when the team I've been put on comes last in the 'Guess Who It Is?' quiz. My team-mates instantly heap all the blame on to me. It's not my fault if they're blind and bloody stupid, is it? Jesus.

It's 4.30 p.m., and outside it's dark; everybody files back on to the bus, then Bob loudly announces: 'By the way, ladies, I hope you've remembered that you'll all be featuring prominently in Seb's new book.'

There is a shocked silence. We all sit there for a few moments. I do wish Bob wouldn't do this; especially use the word 'prominently'. Then I remember that the shocked silence is in fact the merest soupçon of complete indifference all over again.

'Just don't forget Betty and Mim this time,' comes a call from the back.

As we sow our elderly seed around and about Botley, it strikes me that this is an awfully long way to travel just to bus some old folk around. I'm not sure the energy I have been expending is matched by the good I am actually doing here; I fear my carbon footprint is longer than the charitable one I seek to deploy. It's with a heavy heart, then, that I inform Bob that although this has been informative and super fun, I feel today ought to be my last day with the Thursday Club.

'But they want you to come and entertain them,' Bob says. 'To be the entertainment next time instead of just doing the tea.* Don't you, ladies?'

'Yeeeesssss,' they hiss, altogether now.

'Entertain them?'

'Entertain them. I've told them all about your prowess on the guitar and they're terribly excited.'

'My what?'

But, goddamn, I was flattered.

'Well, I suppose I might be able to rustle up something.'

'Just a little something.'

'Something,' the ladies rustle.

'I could play guitar and I have a friend named Owen who could come and play the piano and we could both sing, I suppose.'

Luckily it's dark so they can't see how hard I'm blushing.

'Some jolly old songs.'

'Classics,' the ladies hiss.

'Do you want this for your Christmas party?'

'No, we have an accordionist for the Christmas party already.'

'Oh. I see. So, when . . .'

'In the New Year.'

---

* 'Just' doing the tea! I ask you!

'A knees-up,' hiss the ladies.

'Right.'

'I think you'd better get practising.'

'Don't underestimate us,' I snap. And then apologize. Actually I didn't say that at all, I just sat there quietly and waited for the hissing to stop. But I was thinking it.

Oxfam, Kensington High Street branch
Monday morning

Tonnes of 'white goods' dumped in the UK annually: 350,000
Percentage of the above profitably recycled: 75%

I am in Sally's office, attempting to price a large pile of antiquarian books while simultaneously eyeing Gladys over the CCTV system. The camera in question looks down over the whole till area, so I am able to study her sales technique in detail, and I am coming to the conclusion that her method is a workmanlike take on 'violent despising of all humanity'. Watching her onscreen reminds me of that eerie Japanese horror film *Ring*; I am scared that any minute now Gladys will begin to ooze out of the flickering television screen in front of me and slither across Sally's desk, where she will proceed to nag me viciously to death aided by her giant, steel-grey Ming the Merciless collars. Gladys didn't say hello to me this morning. Instead she went straight up to Sally, still with her coat on, and said, bold as brass, 'Seb's not going to be on the till with me today, I hope.'

'Ah, no, he's going to be working on—'

'Thank God for that.'

Then she took off her coat.

I mean, how would *you* feel after somebody's said something like that right in front of you? It would put you right off your Fairtrade biscuit.

As I dilly-dally and dither over pricing these stupid, mould-covered old hardbacks, the phone rings. I answer. It's an Irishman. He wants to know if we'll take his cooker.

'No electrical goods, sorry.'

'It's a good one. Hotpoint.'

'Really no electrical goods at all, I'm sorry.'

'So what am I meant to be doing with this cooker now then?'

'You could try your local municipal waste disposal centre. Or, I don't know. Can't you sell it?'

'Ah, bejesus. What about all these old clothes and that? Bric-à-brac and whatever.'

'Yes, we'll happily take that.'

'Great, so what time will you be wanting to come round and pick it all up?'

'No, you don't understand. You'll have to bring it in; we can't come and collect anything. We're just a shop. Just a little shop . . . of elderly volunteers.'

There was a pause. 'Well, how about I send it round in a taxi?'

'Would you want us to pay for the taxi?'

'Right.'

'Well, no, you'd have to pay for that yourself – we're not some sort of charity, you know. Hold on – we *are* a charity, but we don't operate, erm, we don't come and pick up stuff. We don't have a car.'

'Ah, feck.'

The conversation continued like this for some time, with the canny Irishman working through all the options that involved us picking up his stuff.

'Someone's died, you see.'

'I'm sorry to hear that, but we really are just a charity shop and we really don't have any means of collecting these . . . items, valid though I'm sure they are.'

'Can't someone just drive around? It's not very far.'

I begin to consider hanging up, but I fear that if I do I might get into trouble. He might be another undercover *Daily Mail* reporter.

'I told you, Oxfam doesn't have a car.'

'You don't have a car?'

'Well, I've got a car myself, yes, but I can't come round and collect your things.'

'Why not?'

'I come in on the bus.'

'What!'

'That's just the way it is. Look, I'm sorry, but I'm not prepared to argue with you any more about this.'

'Holy sweet Mary, Mother of God.'

He hangs up, thank (Mary, Mother of) God.

On the CCTV Gladys gets stuck into a loitering homeless man. I watch them point at one another. Then he disappears from the screen. Then Gladys disappears from the screen. Then Gladys reappears in the office doorway right in front of me. I stifle an urge to scream.

'Looks like a *nice job*,' she spits.

I am unable to reply, so speechless am I. An attempt at a shrug comes out more like a shiver.

'It's all right for some,' she snarls. 'Sitting out here like that, on a chair. I'm afraid you're in my way, I need pound coins.'

I try to scramble sideways but knock over the pile of books, and Gladys tuts like you've never heard *anyone* tut before – a tut coming from the deepest bowels of a joyless and hate-fuelled life. She gets her bag of pound coins and soon reappears back on the CCTV screen and a sudden flash of panic grips my heart: *what if I'm put next to Gladys for the Christmas party?*

Later that morning I muster up the courage to ask Sally whether or not we actually have a Christmas party.

'We have a small bash, yes. We go out and twist the local supermarkets' arms to supply us with free food and booze and just have a little drink-up in the shop after closing. It's mostly for the sake of the oldies.'

I freeze.

'Is everything all right?'

But I'm still frozen.

'Are you worried about Gladys?'

I nod meekly.

'To be fair, Gladys has always been the life and soul. Last year she even dressed up as Father Christmas and handed out presents to everyone.'

'You're kidding me.'

I try to imagine what a present from Gladys would be like. It would probably have concealed razor blades, and a timer.

'I am. Don't worry, she won't come. She never comes. She refuses to.'

Wahey Xmas – bring it all on!

Step Two

My house, Brentford, west London
Teatime

Number of regular bingo players in licensed UK clubs: 3 million
Average length of a British game of bingo: 4.5 minutes

Though by now I was feeling pretty damn righteous working a few days a week at Oxfam, a nagging voice in my head – also a louder one from my wife – kept on that I still wasn't really doing enough to properly better myself; I wasn't sure whether intensely disliking one specific elderly lady was really cutting the benevolent mustard. Online one afternoon, half-heartedly mooching about for perhaps more fundamentally rewarding volunteering opportunities, I stumbled upon an advertisement for a position as a bingo caller in a day centre for the elderly in Hanwell, west London, just down the road. The idea thrilled me, and I fired off an application for the position via email straight away. Even though the only bingo lingo I knew off the top of my head was legs 11 and two fat ladies 88, I considered this to be a perfect thing for me to volunteer to do: fun, asinine, a piece of piss and no Gladys (or at least another newer, nicer Gladys). I was so inspired that I began researching some further bingo lingo so that I'd be up to speed for the job interview. I could buy the bow tie at a later date.

Eyes down for a full house.

> Cup of tea 3
> Garden gate 8
> Coming of age 18
> Overweight 28
> Dirty Gertie 30
> Buckle my shoe 32
> Christmas cake 38
> Steps 39

Naughty forty 40
Droopy drawers 44
Was she worth it 56 (eh?)
Old age pension 65
Saucy! 69
Heaven's gate 78
Staying alive 85
. . . and the exhausted-by-now: Torquay in Devon 87

There are lots more (they go up to 90) but I don't want to bore you too much; plus some are a bit crap: time for fun 41, for example, or four and seven 47, or trombones 76 (which I don't understand, do you?).

Getting a reply to my application proved difficult. Because of various boroughs' data protection policies, no organization was able to forward my details to a different civic body; thus I was constantly thanked and then given another email address to apply to a little more directly. It never really seemed like particularly directly to me, as I was virtually shuffled around the houses for ages until, eventually, I electronically arrived in the right place, only to be solemnly informed that the position of bingo caller had been filled many months ago, and that there were no further bingo calling positions currently available in the borough, though would I perhaps be interested in running a basic computing activity on a weekly basis at our day care centre in Acton for older users? Pardon? All this advanced-level proto-municipal council-speak was cluttering my critical and regional faculties with invalid lexicographical ephemera. I was blinded by the red pen. I replied: Well, OK then, seeing as you asked so nicely.

Turn of the Screw 42.

Oxfam, Kensington High Street branch
Monday afternoon
Oxfam goats sold, 2004: 38,000
Oxfam tree seedlings sold, 2004: 875,000

Anticipatory bliss. Me, on my own, on the till all afternoon, replacing Maureen who's not here (hope she hasn't died – I daren't ask –

we die quite often). I've brought in my own CDs to play over the Tannoy, too. What could be better? At last I'm the king of the shop floor – the punters are gonna be proper doped by my kick-ass tunes shimmying out of our octophonic ceiling speakers, inspired to previously uncharted psychedelic heights of charitable retail splendour. All right, look out!

'Where's that noise coming from?' Gladys is mock-staggering around the shop floor with her hands over her ears. She stayed behind from her morning shift to cash up, and she has deliberately ventured out in order to have a gratuitous go at me. Again. Of course, she can't actually hear the music from the office, she's just come to be nasty and try to embarrass me in front of the customers and it's worked – I am deeply embarrassed; her impression of Munch's *The Scream* is uncannily convincing.

'Is this horrible noise coming from here?' Gladys stands, mock-reeling beside the world music CD stand. 'Or from up there?' She cringes beneath a small ceiling speaker. The music she is complaining about is Funkadelic's 'Maggot Brain', a beautiful wailing electric guitar meditation by axe virtuoso Eddie Hazel that sounds like a Quaalude-guzzling, Buddhist Jimi Hendrix only without the tooth-picking. OK, it's not the Mamas and Papas but neither is it hardcore sodding techno for God's sake.

'It's not noise, it's music,' sweetly comments the customer I am serving. At least trying to serve.

But Gladys ignores this and continues to zigzag around with her hands held to her ears like Richard the Third desperate for the toilet.

'Where's this *noise* coming from?'

I try to ignore her but it's not easy, what with the hysterical yelling and all.

'Is it *you*?' she screams at me. 'Is this what you've put on, this noise? Is it *you*?'

'It's music, Gladys. And yes, I put it on. What's your problem?'

Now she pretends she can't hear me over the rampaging sonic assault, which if you listen to *really* hard, you can just about identify over the general hubbub of the store.

'Oh, *you* put it on! It all makes sense now!'

'There's no need to shout, Gladys.'

'It all makes sense now!' She dramatically retreats out back towards the office, with her hands still clasped over her ears.

'Is that woman always like that?' asks the woman I'm still attempting to serve.

We are all dazed, and rather traumatized by Gladys's crazed performance; it was quite obviously the work of a cruel and diseased mind and absolutely not the sort of thing you want to experience in a retail environment, ever.

'Yes.'

'Poor you.'

'I know.'

'You should turn it up.'

'Oh, I don't think so.'

'Oh, go on.'

'No, I really don't think so.'

Then it starts skipping. Then my next CD skips too, and the next. I give up and replace them with one of the seemingly unskippable official Oxfam world music CDs. *Sudan*, I think it is. It doesn't skip.

'Ooh, what's this music? It's lovely!' enquires a customer almost straight away.

'It's *Sudan*.'

'Isn't it delightful?'

'Oh, come on.'

And she buys the CD.

Our Christmas catalogues have arrived. In it, you can buy a donkey (£50) – not for the garden but for somebody in the developing world. Or you can buy them a camel, or a goat, or a water pump or a classroom or a whole mango plantation if you're feeling flush. A lady customer comes in and sweeps about twenty catalogues into her bag and says she's giving an Xmas party for all her friends but instead of champagne and presents they'll be getting something from our catalogue; i.e. a nice donkey that they'll never actually get to meet. Ha-ha-ha! I'm glad I'm not going to her Christmas party though.

'A what, a donkey?'

'Merry Christmas!'

'A donkey in fucking Liberia?'

'Ho-ho-ho.'

'I'm never coming to one of your parties ever again. Pass the warm orange squash.'

Meanwhile the donkey gets on a plane. I think.

Basic Computing Activity, Age Concern, Acton High Street
Friday lunchtime
Pensioners in the UK: 11 million
Pensioner percentage of UK population: 18%

'Are you ready?' asks Liz. 'Would you like a cup of tea?'

'A cup of tea and I'll be ready.'

The two canteen ladies say they fancy me and Liz tells them off.

'I don't mind.'

'It's unprofessional.'

I sit and drink my tea in the sun-streaming café and wait for the t'ai chi class to end. I'll be teaching in the same room as soon as they're done. I've never taught anything before; my heart is thumping. I pick up a copy of *Mature Times* and try to concentrate on a piece either by or about, or by and about Alan Titchmarsh. Pages and pages of Alan Titchmarsh. Then when it's time I stand and timidly follow Liz into the other room; there are four computer terminals against a wall, each with an incumbent pensioner. Behind them two more pensioners sit politely waiting their turn. Liz introduces me; explains why I'm here.

'Good afternoon,' I say.

'Good afternoon,' they reply.

Although they all talk at once and constantly butt in over one another, I think I do quite well: I restore order and help out with emails to grandchildren and supervise design of a flyer for a jumble sale. Two of them are working through an online touch-typing course,[*] but they can't seem to locate the link for the site so I pull down their favourites menu to see if it might be there. It isn't; instead their favourites read:

> *Online Chat with Nude Girls*
> *NEW VIAGRA at Half Price*
> *Online Sex Poker Rooms*
> *Play Adult Poker*
> *Age Concern England Homepage*
> *XXX Poker XXX Sex XXX Poker XXX*
> *Poker Sex Chat ££££*
> *Welcome to the Alan Titchmarsh Website*
> *$$ Amazing Deals on VIAGRA $$*
> *Poker Sex Chat with Alan Titchmarsh on Viagra*

'The touch-typing course appears not to be here.'
  'No.'
  'Instead there are all these poker and sex sites.'
  'Yes.'
  'Know anything about these?'
  'I don't think so.'
  We locate the course. There's some coughing.
  Maria, from Portugal, says she wants to check her horoscope but has no idea how. I guide her through it, step by step. Many horoscope websites want personal details; personal details and credit card information. I tell Maria to ignore these sites and never to enter her personal details into any of them, but each time I return after checking on the others, I find she's typing her personal details into some lurid, flashing website. On my third pass she even has her bank card out.
  'Maria, *no*. Put your card away, these are rogue sites, they just want to fleece you. You don't have to enter your personal details just to get your horoscope.'
  'But they need my particulars to give an accurate forecast.'

---

[*] 0% of this text is brought to you using touch-typing. 100% index fingers.

'Well, let's go to a well-known site and have a look at their horo-scopes instead.'

So we go to Yahoo. We immediately get a box with Maria's name and whole horoscope. I am staggered.

'What an amazing coincidence!' I say. 'It's your name there, look!'

'And my exact stars,' she replies, putting on her glasses.

I consider this briefly.

'Maria, have you ever been to the Yahoo horoscopes before?'

'I think, yes, maybe.'

'I see. And have you come here and entered all your details pre-viously?'

'I think maybe, yes. Yes, I think.'

'So this site appears to be recognizing you.'

'That's right.' She beams at me.

'You told me you had no idea how to do any of this.'

'Where do I click to find out more about my moon rising in Libra?'

'Your what?'

One of those politely waiting is a very tall, dapper, partially sighted old gentleman named Gregory, who is wearing giant 1970s sunglasses. Gregory wants to know whether, with sight as bad as his, he'll ever be able to email. I bring up the largest font I can find and type out: CAN YOU READ THIS?

'Yes,' says Gregory. 'Can you read this?'

'Yes, of course. I was asking you.'

'I was repeating what's written on the screen.'

'Yes, I can see that now. Well. That's good, isn't it?'

'It's wonderful! Does this mean I can email now?'

'I think so. I worry, though, that you can't see the keys.'

'That's a point.'

We sit there.

'I have to leave now,' he said. 'Will you be here next week?'

'Yes, I will.'

'Good, we can go through everything else then.'

'Yes, everything else.'

The class stumbles onward. Pupils gradually leave until it's only

Maria and myself left: me watching her reading her horoscope on Yahoo. I silently drum my fingers. There are only four lines of text; she must have read this twenty times already. Maria also has a bad habit of clicking randomly, anywhere on the screen, and ending up in strange and unnecessary places.

'What did you click this time?'

She shrugs. Clucks. At 2.30 p.m. I turn off all the computers and leave.

'Goodbye,' says Maria.

'How was it?' asks Faye back home. She has been at work all day herself, of course, only for money. Wage slave! Corporate whore! This does, however, mean that we can eat.

'Actually I loved it.'

'You *loved* it? How come?'

'I'm not sure. It's a strange feeling. I don't really understand, but afterwards I felt all . . . luminescent.'

'Well, I'm very pleased for you.'

'No, don't be pleased for me, be pleased for the pensioners, whom I helped.'

'Are you going to be like this all evening?'

'Yes. In fact I'm going to be like it for ever.'

'I'm going to have a bath then.'

'Don't use too much water. Preserve it!'

'OK, stop this now.'

Oxfam, Kensington High Street branch
Monday afternoon
Public donations to Oxfam's global Tsunami Fund: $278 million
Number of people Oxfam has helped directly with funds above (over seven countries): 1.8 million

We've got a new table full of Christmas treats – piles of cakes and puds. I just know that some cow's going to come in and make a snide remark about them or complain that they're too expensive (they aren't). This happens a lot with the brand-new giant display of children's largely plastic stocking-fillers manufactured in some petro-chemical plant in China. Ethically sourced though, eh? *Eh?*

I'm in a shitty mood today. I didn't want to come in; it's freezing outside; our customers are all bastards; I'm unappreciated, not being paid, and further mature observations along these lines. I become terminally bored after just five minutes: all my previous selfless positivity has been replaced by scowls and pouts. I spend my time thinking up pithy replies to the inevitable barrage of self-righteousness and sick, sick meanness from our middle-aged female customers. The first complaint – about the price of menswear – actually comes from a tramp. I argue with him anyway, though after five minutes I feel pretty stupid standing there debating charity shop pricing structures with a bedraggled man with burst capillaries in a moth-eaten woolly hat. He buys two get-rich-quick books (all tramps buy these sorts of books – I'm not kidding).

Is it me, or is money getting dirtier? Pound coins made of lead, painted gold; notes like dirty old leaves; platinum Amex cards stained with caviar. It's so cold in the shop today. Winter is here. I play Mozart's *Requiem* over the Tannoy but Sally comes out and tells me to put something more jolly on, so it's back to *Sudan*, or is it *Morocco*? All this world music's pissing me right off; do I look like Andy Kershaw?★

They're busy out back today – a number of people have died – and whole housefuls of possessions lie around in boxes; it'll all end up in the bin, or on a bin man's mantelpiece. A person who used to be in *EastEnders* (can't remember their name) comes in, looks at the bric-à-brac for a while and then leaves again. That was exciting! I hadn't seen any celebrities in here before this. It's not surprising though, really: you wouldn't want to be papped coming out of here – not unless you were Gwynnie Paltrow or maybe Natalie Portman. Perhaps Kofi Annan, or David Bellamy.† At 5 p.m. a woman who

---

★ Asante sana. Wapi choo?
† Actually, would David Bellamy get papped? Perhaps not.

looks like Lee Marvin comes in and, at last, complains about the validity of the Christmas puddings. She's around sixty, and wearing black spandex leggings that have 'JUICY' in giant gothic lettering across the arse.

'Hey, all those items are Fairtrade, leave it.'

'But for a mere pudding!'

'It's a really nice pudding.'

'But that! For a pudding! Oh, all right I'll take it,' says Juicy with a sigh, plonking it down on the counter.

I bleep the pud.

'But wrap it,' she demands.

'Pardon?'

'I said wrap it.'

We look at one another. I lift the pudding and peer at its list of ingredients. Juicy continues to stare me down; down to the ground. What the hell, I think, 'tis the season to be jolly, and begin haltingly to 'rap' the individual ingredients in a convincing hip-hop styleee.

'Raisins, nfff, currants, nfff, flour, nfff-wacka-wacka, chopped almonds, nfff, mixed spice, nfff–'

'Wrap it, not rap it, you idiot.'

'I'm sorry but we don't wrap. Only this kind of rap. Also there's a queue of about twenty people behind you and it's just me on the till.'

Exit Juicy, minus pud.

These hot babes, they give me wood.

Freestyle.

Basic Computing Activity, Age Concern, Acton High Street
Friday lunchtime
Year by which a quarter of UK population will be of pensionable age: 2031
Percentage of UK pensioners who have never used the Internet: 81%

Today I mine previously uncharted fathoms of pointlessness. Today I make pissing into the wind look positively like time well-spent. This is absolutely not the way forward. I am not becoming a better person by having experiences like this. Let's just try to get this section over with quickly.

I turn up and there are three waiting post-t'ai chi session: a Polish couple (she with awry hairpiece) plus Portuguese Maria. Nobody else – not even blind Gregory. News of my classroom prowess has clearly spread through Acton's elderly community like a rampaging forest fire. The Poles get on with their touch-typing course, which means I am free to turn all my attentions towards Maria, who doesn't want to look at her horoscope today; instead she wants to 'chat'.

'Chat with me?' I see my role here as part hi-tech support expert, half benign Samaritans-esque counsellor. I give her a warm, sympathetic look.

'No, not with you, *tsk*. Chat on the computer.'

'Chat with who on the computer?'

'Chit-chat, chat.'

'You mean like in a chatroom?'

She nods fiercely even though I don't think she knows why. So, with a heavy heart, I begin to search for a suitable chatroom: a chatroom for a Portuguese lady in her late seventies who can barely read, let alone type, or spell, or keep up to speed in conversation, especially not in an online chatroom. I find somewhere, and read down a predetermined list of chat subjects: government & politics, business & finance, recreation & sports, health & wellness, schools & education, etc.

'What sort of thing do you want to chat about?'

'Just chat.'

'Government and politics?'

'No, I think just chat.'

I find something called 'general chat' and locate a nice, slow room with only one or two people in it. Maria's (excruciatingly negotiated) screen name is lucky874523. We ease digitally into the room and our first conversation goes like this:

`mammoth67:` hi lucky
`lucky874523:` hi mammoth thank yoo foryor messig
   cani tok to yoo! ?

Sadly mammoth67 has departed by the time Maria types all this out.

'What's he saying?' she asks excitedly.

'I'm afraid he seems to have gone.'

'Oh no.'

We stay in the chatroom, alone, for a few minutes. Soon somebody else arrives, and then another. They begin to talk dirty.

'What are they saying?' asks Maria.

'Erm. They seem to be having a conversation between themselves.'

Undeterred, Maria gets going on the keyboard.

`lucky874523:` hi wood yoo liyk too tok to me! ?
`high_voltage:` gonna bend u over the fridge and
   make u moan, u luv it!!!!11!
`luvbug66:` i am luving it already! guess what
   pantys i am wearing??
`high_voltage:` sexy black one's that I will rip
   of usin my teeth
`luvbug66:` yeh go on rip em off and hav me over
   the fridge yeh go on!!
`lucky874523:` hell0 , me nam iz luky wood yoo
   likto chat! ? helo hiy voltig , how arr yoo! ?
`high_voltage:` u got bra on?
`luvbug66:` not any more!!!!11
`high_voltage:` I am so hard 4 u
`luvbug66:` i want u to be hard 4 me, i luv
   it!!!!!

'What are they saying now?' Maria asks.

'Erm. They're talking, uh, sort of . . . sexily, to one another.'

Maria ceases her one-fingered typing and fishes into her handbag for her glasses, and sits there quite happily for about twenty minutes.

'OK, that's probably enough now, let's wrap things up, shall we?' The Poles went ages ago, and sitting watching Maria read her horoscope over and over is one thing, but sitting watching Maria watching two strangers' online sex chat for half an hour is quite another.

Liz spots me on my way out; she looks at her watch. 'Finishing early?'

'There were only three today and they're done already.'

'OK for next week?'

'You really want me back again next week?'

'If you can stand it.'

Maria follows me through into the corridor, still smiling from all the passive hardcore pornographic chat.

'Now I must buy you a cheese on toast,' she says.

'But I have to run, honestly.'

'Well, I buy you cup of tea then.'

'Things to do.'

'I buy you cup of coffee.'

'Places to go.'

'I buy you hot chocolate and that's the end!'

We sit and drink hot chocolate together and agree that yes, Sebastian is a really lovely name. I feel soiled. And cheap. Cheaper. I steal a copy of *Mature Times*. That's better.

Oxfam, Kensington High Street branch
Monday afternoon

Sally is beginning to enjoy taunting me about Gladys. This springs from a specific incident that took place this afternoon. I was serving on the till, which is getting pretty hectic now with Christmas just around the corner, when out of the corner of my eye I spotted Gladys speeding out towards me from the direction of the office. I braced myself.

'I've got something to say to you,' she cried.

I winced and stumbled backwards a little into the wall. My

handful of change flew everywhere. 'What do you want?'

'I've been cashing up last week's takings and everything's all over the place. It's terrible. Out by hundreds. Except for Monday, the day when it's just you and me on the till. Monday's spot on. I just wanted to say well done. I doubt it will be spot on again this week, but well done for last week.'

I regarded her with open-mouthed shock. She stalked back to the office.

'Gladys *likes* you,' taunts Sally. 'She *loves* you.'

'She's clearly trying to lull me into a false sense of security. There'll be some terrible masterplan behind this, I'm certain.'

'She thinks you're *brilliant*.'

'You put me next to her at the Christmas party and I swear to God, I'll kill you. Or even, OK, I'm not kidding, I'll resign.'

Sally looks as totally not fussed as it's probably possible to look. 'You're Gladys's *favourite*.'

This is all very immature coming from the manageress, I think.

I realized today that the thing I like the most about this job is that it allows me to kid myself that I'm actually some sort of groovy hipster DJ. I actually take the music that I play over the Tannoy more seriously than anything else to do with the job. This tragic awareness embarrasses me, but I cannot escape the truth of the matter. At home before every shift I earnestly browse through my CDs and pick out four or five that I think might be suitable, i.e. without bad language, overt Satanism or too much atonalism, and put the chosen discs into a small CD holder wallet thing especially.

When I get to the shop, Sally always ever-so-slightly mockingly asks: 'Have you brought some music with you?' to which I maturely reply: 'I might have,' while hiding the CD wallet behind my back and sidling out on to the shop floor. Then, all puffed-up and self-righteous, I put on the first CD (something like the Modern Lovers or *Forever Changes* – very dangerous and cutting-edge, I think you'll agree) and feel incredibly proud of myself for 'enlightening' everybody, even though there's no one listening except me and the posh woman harrumphing over there and that out-of-it trampy-looking guy, but look, he's tapping his mouldy old foot, he's loving it!* The CD player still skips everything anyway, so my gleeful moments of disc-jockeying triumph are fleeting to say the least. This situation drives me to an almost constant level of helplessness and despair, especially when Gladys always chooses to come out at the worst possible moment – i.e. during the backwards sitar solo or whatever. And she just stands and . . . *stares* at me with this undisguised malevolence. Or disguised malevolence even. *Sudan* still doesn't skip, even though I've deliberately scratched it to pieces. Nor does *Tango*, nor *Flamenco* nor *Morocco* nor *Salsa* nor whoever's *Abba Gold* that is, nor the Elvis bloody Christmas album.

I'm all shook up.

Basic Computing Activity, Age Concern, Acton High Street
Friday lunchtime
Percentage of UK pensioners unhappy with their quality of life: 30%
Percentage of UK pensioners who don't get out of their homes more than once a week: 13%

I am sitting in the café drinking my pre-lesson cup of coffee when Liz comes in and walks up to me. She's wringing her hands and she says, 'Bad news, I'm afraid.'

'Oh?'

'There's nobody here for your class today.'

'*Nobody?*' It takes me an hour to walk here, for God's sake.

'I'm so sorry.'

'Not even Maria?'

'No, not even Maria.'

'But what about that woman who just walked past?'

'Someone walked past?'

'Yes, in the direction of the computers.'

We go to investigate and, sure enough, it's Flo, sitting at her terminal, smiling.

'Flo, thank God!'

---

* Actually that's Arthur Lee. (This joke was written before Arthur Lee died.)

Liz flees.

Flo's good – she can do stuff; some of it better than I can. I show her some basic word processing things that she already knew how to do and then, phew, blind Gregory stumbles in. (Oh, and two more new people who say they just want to sit and play computer solitaire. They sit and play computer solitaire. They are quite smelly.)

'Hello!' booms Gregory.

'Gregory!' I cry. Gregory's brilliant: seven feet tall, posh and liver-spotted and slightly confused but damn righteous with his wavy grey hair and oversized tweed jacket and giant sunglasses. He waves a CD at me.

'You want to listen to some music?' I ask.

'No!'

'You want to look at photographs?'

'Right!'

'Take a seat! No, not there, that's Flo. That's better, oh, hold on, whoa, oops, oh, oh, that's fine, just carefully now . . . OK.'

The photos scroll through as an onscreen slideshow: it's a group of disabled people holidaying in Rome and the Vatican, followed by the same group of people holidaying in Lourdes. Taking the cure. Gregory sits with his nose pressed up against the screen, still with his sunglasses on, watching the images creep along. He asks if he can print some of these out but our printer doesn't work so I tell him he can take the CD along to a photo shop and get them done there; we just need to write down the ones he wants printed, which should be straightforward as somebody's already captioned them.

'What's this one?' asks Gregory. It's a long-distance, blurry photograph of Pope John Paul II, waving.

'That one's captioned "Pope 22".'

Gregory shakily writes Pope 22 on a sheet of paper.

'But to be honest, Gregory, numbers 14 and 19 were better quality Pope photographs – more in focus.'

Gregory nods and writes Pope 14 and Pope 19 on top of where he's written Pope 22. Next up is a photograph of Gregory himself, looking startled, wearing sunglasses in a piazza surrounded by disabled women.

'What's this one say?'

'The caption is "Gregory and His Groupies".'

'I'll have that one too then.'

He writes Gregory and His Groupies over where he's written the popes; then leans forward and watches a dozen or so more, many of which are of the Pope.

'Hmm, I think that's everything.'

'Are you sure?'

'Are there any more of me?'

There are a few more. We make a note of them. Then Gregory gets up to leave and we shake hands earnestly.

'Thank you so much. Are you here next week?'

'If you are, then I will be too.'

'Well, I'll see you next week then.'

'Brilliant.'

We say goodbye. I love Gregory. I love it here. You have to take the ups with the downs. The ups being somebody in my class.

OK then, class dismissed.

Oxfam, Kensington High Street branch
Monday morning

Century since which the C-word has been in common usage: thirteenth
Less contentious C-words include: clock, camber, caper, cudgel

Christmas shopping means that the till needs double-teaming, and as it's Monday morning, guess who I'm double-teamed with? That's right.

'I told you not to put that there!'

'Put what where?'

'The pen! There!'

'Why not?'

'It keeps rolling off! Look!'

Gladys throws the pen on to the floor.

'Please can I just pay for these scented candles?' asks a customer.

This is probably what it was like in the gulags, except I doubt the gruel was Fairtrade.

A middle-aged Kensington woman called Sally the C-word today. For having had the cheek to tell her sorry but dogs – yes, even incy-wincy, darling, cute-as-pie pooches like Trixie here, cradled in your fat stupid arms – aren't allowed instore because we sell food. The C-word! And then later that afternoon she was called a 'cocksucking bitch' by a man about to steal some books. We know that he was about to steal some books because he'd just bragged about it to another customer, who came and sweetly informed us of said gentleman's intent. Sally took being called a cocksucking bitch on the chin* and stood and stared the man down; he stood and stared Sally right back in the same direction.

'You *middle-class* cocksucking bitch,' he continued.

However this was an adjective too far for Sally. 'Out!' she trilled. 'Now!'

He exited, and without even having stolen any books. We all stood out back and drank coffee and talked about this episode for a while and about how it was never like this in the olden days.

It's very strange, this working for no money lark. None of the usual rules apply: should one feel guilty for turning up to work late? Yes, because people are relying on you to be there and you're letting them down if you don't show up; your salary is just something that shows up in your bank account every month: you shouldn't work directly to it, right? But what about coffee breaks? Salaried coffee breaks, lunch breaks et al. are always taken without fail – you wouldn't even question it – but when you're a volunteer? To reproduce the usual dossing shtick would be letting yourself down, letting Sally down, letting Gladys down and don't forget letting those needier down too. Therefore volunteer coffee breaks are never very relaxing – a minute or so's chat before the guilt begins to bite: what are you doing standing there chatting? You're not getting paid; why are you here exactly? Get on with the work! Some of our lady

* As it were.

volunteers like to natter 'n' patter for as many as ten minutes, which is OK as this is more of a social thing for them, but for me? I can't think of anything more self-indulgent than ten minutes' coffee gossip, and I usually neck my caffeine on the job, keeping my conscience as clear as possible. And how about leaving on time? I always leave dead on the dot at the end of my designated shift; sod that, I'm straight out the door, see you next week, yeah whatever, bye now.

Basic Computing Activity, Age Concern, Acton High Street
Friday lunchtime

I am sitting in the café drinking my pre-lesson cup of coffee when Liz comes in and walks up to me. She's wringing her hands and she says, 'Bad news, I'm afraid.'
'I see. Is there nobody here for my class?'
'I'm really sorry. And I'm sorry we can't pay you either; we used to have a young man who came and did this and he was very good and we used to pay him rather a lot actually, but we couldn't really afford him so he left and now we've got you, who we can't afford to pay either. I really am so sorry.'
'Well, that's fine, I don't want paying anyway. I'm here because ... I don't, erm, want any paying. You know. And anyway, if there's nobody in my class then I'd feel pretty bad about you paying me for nothing.' *Even though it took me an hour to walk here*, exclaims the self-righteous voice in my head.
Gregory comes in, but he can't see me (honest) and walks straight past and exits via the far door. My heart sinks.
'Shall I just go, do you think, or should I hang on in case somebody comes?'
'Actually I really don't think anyone's coming today.'
'So I should just go home?'
'That might be the best thing. Would you like a cup of tea before you go? Come on, have a nice cup of tea.'
I say no, because I think that would be more humiliating. But then, in a strange, even more humiliating development, Maria

makes a late, Shakespearean, shuffling entrance. She spies me and her eyes light up; she's so delighted she drops all her carrier bags.

I sit and watch while Maria reads her horoscope incredibly slowly and then says, 'It's all so true.'

'What's true? Are you going to be lucky in love?'

'*Un*lucky in love.'

We sit there. I am unsure whether or not to sympathize.

'Oh well. There are plenty more, erm, fish in the, erm, websites to look at.'

We look at more horoscope websites while I sit watching and feeling faintly suicidal. Then Flo comes in, who is always technically competent except she's trigger-happy and must click *somewhere* on the screen every ten seconds or so, after which she yelps and I have to mop up the pop-ups. Unfortunately, one of her grandchildren has emailed her a musical animated Christmas card. She opens it up and a bunch of dancing snowmen blare away annoyingly for about two minutes while I am in the middle of trying to stop Maria entering her credit card details on to the Chinese horoscope section of Russell Grant's online chamber of Horos. Flo and Maria are delighted by the moronic singing snowmen – they've never seen anything like it before – indeed, they think it's some sort of miracle, and now Maria is demanding that we find one for her to send to her friends, even though a) she hasn't got any, and b) really, none at all. She tells me she likes Rudolph (the red-nosed reindeer): can she have a musical, animated Xmas card featuring Rudolph?

'No.'

'Why no Rudolph?' She pouts.

'You just can't. Read your horoscope and be quiet.'

'How about chat?'

'No chatting either. Just read your, read that, read your horoscope again. Look how interesting it is. Look. *Look*.'

Flo asks if I can explain Microsoft Excel to her and I say no, I can't. No, you don't understand, really, I can't. I know I'm the teacher but I just don't know how to do that. *I'm sorry, OK?*

For fuck's sake.

Class dismissed, yes.

On my long walk home, I make up my mind never to return to Age Concern in Acton ever again. At least until I'm a little older and need to utilize their admirable facilities. Sorry, guys. They might all be dead by the time you read this. We might all be dead. Let's hope so.

'What happened to the luminescence?' asks Faye.

'There is a light that never goes out.'

'You're doing that thing with the song titles again.'

'Sorry. But nobody ever shows up to my class. What am I supposed to do? I'm beginning to feel like I'm just wasting my time with this. I need a new challenge. Perhaps something not involving so many old people. Or if it has to involve old people, then I'd like them at least to be present.'

But she'd gone.

Oxfam, Kensington High Street branch
Tuesday morning

Xmas is only four days away and our Fairtrade chocolate advent calendars are knockdown half price, as are the advent candles and other advent items. The Christmas party has been cancelled because nobody can make it. So far as I can tell, nobody cares. Gladys talks constantly about how much she hates Christmas and all right, already, we believed her the first time. The customers believe her too. It was never supposed to be like this.

Merry Xmas, readers.

Step Three

Marine Mammal Sighting Scheme
Hampshire and Isle of Wight Wildlife Trust
Number of marine mammal species: 115
Number of marine mammal species considered 'endangered': 21

The literature states that the Marine Mammal Sighting Scheme encourages volunteers in Hampshire and the Isle of Wight to report sightings of 'seals, porpoises, dolphins and whales. A Dolphin Encounter Guide has been produced, and events are planned.' In the space between steps two and three, my wife and I have moved from west London to Hampshire – a tactical manoeuvre, as Faye is several months pregnant, and we've decided to attempt to raise our child* amid rural perspectives rather than those of the M4's elevated section. And seeing as there are no old people anywhere to be seen, yet, marine mammal sighting seems like as good a place to start volunteering as any. So, hungry for a fresh start under the Oxfam witness protection programme, I email and am accepted gratefully into the scheme.

Unfortunately we have moved to ye olde and ancient city of Winchester, which is ten miles north of the coast, so the chances of spotting a porpoise or a whale are rather slight; though I bet that's what central Londoners probably thought too until recently, when a whale swam right up to the Houses of Parliament and was briefly famous before it died spread-eagled on its rescue raft in front of thousands of dismayed spectators. Because of this, marine mammal sighting has never been so in vogue; plus we do have a river – the Itchen – in Winchester, so I consider my duties to involve checking the Itchen (which handily runs through the city centre) sporadically for marine mammals. I haven't seen any yet. Swimming dogs

* I'd just like to take this opportunity to apologize to my son Reuben for his first ever mention in print being a footnote in a passage about my failure to sight marine mammals.

don't count. And I don't think ducks are mammals, are they?

What about swans?

Winchester Litter Pickers
Monday afternoon
Annual cost of litter clearance by UK councils: £500 million
Fly-tipping incidents per month in the UK: 90,000

The phone rings. There's coughing.

'Mr Hunter?' It's an extremely elderly, extremely upper-class gentleman.

'Yes?'

'Alistair Forbes-Watson,' he gargles. 'You telephoned.'

'Ah yes, I was calling to enquire about your litter-picking activity.'

'That's right?'

'So do you still . . . are you still, picking . . . the litter?'

'Litter picking? Yes?'

'Well, I want to come and join. In.'

'What?'

'Well, I believe that maintaining our cities' civic spaces', erm, hygiene, so to speak, fulfils an important and valuable role in, erm, the core values in contemporary society, or something. It's great. You know?'

'Really? Well then, that's marvellous. Do you have any tongs?'

'I'm afraid not.'

'Ah, right, I expect Hermione will come and drop you some tongs. Where do you live?'

I tell Alistair Forbes-Watson where I live.

'Hermione will drop you in some tongs. Hermione's the co-ordinator now, not me, I'm too old.'

'I see.'

'Righto.'

Three minutes later the phone rings again.

'Mr Hunter?' The voice is female, elderly and extremely upper-class.

'Yes?'

'Hermione Rudd,' she brays. 'Winchester Litter Pickers. I gather you're interested in joining our merry band.'

'That's right.'

'And I gather you need some tongs.'

'I believe I do, yes.'

'One pair of tongs costs £7.'

'Goodness – £7!'

'Do you want a badge too?'

'How much is a badge?'

'Also £7.'

'I think I'll make do with the tongs.'

'Very well. Can you make it along to the main entrance of the railway station for nine o'clock sharp next Monday morning?'

'Yes.'

'Marvellous. I'll bring along some tongs and then we'll be able to get you started, even though you'll be without identification. One last thing – I didn't catch your Christian name.'

'It's Sebastian.'

There is a brief, rapturous pause. 'Oh, *good*.'

'Yes?'

'Goodbye then, Seb*astian*.'

'Goodbye.'

It's like the 1950s, 1960s, 1970s, 1980s, 1990s and most of the 2000s never happened. It's like *Goodnight Sweetheart* but without a time machine or Nicholas Lyndhurst. Maybe the station can't afford cleaners, post-privatization and all. Little bit of politics there.

Winchester Litter Pickers, Winchester Railway Station
Monday morning, 9.27 a.m. sharp
Most littered item (worldwide): cigarette butt
Largest volume component of litter (worldwide): beverage
container

As I almost jauntily make my way to the railway station, I realize with a sudden flush of horror that my wallet is empty and I don't have the £7 for the tongs. Worse, there's no cashpoint along my route and I haven't time for a diversion. Worse still, as I pass the entrance of the station car park, I spy several elderly people decked out in skewed bibs already hard at work with tongs in one hand and plastic carrier bag in the other, and they all glare at me suspiciously, as if I'm about to drop litter of my own, little knowing that I'm actually here to join them, albeit without my own bib or, silly me, carrier bag either. Lurking by an idle line of taxis is yet another small group of upper-class elderly people in Barbour and bibs and I boldly approach them.

'Hello there, my name's *Sebastian* and I'm a new recruit.'

'Oh good!'

'We do like new recruits,' says another, mercilessly crushing a dewy plastic Lucozade bottle with a vice-like pair of tongs. Team leader Hermione approaches. She looks fabulous – like Twiggy'll probably look at eighty-five. Her floppy green hat matches her diamond-cushioned Barbour perfectly. She holds up one of those cheap mechanical grappling devices that old people use for picking the remote control off the floor, which I suspect are my tongs.

'Look, I'm really sorry but I forgot to bring any money and I need to find a cashpoint before I can pay you for those tongs.'

'There's one over here, look.'

Hermione accompanies me to the hole in the wall of the station and we step in to queue behind an alternative youth with a skateboard who spits continually on to the pavement. Our uneasy small talk is punctuated by his machine-gun flobbing two feet from where we stand; and when my turn arrives at the machine Hermione is unwittingly standing in the middle of his foaming bronchial puddle.

'Hermione, do you have change for a £20 note?'

'Absolutely not.' The insinuation is that only common people carry money. I feel ashamed of my bright, vulgar £20 note and shove it back into my pocket; but Hermione kindly hands over the tongs anyway and says it's acceptable for me to pay next week instead.

'I haven't got a plastic bag either.'

She hands me a plastic bag. I think I'm ready now.

Hermione suggests I stick with her today and she'll show me the ropes. The ropes consist of us walking around in the station car park picking up litter with our tongs. Other litter pickers wander about in other parts of the car park, along railings, beside the bus stop, in the subway, by the hedge, picking up litter with their tongs too. I find that I am a good tonger.

'Does one pick up the fag butts?' I ask Hermione.

'One can if one can be bothered.'

One can be bothered for the first four or five, but after that one reasons that they're probably bio-degradable, so one kicks them into the road instead. I tong a whole bunch of crap* into my carrier bag: chip forks, squished chips, greasy paper, mashed cold green chilli peppers: yes, readers, I am tonging outside the kebab shop. I don't tong the beige cowpats of puke.

'Hermione, why do we meet specifically here every week?'

'The railway station is vitally important because this is the first thing visitors see when they arrive in the city,' sings Hermione, flinging a wet, soiled nappy† into her bag. 'And we want it to look nice for them; we don't want it to be all filthy.'

'Ah yes, of course.'

'We cover other areas too, you know.' She slips her tongs under an arm and thrusts a slip of paper into my hand with the Winchester Litter-Pickers' schedule typed out on it: 'Our members gather at as many of these rendezvous as they can manage.'

And then, even though I've only been tonging for about ten minutes, I think we've finished, as a large group of us are now jovially huddled outside the automatic doors to the station entrance which we keep setting off, as well as getting in the way of all the passengers and station staff. I shake a number of mucky hands as, one by one, I am introduced to the rest of the litter

---

* Not literally.
† OK, this is literally now.

pickers* until we're all now properly acquainted and it's time to wend our weary way back home again.

'Will we see you again next week, Sebastian?'

'Oh yes!' I wave my tongs happily in the air and accidentally whack the brim of Alistair's deerstalker and apologize; he's fine about it. I arrive home at three minutes to ten. That can't be right, I think, but it is.

Short, sharp shock and awe.

Winchester Litter Pickers, Winchester Railway Station
Monday morning, 9.27 a.m. sharp
Maximum UK fine for littering: £2,500
Average annual UK local authority spend on clearing up chewing gum:
£13,000 (maximum £200,000)

Last week there were about ten of us; today we're just four — Alistair: seventy-something, ruddy, capped and Barboured, pushing a street-cleaner's trolley; George: seventy-something, ruddy, capped and Barboured, pushing a street-cleaner's trolley; and Gillian: sixty-something, friendly, giant flapping bib. I cover the front car park and my bag is overflowing after just five minutes. The car park's on the edge of a steep scrawny slope leading to a fence and a road, and for some reason I break rank and slither down through the dead leaves to the bottom. There is so much litter down here I am fast overwhelmed; this trough is clearly not part of our remit; it's freezing cold and the wind is whipping icy cold rain directly into my ears. Maybe this is why there are just four of us. I tong until my hands are filthy and numb and I am a dead ringer for Stig of the Dump, only less charismatic.

On the pavement on the other side of the road, a group of passing schoolchildren begin to shout things at me, and after they've passed they get braver and braver until finally I get: 'Wanker!' And: 'Oi, twat! Oi! Oi, wanker, twat, here!'

---

* As well as Barbour, there's tweed, houndstooth and a blazing rainbow of paisley headscarves.

Step Three

The cheeky scamp theatrically drops his Coke can on to the pavement, from where it slowly rolls into the road and is crushed by a passing car.

'Ha-ha! Wanker!'

Poor me, eh, readers? But don't worry, I've memorized their faces and if I ever see them again, I'll punch them in the mouth (as soon as they've turned sixteen). In the meantime, there are damp cigarette packets to tong, and lager cans and crisp packets and *insert your own refuse item here*. I decided to make this section interactive. Tong it into my plastic bag; there, that's right. Isn't that fulfilling?

When I clamber – Lazarus-like – up out of the pit and into the car park again twenty minutes later, Alistair, George and Gillian have gone. It really is freezing bloody cold so I can't say I blame them. This appears to be one of those 'rather thankless' volunteering opportunities. Self-pity descends. On my way home I spot Alistair, head down, tonging in the car park over on the other side of the tracks. He hadn't gone home after all. I scuttle around the edge of the car park so that he doesn't see me. What, you reckon Mother Teresa never glossed over the occasional leper?

Winchester Litter Pickers, Winchester Railway Station
Monday morning, 9.17 a.m. sharp
Cause of bubonic plague of the mid-1300s: litter (thus rats)
Total cost of UK fly-tipping clearance and disposal, 2005:
£100 million

Although, yes, the early bird catches the sodden empty packet of ten Benson & Hedges, a problem with starting this early is that commuters are still pouring out of the station: you're in their way, and they all stare at you – indeed I am certain they assume I am performing community service. Oh, how I wish I'd spent another £7 on a bib or a badge or anything to demonstrate that although this is of service to the community, correct, it is certainly not being undertaken in lieu of a custodial sentence. Saying that, I find a threatening curl of the lip deters the most starey of these despicable commuting folk.

Somewhat exhausted by these intimidating facial contortions plus the relentless chomping of tongs, I am cheered when Hermione approaches and hands me a copy of the Pickers' latest newsletter: *Dear Fellow Litter-Picker,* it cordially begins, as I stand and read it before the open-and-shutting station electric doors. *Amazingly this year it will be ten years since three of us started the Winchester Litter-Pickers. Little did we think then that we would grow to over one hundred members . . .* 128 members to be precise; so how come there're only ever just a few of us at the station every week, eh? It must be easy to be a Picker if you never come out to bloody pick – sitting at home and lazily leafing through our newsletter with a log fire, gin and tonic and your rusty tongs gathering dust on the mantelpiece – it's all right for some of these pickled Pickers. The newsletter continues with some fond reminiscence over the Pickers' first attempts at a publicity stunt – back in 1997 – when a 'live King Alfred'* 'raised his tongs'† 'in a peaceful gesture, as on our logo'.** That's the end of the reminiscence.

Today in the car park there are several piles of empty cans of lager and rainbow dollops of sick. Straining to picture all the fun the young people must have had standing around in the car park drinking the lager makes me feel more charitable about cleaning up after them. Towards the end, Hermione approaches again.

'How's it going?'

'Brilliantly.'

'Would you like to help out doing some more tonging down in the cathedral grounds next week?'

'Yes.'

'Super.'

What's wrong with 'no'? I think afterwards.

---

* King Alfred's statue is Winchester's Eiffel Tower; her Big Ben; our proud international symbol. It's at the bottom of the High Street.
† As opposed to his sword.
** Erm, right, the logo is a picture of the original statue. All clear? Good.

Marwell Zoological Park
Colden Common, Hampshire
World's oldest zoo: Vienna (est. 1752)
Marwell Zoo founded: 1972

'There's absolutely no contact with the animals.'

'OK.'

'There's not even to be any touching of any animals.'

'Yes, OK.'

'You will not be involved with the animals at any point as a volunteer at Marwell Zoological Park.'

'I think I understand.'

'Right then. Now that's out of the way, we can move on to taking down your details. What's your name, please?'

This was my first telephone call to the zoo to offer my services. Why should just the human race benefit from my newfangled benevolence? Animals – *it's their world too*, remember?

'Most people don't even make it this far,' explains the lady on the other end of the line after I've donated my particulars.

'What, beyond being told not to touch the animals?'

'That's right. They think they'll be . . . *fondling* the animals, but, of course, they mustn't go anywhere near the animals; we have professionals to do all that.'

'Yes, yes, all right.'

'So you're still interested?'

It was tempting to yell hoarsely: 'No fondling?!?' But instead I just said yes and so we proceeded with my application. But then at one point another of her questions was: *Do you like animals?* A trap?

'I like some animals. I mean, I'm interested in animals generally, that's why I'm here, indeed, but I'm totally not fussed about touching them. Or anything. At all.'

This was exactly what they wanted to hear; and so it came to pass that I was admitted into the famous zoological park. Though when I say admitted, what I mean is sent a terrifying application form and then a date for an 'informal' interview. Marwell appears determined to stamp out any thoughts of animal fondling whatsoever.

Even though they're so cuddly.

Winchester Litter Pickers
Monday morning, 11.17 a.m. sharp
UK litter prosecutions, 1990: 2,543
UK litter prosecutions, 2002: 713 (17,428 spot fines instead)

This heading is a minor white lie, in that I didn't actually go litter picking this morning. I don't have an excuse really – it wasn't particularly cold, or raining; it wasn't even that I was reluctant to get out of bed – I just could not be arsed to leave my house to go and clean up the youth of Winchester's boozed-up trail of destruction. (This seems to be one of the fundamental flaws with volunteering actually – sometimes you can't *quite* be bothered to go out and do any of it. And no one's ever going to *make* you.) Instead I tootled about, drank tea and decided to get on with a spot of decorating upstairs.

So come eleven, there I am, whistling, up a stepladder with a paintbrush in the nursery, when I hear the creak of my garden gate. I glance down from my position near the window and spot a grey-haired lady moving determinedly towards my front door. In fact it's Gillian, from the Pickers. Oh shit – she's come to bawl me out for the no-show. I throw myself against a wall, out of sight, as I hear the doorbell ring, which needless to say I don't answer; instead I get paint all down my side. Then I hear the letterbox clatter, and the gate squeals again and I peer out to see Gillian departing up the road. She looks really angry, I think; indeed, she looks positively apoplectic. Maybe there were rivers of alcopop puke out there this morning and she had to clean it all up by herself? Guilt washes over me like a three-for-two pitcher of Bacardi Breezer.

A few minutes later I gingerly tiptoe down the stairs to the front door, to see what despatch of bile she's deposited on my doormat – it can't be another newsletter, I think, as I had that last week and they only produce them once every six years or so. But there's something; it's blue and white and large. Neatly folded. I pick it up, unfold it, and then almost drop the thing in horror. *Can You Help Winchester Conservatives?* No, I can't, I think, panicking. I have stumbled unwittingly upon an artefact with the potential to make me into a much *worse* person rather than a better one. *A Message from DAVID CAMERON*, it continues. I ignore David Cameron's terrible message and turn the flyer over: several paragraphs of malevolent right-wing propaganda regarding various local issues plus three large photographs of Gillian 'out and about' in Winchester, surrounded by candelabra and pentagrams: not only is she delivering these things, but she's actually *standing for council election herself.* So she hadn't come round to tell me off about my litter-picking absence after all; the truth was far, far worse: Gillian was a hardcore Tory activist. *I am horrified by the awful state of most of the pavements in St Paul's ward*, howls Gillian. *Many of the residents have spent time and considerable amounts of money making their front gardens attractive. But beyond the garden gate lies ugly, patched tarmac, which is dangerous, unsightly and a menace for pedestrians when it rains! Isn't it about time for some scheduled upgrading of pavements in the St Paul's ward? I certainly think so.*

Next stop: rivers of blood etc.

The very next morning, the same thing happens, almost, again. I'm painting away when I hear the gate creak; I look down and this time it's Hermione striding up my garden path, letter in one hand, metaphorical pitchfork in the other. Why can't these nefarious disciples of Lucifer leave me alone? I wearily descend the stairs, expecting to be confronted with Hermione's own rage at the state of the pavements and a couple more paragraphs of neofascist propaganda, but instead it's a sweet letter informing me of my new shift-work picking in the Cathedral Close. Plus a thinly veiled suggestion/threat that I really ought to invest in an official badge else I might be perceived as 'just another itinerant do-gooder'. Can you imagine how awful it would be if somebody did actually think that?

Winchester Litter Pickers, Winchester Railway Station
Monday morning, 9.27 a.m. sharp
Most common litter-dropping situation: while driving
Maximum penalty (UK) for dumping of waste:
12 months' imprisonment

Remain a while amid any organization and even the best disguised internal schisms will eventually reveal themselves in all their bitter, misanthropic glory. Take Alistair, today, and his Dictaphone. After I told him I'd seen Gillian picking over on the other side of the station, I thought I saw him speaking oddly into a mobile telephone, perhaps dissecting the intricacies of picking strategy with Gillian, but no: closer inspection showed him to be covertly muttering details about today's attendance into a hi-tech voice recorder.

' . . . and according to probationary Picker Seb Hunter, Gillian Allen is also allegedly in attendance,' he discreetly murmurs as we all sway uneasily in the station car park, eyeing one another with rank hostility. *Allegedly?*

'Just making a few notes on who's here . . . or not,' he says as the contraption is shoved back into his pocket. Earlier Bill had ignored my waved greeting; as had George. They don't like me, I can tell. It's obvious. Even though I *always* do this one, specific section of the car park, George follows insultingly behind in my footsteps, like I'm not even there. I wave my tongs to say *hey, back off my patch, man!* but he keeps coming, mooching along in my pristine god-damn slipstream. At the end, Hermione tells our grimy, gathered group that the cathedral wants to erect a new snack bar in its grounds.

'Over my dead body,' says Alistair, and everybody haws their approval.

'What's wrong with a new snack bar?' I enquire.

'Well, for a start, more litter,' says Hermione. 'And secondly . . .' She has a small think; the others egg her on with their wild, snack bar-loathing, anything new-loathing, rheumy eyes. 'Secondly, it'll harm the business of the other, snack-providing establishments in the surrounding area!'

'Bravo, Hermione!'

'We'll put a stop to that little plan, don't worry.'

'Oh no, they *won't*.'

'Over my dead body!'

'And mine!'

'Mine' – a polite cough – 'too!'

If the snack bar gets the green light from the local authorities, it will be over the dead bodies of virtually all the Winchester Litter-Pickers, who by that time will probably all be dead anyway.

Storm clouds gather. Let it come down.

Marwell Zoological Park
Colden Common, Hampshire

Name of giraffe involved in famous 1977 Marwell Zoo media furore: Victor
Organization brought in to attempt to assist Victor in his peril (he had fallen
over): the Royal Navy

The 'informal' interview takes *two hours*. After about one hour, I am asked how Marwell might benefit from having me as a volunteer.

'I'm enthusiastic! I'm energetic! I love working with people!' They'd be crazy to deny it! Let's have a party.

'Is there anything you might be able to bring to Marwell other than your, what, "enthusiasm"?'

I am shocked and quite hurt by the sneering suggestion that this might not be sufficient; what other skills do you need, exactly, for directing thick tourists to the ice creams and toilets?

'Have you ever, say, been on safari?'

'On safari?' I gaze thoughtfully out of the window. 'Never.'

Ruth, assistant volunteer co-ordinator in a special blue Marwell sweatshirt and badge, scribbles negatively on to my application form.

'But I'd love to go on safari one day.'

The scribbling becomes more negative.

'I really would like to do that.'

71

The scribbling becomes block capitals.

'For example in Africa, on the plains, with, erm . . .' It was lucky my sentence trailed away, as I had been about to say 'an elephant gun'.

Ruth drops her pen in exasperation. 'Can't you think of any other reasons why we might want you here? Any particular skills you might be able to bring to the position?'

I panic. I hadn't been expecting any of this; I thought they'd just hand over the keys to the hippopotamus enclosure immediately. I stare wildly out of the window.

'I love red pandas!'

Ruth looks at me. 'Red pandas.'

'When I was a kid I used to be obsessed with red pandas; I even invented an animal bingo game that featured red pandas. Prominently.'

Ruth looks at me. 'Volunteers have absolutely no—'

'No contact with the animals, I know, I'm sorry, I got carried away. I didn't mean it.'

'So there are no other reasons why we might select you as a volunteer?'

Because I'm bloody offering?

'No, none. Although my wife is pregnant?'

She pushes my form distastefully across the desk and I'm told to come back the following Thursday for a second interview. How much do they need before they'll allow you to come back and work for no money? On the long walk back to the car park I spot a giant rhinoceros's arse bulging out of the barn door of its enclosure. Never having been able to resist the romantic lure of the rhino, I surreptitiously sidle into the viewing area and deliriously watch four rhinos being fed their dinner, thrown out of buckets, for around ten minutes. They bump about and snuffle their supper off the concrete floor with such delightful hefty charm; I am fantasizing about cuddling them; if not an entire rhino then perhaps just a wrinkly leg. Then after that I see some kangaroos and a tapir and even a baby snow leopard and *I want to cuddle all of them.* No touching the animals? *Just try and stop me.*

Winchester Litter Pickers, Winchester Railway Station
Monday morning, 9.27 a.m. sharp
Average cost of litter bin (UK): £600
Average cost of spot fine for not having used one: £75

I pick up litter for three-quarters of an hour and then go home.*
Later that afternoon, I give my mother a lift to the hospital. She had slipped on a discarded kebab in the Cathedral Close and injured herself.† As I open the car door to let her out, she says, 'Hospitals always need volunteers, you know. There will be all sorts of things you could do at this one here, for example.'

I look up at the hospital. It is a hospital. I hear wailing.

'Like mopping up blood? *No thanks.*'

'There are plenty of things, not just that! How about hospital radio, for example? They're always desperate for volunteers. You could play them all your . . . interesting music.'

I open my eyes wide. My mother is a genius.

---

* This undoubtedly worthwhile volunteering activity is shedding some of its feelgood factor and I'm not sure how to go about trying to reclaim it. I'm considering resigning from the Pickers except I haven't done a single shift in the (permanently adolescent-and-litter-filled) Cathedral Close yet, and I promised I would, so I'm kind of stuck with it. I'll probably carry on but, for your sake, just stop writing about it.

† Well, this certainly *could* have happened. In actual fact, my mother is a longtime sufferer of Crohn's disease, and had an appointment to see a specialist.

Step Four

Winchester Hospital Radio
Royal Hampshire County Hospital

UK's first hospital radio station: York County Hospital, 1925
Number of loudspeakers installed in York County Hospital in 1925: 70

'Can I be a DJ?'

'Yes.'

And it's sorted. No four-hour, split-legged interviews here, thanks very much. Let's just get on with entertaining these patients, whose average age is, I'm told, around sixty-five.

'Do you think they'll like experimental German music from the 1970s? As I have to say that's one of my speciality areas.'

'No,' says Anna, station kommandant. 'They're sixty-five.'

'So one would imagine they'd be quite open-minded?'

'I'd think more along the lines of Glenn Miller, Johnny Mathis, Daniel O'Donnell, Cannibal Corpse.'*

'Must I?'

'You're here to please the patients, not yourself. And you'll mostly be playing their requests. To be honest, you'll entirely be playing their requests.'

'And reading the news?'

'No.'

Anna shows me their charts. Daniel O'Donnell is at number one. I don't even know who Daniel O'Donnell is. Bing Crosby is coming up fast on the inside, however, and probably Engelbert Humperdinck and things like this. I'm not sure, I was so furious and everything had gone spangled and blotchy.

After I calm down, Anna takes me on a guided tour of the station, which is housed in a prefab building adjoining the orthodontics ward in the grounds of the giant Royal Hampshire County

---

* God, I'm laughing so hard I can barely see the screen.

Hospital, opposite Her Majesty's prison. Hospital radio volunteers are in alarmingly short supply at the moment, so tonight is part of an ongoing recruitment drive – a special volunteers' induction evening, though sadly I am the only person here. Anna introduces me to Nigel, one of the station's engineers. Everyone who works here – Anna included – is a volunteer; nobody gets paid; just dues.

'There's this myth that says there are certain songs hospital radio stations will never play, that are banned, but it's complete bollocks,' says Nigel, who looks a bit like eighties darts legend Dave Whitcombe. 'We'll play "The First Cut is the Deepest", for example.'

'You will?'

'Very much so. And "Suicide is Painless".'

We leave Nigel and head down the corridor to the actual broadcasting area. An illuminated red light above the studio door means the team inside are going out live to all wards, calling out around the world, are you ready for a brand-new beat?

'Often the computer plays the records all by itself, automatically,' says Anna. 'If there's no one around to present, then we can just programme it to play whatever we want, even the jingles.'

'There are jingles?'

'Chin up, things like that.'

'Is this the computer live on air at the moment?'

'No, it's Sarah.'

We pop our heads around the door and say hi to Sarah, and young Andrew, assisting. Sarah blushes. I blush. Andrew blushes. We all blush. We decide to leave them to it, and I am taken into an anteroom where I am shown an induction video, which has lots of elderly patients rhapsodizing about how happy listening to hospital radio makes them, especially when they haven't got any visitors or they're in a lot of pain, or quite often both. I am moved by it. At the end, Anna asks whether I'd like to join them (the radio team, not the patients).

'Can I be a DJ?'

'I already said you could.'

'Yes, but do you promise?'

'I promise.'

'OK, I'll join then.'

'Good.'

Here come the backwards sitars: Gladys, screw you.

Marwell Zoological Park
Colden Common, Hampshire

In 2003 further media furore occurred after one of these animals managed to escape: a leopard

The leopard sadly died, and then its replacement's own newborn cub sadly died too

It's two days before my second interview and I've been in the city centre shopping for pith hats, except nowhere seems to stock them, so I buy a safari jigsaw instead, and make a few notes. I arrive home to be greeted by a letter from Marwell on my doormat. Promotion already? It was a typed missive from Ruth.

Dear Seb,

Thank you very much for coming in to see me last week. It was a pleasure meeting you and having the opportunity to discuss your exemplary application. While we appreciate the enthusiasm and time you are able to offer to volunteering, a particular interest in wildlife and appreciation of conservation issues are also needed to help further the aims of Marwell. Therefore after careful consideration I regret to tell you that we are unable to offer you a place on the volunteer team. Basically go fuck yourself.

Yours sincerely etc.,

Ruth

I see. I look down at the jigsaw; the elephant on the front gazes at me sympathetically with his tusks, and I remember my old rhino pal at the zoo. Goodbye, my good rhino friend, I shall never cuddle your leg after all, as your boss is a right jobsworth and I've never been on bloody safari. Jesus H Christ, what a joke; you try to play down your animal passions out of fear of being rejected as some kind of bestialist and this is how they reward you.

I have decided I'm going to be boycotting Marwell after this. I might log on to their website and post negatively on their web forum. Yes, that's what I'll do. See you later.

Well, it turns out they haven't got a web forum.

Winchester Litter Pickers, Winchester Railway Station
Monday morning, 9.27 a.m. sharp

Spring is here. No more coats, scarves, gloves or deerstalkers – our ruddy features are fully exposed for all the world to see; especially when we line up on the station forecourt to have our photograph taken for *Hampshire Life* magazine this morning, even though Alistair's holding his camera the wrong way around. He takes a few close-ups of the bridge of his nose before noticing our shouting and flips it the right way around.

'I've got it, now say cheese!'

'Cheeeeese.'

'Right. Say cheese once more. And again. Just one more. That's it, cheese. Again, cheese, come on. Cheese, yes, yes. That's right, cheese, come on. Right, yes. That's enough cheese now, come on all of you.'

Some of us are aggrieved at the lack of a professional photographer. Hermione had telephoned us over the weekend, urging all Pickers to show up on Monday for this publicity opportunity – thus our numbers this morning are vast: there're about twelve gathered for the photo shoot. A couple of Pickers I've never seen before push to the front of the group and raise their (pristine) tongs, while we station vets lurk tutting bitterly at the back, giant white plastic bibs flapping in the spring breeze as we attempt to maintain these rather unnatural tongs-ahoy poses. We also moan about having to wear the bibs in the first place. Alistair handed them out and insisted we put them on for the photo; we did so with much ill grace while we grumbled about the opportunistic, publicity-hungry new arrivals.

'You look like a knight with that thing on,' says Bill, pointing at my billowing plastic singlet; and instead of answering that I actually feel more like a complete twat rather than, for example, Sir Galahad, I say, yes, and look, my tongs here are, like, my *lance*. My plastic carrier bag is my trusty steed if I hold it like this, look . . . yet Bill has walked away. I sigh; tong.

The twelve of us scour the forecourt* until you could even eat your dinner off it, if you had to; if you like kebabs it's all here. As always we regroup before the electric station doors and they flap open and shut while Hermione thanks us all for coming, and says *well done*. As I begin my stroll home, through the station's pedestrian tunnel under the tracks, right at the bottom of the steps to the car park is a veritable mountain of garbage: sodden newspapers, cans, chip paper; it's a filthy, disgusting mess. As this is on the 'other' side of the station, we Pickers don't appear to give a shit; it can all pile up here and nobody cares because most of the tourists emerge on the nice side. I stand before the rubbish mound and think things through for a little while and then – with my internal jukebox cranked up to self-righteous stadium max – determinedly shake out my spare carrier bag and tong it brimful (of asha), up to forty-five (items). Everybody needs a Picker for a pillow.

The Mid Hants Railway, Ropley Station platform
Sunday lunchtime

Number of preserved steam trains still active in the UK: 186
Litres of saliva the above can be relied upon to provoke in UK railway enthusi-
asts (monthly): 8.6

It occurred to me that one way of becoming a better person might simply be to help other people feel better about themselves when out and about involved in leisure activities such as, say, visiting a steam train line. Everybody likes steam trains; well, some people like steam trains – trains in general, really. I refer here to that infamous sub-stratum of humanity, the tragi-compulsive ranks of the Railway Enthusiast, a portly battalion of whom run and maintain the heritage steam loco-

---

* SOME PERHAPS MORE CAPABLY THAN OTHERS.

motive attraction, the Mid Hants Railway, better known as the Watercress Line, which runs a regular service back and forth from Old Alresford to Alton, ten miles away. I have been stationed (geddit?) for duty at Ropley, one of the three interim stops (no one else wants to do Ropley, you see, and we shall discover the reasons for this in a minute). This is the first time that nobody has asked why I want to come and work for free for their organization; this is presumably because the only people who are prepared to give up their time and dress-sense to mess about in authentic period costume (uniform) with steam trains must feel as obsessive-compulsively about steam trains as they do. Thus my job interview is pleasantly straightforward: I sit in the stationmaster's office halfway down Platform Two and drink tea out of an old British Railways mug in front of a roaring fire (it's 23°C outside, but hey) while being regaled with anecdotes about the good old days, and strategies pertaining to reconnection with afore-mentioned days through accurate historical recreation here at Ropley Station and the Watercress Line generally. The only question I'm asked all afternoon is to do with my choice of overcoat button livery. Do I want late Southern Railways buttons on my railway overcoat or would I prefer early British Railways? Stewart, Ropley's stationmaster, looks (and remains) perplexed when I answer that I don't really have a preference, that either will do.

'We've got a funny one 'ere,' he quips to Station Assistant Bert. 'Says he don't care what livery he has on his buttons!'

Bert finds this hilarious; but I get the job anyway.* My position is 'railway porter'. Everybody starts as a porter, then works their way up to heights as dizzy as, for example, guard or signalman.† I'm escorted to the back of a prefab hut in the station car park, where I am loaded up with kit: a white British Rail shirt (still in its crinkly wrapper), a navy blue woollen British Rail jacket, a pair of black trousers, an antique woollen British Rail waistcoat and a heavy

---

* FYI I didn't ask whether or not I'd be allowed to fondle the steam trains; though had I, I'm pretty sure the answer would have been 'Of course!'.

† There aren't any women. Neither, I fear, are there any waiting at home for those regularly volunteering on the Mid-Hants railway.

woollen navy blue overcoat. With these clothes on, I'm certain that I could besiege Moscow. If it rained, I would weigh six tonnes.

'All right f'ya?' asks Stewart.

'Do I wear this all at once?'

'Problem with that?'

Over the mountain of itchy fabric piled high in my arms, I mumble, no, I haven't.

'We'll see you in a few weeks' time then, for your first shift proper.'

Before I go, Stewart hands me a leaflet regarding safety on the railways; particularly with regard to not stepping on the electric rail when crossing the tracks.

'But you can ignore that bit,' Stewart proudly advises. 'No electric rails here, thanks.'

He begins to say something else too but his words are drowned out by the arrival of a giant steam locomotive (with a tail of heritage carriages), which toots throatily as it puffs into the station emitting enough steam to power several thousand Roman baths. *Flaming heck, a real steam train!* I think, and turn to face Stewart with bulging wide eyes, but he's whipped a pocket watch out of his waistcoat and gone trotting down the platform to blow his whistle and probably wave a little flag.

I drive home and exclaim to my wife that I've just seen a *real-life steam train!* She merely turns up the wireless and continues with her knitting with her hair up in rollers, just like the good old days; we'll meet again. Powdered egg.

Winchester Litter Pickers, Winchester Cathedral grounds
Thursday afternoon, 5 p.m. sharp
Winchester Cathedral founded in: AD 642
Winchester Cathedral's highest chart placing, in the New Vaudeville Band's song 'Winchester Cathedral' in 1966: #4

'Are you intimidated by rude and sarcastic groups of young people?' asks an obviously concerned Hermione as we shake out our carrier bags in the late afternoon sun and fix the heaving cathedral grounds with our steely gaze(s).

'Of course not!' Although actually I look frightened, flinch and then splutter, 'Yes!'

'Ha! I'm not – I give as good as I get,' spits Hermione. 'Come on, let's get started.'

We waddle boldly into the cathedral grounds and I start to tong on the right side of the path while Hermione selflessly covers the left – the area with most of the groups of young 'uns with baby-dreads, acoustic guitars and thick clouds of marijuana (dried banana skins) smoke. There is a large Indian family group wandering around over on my side, and they spot my (new, official, laminated, oh yes) Cathedral Volunteer badge and come over and start asking me questions.

'Who is buried in all these graves?' they ask.

'Doesn't it say on the tombstones?'

'Are there kings and queens buried here?'

'Doesn't it say on the tombstones?'

'Where is Jane Austen buried?'

'Inside the cathedral! Inside!'

They reluctantly begin to follow the point of my outstretched finger.

A group of footballing young 'uns present me with my next moral conundrum: since ballgames are banned, I don't know what to do when their stray football rolls towards me and one of the kids calls, 'Pass.'

I check Hermione's not looking and then slice a cheeky pass into a group of picnickers, upsetting their bottle of squash.

'Oh, *nice* one,' mutters everybody, while I timidly creep towards the far wall and its yellowing slew of McDonald's debris.

Then a circle of six or seven baby hippies calls over to me. I pretend I can't hear them but they carry on calling, so reluctantly I slowly sidle over.

'Yes, what do you want?'

'So sorry to bother you, but we've got some litter here; do you mind if we put it all into your sack?'

'I suppose.'

They politely put all their drinks cans etc. into my bag and then even say thanks very much and smile really sweetly and I'm thrown, completely *thrown*.

'The Youth of Today,' tuts Hermione at the end.

'They seem nicer than the youth of yesterday; for example the youth of my own, youth.'

'I'm sorry, you'll have to speak up.'

'I'm saying my own generation were probably even worse.'

'Half past five.'

Winchester Hospital Radio, Royal Hampshire County Hospital 7.30 p.m.

Number of UK hospitals served by national charity the Hospital Broadcasting Association: 406
Combined weekly broadcasting time of the above: 9,072 hours

'Excuse me, madam.'

My fellow DJ Ian and I are standing at the end of an elderly patient's bed, clasping our WHR clipboards, smiling.

'She's asleep,' I whisper through glinting teeth.

'*Excuse* me, madam.'

'I'm virtually certain she's asleep.'

'You're right.'

We move to the next bed. Its elderly occupant is bedecked with tubing, and also asleep. We stand and smile at her anyway.

'Time for the next ward,' says Ian, and we stride out under the fluorescents, halting briefly to scrub our hands contractually under the alcohol-rub dispenser unit that stops our germs killing those we are endeavouring to rouse with our broadcast (tonight's daily request show, *The Sound Remedy*, 8–10 p.m.). Ian retired from thirty-five years in the army just a few months ago; he says he's enjoying civvy street except for the fact he now has to choose what clothes to put on every morning.

'It used to be so easy.'

He smiles ruefully as we hare along the corridors just like real doctors; or at least real hospital porters – whatever, I'm trippin' on the vibe. And lost. As this is my first day on the wards, I'm shadowing Ian tightly as we stalk the wards for requests. After we've collected them all, we're to head down to the studio and attempt to unearth the requested tracks before scampering back up to the wards to present the show live via some *'Allo 'Allo*-style outside broadcast equipment cunningly fitted into a brown leather suitcase. In the meantime, we could do with some requests from a few of these patients (in case of request-free emergencies, a contingency plan comes into action, which consists of: *Quick! play some Daniel O'Donnell*).

'System of a Down,' says a young man named Barry with an earring. 'Or Korn or something like that; whatever really.'

Ian perks up. 'Great!' But then frowns. 'I'm not sure whether we've got any of that downstairs. Is there anything else you'd like to request just in case we're out of System of the thing or the other one?'

'Korn,' says Barry.

'Or any Quorn.'

'Rage Against the Machine,' says Barry.

'We'll see what we can do. Would you like to dedicate your song to anybody in particular?'

Barry sits on his bed and thinks. 'Just to me.'

To Barry, I scrawl on the request slip.

'OK, we'll do our best – bye!'

The next three patients are asleep; but a nice rather haggard and weather-beaten Scottish man with a drip coming out of his nose plus some other stuff requests Joan Baez.

'We'll definitely have some Joan Baez.'

'Och, that'd be *great*.'

We've only been going five minutes and already I feel all fuzzy and emotional. All this ridiculous smiling is real.

'This is brilliant,' I say to Ian.

'I know,' he replies. 'And it's addictive.'

Back down in the studio (the hospital's old cardiology unit), Dave the producer – an alarmingly young, ponytailed dude in a heavy metal T-shirt (everyone here seems to have a secret passion for heavy metal) and glasses – laconically belittles the evening's requests. It's quite easy to do this; so easy, in fact, that I refuse to stoop that low, for now. Instead, just as I'm beginning to get to grips with the record library cataloguing system, Ian tells me it's time to grab the OB suitcase and dash upstairs to start our show live from Clarke Ward.

Up and out of breath on the ward, we don headphones, plug our kit into the wall alongside the nurses' station, and prepare to hit the airwaves. Dave continues to belittle the requests through our head-phones as he cues up the tracks and the news and the jingles and tonight's Brain Tickler; and Ian and I grasp our microphones and nod at one another with gravitas. Ian looks down at the running order. I wink at the nurses. The nurses scowl back (we get in their way).

'Ten seconds,' says Dave through the cans. 'Nine, eight.'

'Am I going to be saying anything?' I whisper to Ian.

'No,' he replies, and then Dave says no too through the cans, then the nurses, and finally Mr Ellingham from Clarke Ward on his way to the lav and who *reeks* of piss. Thanks, guys.

'*Winchester Hospital Radio. The Sound Remedy*,' croons the jingle; I notice Ian's hand holding the mic is shaking slightly. We're on.

First dedication is to Jean. 'Hello, Jean, it was lovely to meet you earlier. You mentioned that the view from your hospital window is lovely. It really is, isn't it? And your request for tonight was Petula Clark, and her famous "Downtown". What a great tune. Well, here it is especially for you, Jean. I hope you enjoy it.'

Cue 'Downtown'.

'Well done,' says Dave down the line. 'You guys nailed that.'

And we really did. Twenty minutes later it's time for the Brain Tickler. I read the Brain Tickler from the script on the piece of paper Ian's holding. I get a bit cocky and ad-lib a little as I read; I sense Ian beside me becoming a little uneasy. The Tickler itself consists of my reading a song lyric. The patients have to guess the song. There isn't a prize, it's just for fun, I remind everybody at the end. The answer is 'Daniel Bedingfield'.

Having had their brains well and truly tickled, many of the patients now go to sleep. Those who don't are treated to the more cutting-edge part of the show, the bit where we'll play any rock tracks that have been requested, plus maybe a little Daniel O'Donnell to get things movin'. Ian and I leave the wards and head back down to present the rest of the show from the studio. Or rather, Ian does, as halfway down the stairs I am informed that I can go home now; I'm not needed for the second half of the show. Thanks, though, I was brilliant. I nailed it.

I nailed it.

The Mid Hants Railway, Ropley Station, platform 2
Tuesday morning, 10 a.m.
The official word for somebody (a man) with a devout love of railways:
a ferroequinologist
Number of ferroequinologists currently active in the UK: 25,496

The clothes I've been given and that I'm currently wearing don't fit very well: the starchy shirt collar rips into my neck; the waistcoat's too tight; the jacket is too big; the overcoat barely squeezes over the top of it all and my shoes are a size too large so I keep tripping over my own feet as I clump dismally up the abandoned platform to the stationmaster's office to report for duty. My red tie, however, is dashing as fuck. I am going to bring holidaymakers/ferroequinologists much joy today, I can feel it in my heavy, Southern Railways-regulation Y-fronts; at least, I can certainly feel *something* in there. I wonder who had these last?

'Where's your hat?' demands seventy-five-year-old Watercress Line veteran Peter, who I am 'shadowing' here at Ropley today. Nobody had told him I was coming, thus Peter's demeanour is initially rather uneasy; poor guy thought he'd be pottering around

Ropley Station all day in blissful locomotive reverie but instead here's me trussed up like a navy blue woollen chicken with a hideous Yuppie ponytail, demanding to be trained and made a cup of tea and full of questions that I already wish I hadn't asked, for example: 'What got you into trains then, Peter?'

I sit and listen to his answer for three-quarters of an hour until suddenly a bell somewhere goes *ding* and I'm so relieved I can't begin to explain.

'Action stations,' says Peter, rising unsteadily and patting his immaculate kit into shape.

We file out on to the platform, where a steam train is approaching in a picturesque fashion. As it chuffs into the station, the coal-blackened driver eyes me suspiciously; as does his fireman assistant, the train's guard, and then all the passengers through the windows. Perhaps they have mistaken me for Marty Pellow.

'What shall I do now?' I ask Peter, who is standing looking important with a whistle.

He replies, 'Make sure everything's OK.'

I squint up the steamy platform. 'Things look fine, but then I'm not really sure what I'm supposed to be looking for. Nobody has fallen out of the train or anything. I can't see any trouble. Not yet.'

'Good work, that's it, that's it.'

The train guard saunters over. 'Who are you then?'

'He's a new recruit,' replies Peter.

'New recruit?'

'That's it.'

The guard hoiks his thumbs into his trouser pockets and gives me the once, twice, three times a going-over. The guard and Peter then discuss the precise minutes and seconds of the train's departure while looking at their watches, waiting for this event to occur.

Meanwhile some passengers get off: retired men with rucksacks and waterproofs. As they walk past, they smile broadly at Peter but stare at me in confusion – clearly not 100 per cent convinced that I'm out of the 1950s.

'Welcome to Ropley,' I say, but they scuttle away over the footbridge to eat their sandwiches and stare at me disapprovingly some more.

Ropley's in the middle of nowhere – a tiny village with this renovated old station at the top of the hill behind it. After any passengers alight here, they wander around for two minutes before realizing there's sod all else to do except hunker down and wait for the next train to arrive to take them far, far away from Peter and me, just standing here hopefully, in our navy woollen kit with our little flag. Often they approach and ask what time the next train the-hell-outta-here is due.

'Twenty-six minutes and forty-five seconds,' says Peter, studying his pocket watch meticulously as the previous loco (we call them locos) eventually departs in a shroud of acrid puff and some tooting. 'And it'll be the diesel this time.'

'The *what*?'

You see, the diesel is a source of much controversy, as it's a diesel and therefore not a steam train. Passengers expecting only steam trains get quite traumatized when they see the diesel pull into the station. Occasionally they even ask for their money back. I say to Peter that I'm not wholly surprised by this, that diesels don't perhaps have the same nostalgic aesthetic tug that steam trains seem to possess. Peter replies that actually diesels have a magic unique to themselves and that people should respect this a little more; and then we talk a little more about diesel engines and I guess I ought to break in here momentarily just to inform you that I was once – back in my distant and naïve youth – how can I put this? A train-spotter. (When I was eleven. It took AC/DC to bring me out of it.)★ At the time, I took it enormously seriously, and for some reason (the curse of memory), I can unfortunately still remember all the train facts and whatnot that I picked up. I recite all this information to Peter as best I can, and he blinks not an eye. Why wouldn't I know all this, seeing as here I am volunteering on a steam heritage railway line? Even so, I feel proud to know at least something (information regarding diesel locomotive class 47s and 73s

★ For details, see my superb book *Hell Bent for Leather: Confessions of a Heavy Metal Addict*.

and 33s and – rare! – 56s). Plus I think we've bonded now.

Peter relaxes; shows me around the station and the loco yard and how to change the hand towels in the loos and where the urinal soap is kept. In the urinal. Then we go and sit down again in the sta-tionmaster's office and drink tea and Peter peels a banana and con-tinues with his interminable tales of the olden days. And though I maintain a vigilant array of fascinated facial expressions, beneath the woolly veneer I am bored senseless, and this goes on for about four hours, and I forgot to bring a packed lunch, too, so I'm watch-ing this banana like a hawk.

The Mid Hants Railway, Ropley Station, platform 2
Tuesday afternoon, 3 p.m.

And then after these four, long hours are up, I'm taken along to the end of the platform to sit in the small signal box with Bill, the also immaculately kitted-out seventy-year-old signalman, for a further two hours of brilliant shadowing. Bill's own signal-related pro-nouncements are so excruciatingly dull, and confusing, that after just ten minutes, I'm pining already for Peter's newly fascinating locomotive reminiscence. Bill stands me in front of the long line of multicoloured signal levers.

'OK, having listened to all I've been saying and with a train approaching *up* the line, which one of these signals do you pull now?'

'That one.'

'No.'

'That one.'

'No.'

'That one.'

'No.'

'This one?'

'No.'

'This one.'

'Right. Now go on, pull it.'

I pull it. Bill says well done. Twenty minutes later another train is coming through or whatever.

'OK, which one do you pull now?'

'That one.'

'No.'

'That one.'

'No.'

'That one.'

'No.'

'This one?'

'Getting warmer.'

'This one.'

'Right. Now go on, pull it.'

I pull it. Bill says well done. Peter now enters the signal box.

'How's he getting on?'

'He's a natural.'

'I suspected as much.'

By this time I am incredibly grumpy and pulling at the levers like a spoiled child; and then, another three or so hours later, finally it's time to go home and I storm out of the signal box in a huff and trudge back to my car and drive home. My neck is chafed to pieces and the thought of having to come back to Ropley Station ever again is more than I can bear, *plus* I'm not sure whether anybody (myself included) has actually benefited from my volunteering here today; except for a carriage-load of very young disabled kids and their carer-teachers who I helped disembark at about 3 p.m., and then chaperoned across the tracks to enjoy a nice though chaotic picnic over on the grass; later I leaped back into action and helped them back across the line to be escorted home in the diesel train which, thinking about it, they didn't appear to have a problem with, which made a pleasant change. Actually that bit was cool. That bit felt good. Never have I pined for a carriage-load of disabled kids as much as I did for the entire latter half of this afternoon, or a banana.

Or, indeed, death.

Step Five

Appleby House (homeless drop-in centre), Staines
9.30 a.m.
Number of single homeless people (UK): 380,000 (approx.)
Entire households accepted as homeless by English local authorities, 2005:
100,170

Right at the outset of this philanthropic, increasingly psychotropic odyssey, I had figured that at some point it would involve helping the homeless in some shape or form. Having been borderline homeless myself some years back,* I've always been particularly empathetic towards those forced out on to the streets. I know how easily it can happen. And how hard it can be to bounce back. One of my friends told me about this place a few miles up the road – in Staines – a place where the homeless and/or thereabouts can come to get fed and watered and hosed down and rebooted sufficiently to be able to face the rest of the day (and night) in relatively good fettle. This place turned out to be Appleby House – what's known as a 'drop-in centre'. Most cities and towns have them. They don't advertise, but those in need usually manage to find them. I had a little trouble myself, but then I'd neglected to bring along a map. These places don't have neon signs.

It's early, and I'm sitting in manager Brian's office, in a cramped attic office space, and he's taking me through the list of the High Risk clients, of whom at the moment there's just the one to be really concerned about and his name is Knuckles. I don't enquire as to the specifics of Knuckles's particular misdemeanours; merely nod gravely at the news that Knuckles is not long out of prison, is expressly banned from being alone with any female members of staff, and is potentially rather dangerous all-round.

* See previous footnote.

91

Obviously I'm eager to lay my eyes upon such a brute, and my vulgar curiosity is rewarded after being led back downstairs for the day's opening of the centre's doors to the town's waifs and strays at 10 a.m. Knuckles is soon over the threshold, and he's *incongruous*, just a guy in an overcoat, smiling at the floater at the door. I believe this just goes to show. Knuckles saunters past smiling in greeting and I'm sure my terrified expression becalms and warmly welcomes him to the centre and today's multitudinous goings-on, about which I have absolutely no clue whatsoever; thus I continue just to stand here staring at everybody, making everyone feel really really comfortable.

I learn that the job of floater is supremely important. Today's floater Kate's job is to 'float' in the Appleby House entrance hall – to meet 'n' greet; she assiduously logs all entrants, checks their bags (for drugs, booze, weapons of mass destruction), checks they're not under the influence of drugs, booze or mustard gas and then waves them through to the large day room at the back of the centre, where they all sit around and smoke and natter and wait for lunch playing pool on a table that could've been used as a prop in *Nuclear Destruction Derby VII*. The balls do not run true; nor are they particularly spherical; indeed they resemble vaguely pigmented rocks; those that have not been stolen or applied as projectiles, that is. There is a heavily stained dartboard which, though it's seen no actual darts since the summer of 1997, occasionally hosts an impromptu game using syringes. And then there is the ping-pong table, upon which I'd wager it's actually against the basic laws of physics to be able to play a game of ping-pong. Later I watch people try, and it's a bit like watching a miniature game of rugby. But then somebody nicks the ball and then someone else falls asleep on the table with his/her dog on top of him/her. And so, this is the day room – a room not unlike 'the streets', in that our largely chaotic visitors are able to behave as if they were on 'the streets' inside it: i.e. without having to utilize too many social skills beyond swearing while eking out roll-ups. But enough about me.*

* Have I used this gag already? What the hell - it's such a great one!

We serve lunch – prepared by chef Leanne, a formidable presence in the kitchen (think Popeye, only replace the spinach with a hundred tins of Sainsbury's Basics baked beans)★ – at 12.30 prompt, so until then my time is spent shadowing Kate and getting to know the clientele and their needs, which can range from showers and laundry, to phone calls and housing and medical advice; although most of the time Appleby's primary role is in providing a non-judgemental, neutral zone for those down on their luck to relax in and enjoy a free hot meal. So long as you're not fussy about eating organic or anything.

Today, one of our female visitors has an issue with a puppy she's decided to take under her wing and so, after a brief staff discussion, we agree that puppies shouldn't be fed on old hamburgers and crisps after all, and Appleby's coffers are prised briefly open in order to purchase some bonafido puppynosh. The puppy also needs a bed, so a large empty box of condoms is requisitioned and utilized, and everybody's happy; thus Puppygate's over before it's even really started, and all the while the staff are chatting and diffusing and coaxing and advising, *and* having to reply to all my stupid questions, such as: 'Ooh, where did you get that lovely necklace?' I'm impressed.

As lunchtime approaches, more people arrive, until we're holding around fifty. They're not allowed out again in case they go to drink, deal drugs, or hotfoot it back to the *Daily Mail* to file their copy.†
They mill in the day room and in the corridor; and we mill among them, having a chat, having a laugh, and avoiding Knuckles as much as possible, despite his constant (or is it my constant?) eye contact and subsequent Hannibal Lecter (in my opinion) sinister rictus grin (friendly smile).

A chubby-looking guy in a battered leather jacket called, let's say, Smasher, approaches and makes conversation with me. The conversation swiftly mutates into Smasher 'teaching' me weird mind games and tricks, which I suspect he's actually playing on me as he teaches

★ Later in the day I witness Leanne physically assault a malfunctioning fridge, and I *mean* assault.
† See Step Two.

them. I begin to get a bit freaked out, and realize that my keen-to-be-liked agenda doesn't always work out quite the way I'd like. But then it strikes me that I'm doing this right – that my role as assistant-to-floater-Kate is exactly this: to help all these dudes to chill and relax and feel less persecuted in their lives generally. Thus I let Smasher continue to mess with my head right up until the moment he suggests we go into business together, as a joint farming co-operative.

'I, uh,' I stumble as Smasher looks at me all excited. 'I can't – because you see I've got a baby.'

Smasher's face falls, but then soon lifts as he remembers another trick. Now he points to the wall and says, 'There's a nail.'

It looks to me like an empty piece of wall. 'There isn't a nail.'

Smasher's voice rises. 'There's a nail. I'm pointing at a nail.'

At what point, I wonder, does-the-fun-and-games stop and the paranoid psychosis kick in?*

'Ah, *that* nail.'

'You've got it, yeah?'

'I've got it.'†

'It's a good one isn't it?'

'Yes!'

I wander casually away. Smasher watches me. Kate sidles over.

'You shouldn't have told him you have a baby.'

'I shouldn't? It's true though – I wasn't *lying*, Kate.'

'It's safest to keep all personal details secret. In all the time I've been here, all I've ever let be known is that my name's Kate, and that I'm married.' Kate flashes me her wedding ring. It's overt.

'But hey, guess what? I'm married too!'

Kate looks at me. I'm doing it again, aren't I?

The clock strikes 12.30 and lunch is finally served. My year-and-a-half's previous employment experience as a dinner lady comes in handy – as I knew it would one day – after I'm stationed in the

* I'm talking about Smasher here, not me. I'm still just about in control.
† I haven't. There isn't a nail and I'm frightened. I figure out later he was possibly talking about his *finger*nail.

food hatch, on vegetable-serving duty. As a disorganized, heckling queue forms along the dining room wall, I don a pinnie, lift a giant stainless-steel serving spoon and wedge a metaphorical fag into the corner of my mouth. Kate, standing alongside, serves up portions of 'Cajun chicken'* and burned† jacket potatoes.

'Cabbage?' I offer, smiling sweetly.

'No thanks.'

'Sweetcorn?'

'No thanks.'

Client user shuffles off to a table with his stark plate of chicken and blackened potato. Here's the next guy; first he gets my winning grin.

'Some cabbage?'

'Och, nae.'

'Sweetcorn?'

'Hoots mon, yeuch!'**

Client user shuffles off. It would appear that these guys generally have a kind of fundamental and instinctive fear of anything that might actually be good for them. Had I instead been offering a ladle of: 'Battery acid?'

'There's a moose loose aboot this hoose, pile it on, big man!'

Thus we end up with a significant cabbage surplus; and those who actually wanted some are complaining I've put so much on their plates they cannae see their chicken for it. This isn't such a bad thing, I want to say, but Leanne is standing directly behind me with her arms folded, eyes narrowed and speaker-shredding Radio One over her shoulder, daring anybody to complain about the burned potatoes.

Once everybody's munchin', Kate turns and says: 'So, Seb, are you hungry? You must be after all your hard work this morning.†† Would you like some lunch? Help yourself!'

I glance at Leanne; she hasn't moved a muscle.

---

*Much as I'd like to make a joke or two at the Cajun Chicken's expense, I'm actually much too scared of Leanne to be rude about it.
† But not that scared, obviously.
** That's right, he's a Welshman.
†† Verbatim, ladies and gentlemen.

'Thanks, Kate, yes, I'd love some; mmm, delicious.'

I take a plateful, bury it in cabbage and move on through the dining room, where I sit myself down at a spare place at one of the tables. Conversation immediately stops. Two people get up and leave. I've seen this sort of behaviour before – in prison films and an episode of *Porridge*. I fear they might have mistaken me for a 'nonce'.

'I'm happily married, and I have a baby,' I offer to the table's one remaining and bearded diner, who is sitting staring miserably down into the plastic tablecloth. He continues to do this, despite further illuminative small talk from my direction, so I take a deep breath and eat lunch on my own, and the Cajun chicken turns out to be so Cajunny that it reminds me of my childhood in the Deep South; of England.

Keeping it all down, I repair hurriedly to the kitchen with my dirty plate where Leanne stations me on dishwasher machine duty. Let me tell you, nothing I've done in my life has been more fundamentally grounding than collecting, scraping and washing up these folks' dirty dishes. It felt like the *cosmically correct* thing to be doing. Everybody should have a pop at something like this, just to remind themselves that nobody's ever too big to scrape tramps' scraps into a bulging plastic bin-liner. Bring on the Cajun remnants; bring on the dirty cups with weird-looking shit at the bottom: I'll do it – somebody has to, and why the hell shouldn't it be me? Glorious waves of golden, enlightened self-righteousness flood through my synapses; I am in love with the world, and these people and this kitchen and this banging, clanging washing-up machine. I am becoming better before my very own eyes! I grunt with pleasure as I work and Leanne regards me with suspicion.

'You all right?'

'Oh yes!'

'You sure?'

'Oh, quite!'

I guess this is how missionaries must have felt as they massacred and enslaved indigenous tribes throughout Africa in the nineteenth century: all fuzzy and pious and drenched with the blood, spittle and Cajun gravy of the great unwashed. When we're done and the kitchen's spotless and gleaming,[*] I stride back out to the corridor grinning from ear to ear.

'Enjoy that, did you?' asks Kate sarcastically.

'Oh yes!'

'Well, close your mouth. It's time for the post-wash-up debrief.'

We gather in the Quiet Room. Tea is distributed. The day's particulars are painstakingly raked over, and it's impressive stuff: those seemingly innocuous, fleeting chats with passing fellas in the corridor turn out to have been less passing banter, more vital and forensic information-gleaning. Pretty much all of today's fifty-odd clients have been assessed, chatted to, aided somehow or other, provided with advice, or a phone call, or a quick chat. I'm hugely impressed, both by the ruthless pincer-glean as well as the astonishing depth of knowledge regarding each client's individual circumstances. And I forgot the compassion – there's also a *lot* of compassion. And caring! They are super-beings; I love these guys! This has been the most humbling and rewarding day of my whole life. I feel genuinely inspired. I check my palms for signs of stigmata. And then the meeting finishes, and manager Brian says, 'You can go now.'

'But I really—'

'Please, it's time you went. We've all got really important stuff to do.'

'All right, but I'll see you next week; same time, same place – i.e. here!'

'Yes, OK, just, look, there's the door.'

Hampshire Volunteer Park Rangers
Somewhere on a hillside near Petersfield
Official 'Areas of Outstanding Natural Beauty' in England: 35
As above, in Wales: 4

The countryside's pretty, isn't it? As we drive full-pelt through doggedly quaint villages, we occasionally pay distracted heed to the rolling fields, elegant valleys, winding rivers and mossy downs that scroll by as we angrily sneer along. Who do you think it is that

---

[*] To be fair, this kitchen's clearly never been either.

looks after all this stuff? How come it always looks so nice? Fields don't mow themselves, you know. So who is it who makes sure the English countryside maintains its idyllic veneer at all times?

Farmers.

Dan (rugged professional* Park Ranger), Zed (rugged professional† Team Leader Park Ranger), David (keen old duffer in off-white shorts and unpaid) and I** (see David) are lounging on a hillside watching a train cut through the valley below us.

'Ten carriages on that train, count 'em, look,' says Dan. We raise ourselves on to elbows, squint into the sun and watch the train cleave through the fields. It's a lovely day to be lying on a grassy hillside not really doing anything of specific merit, so far as I can tell. The train disappears out the end of the valley and we return to what we were doing, which was, erm, looking at some grass. But it's not *just* looking at grass – it's looking *really closely* at the grass: David even has a steel-mounted eyeglass so as to look at it particularly closely; while we sit here in the sun saying, *Isn't this nice*. Zed's dog Merlin is here too. He's friendly. So we're all sitting on the grass, looking at the grass, with Merlin the dog. It's a hard knock, life. Is it time for lunch?

When we all met in the car park of Queen Elizabeth Country Park an hour or so beforehand, the small talk was rather uncomfortable, as I had been expected to show up the week before; thus I had to mumble through my excuses, which were quite poor: I was there, I had just gone to the wrong car park.†† It was embarrassing. But Zed and the guys accept my apology, and off we set in Zed's Tonka

---

* i.e. paid.
† See Dan.
** Hi.
†† I'm still quite bitter about this. Zed had said to go to the Butser Hill car park, which I did, only to learn (much) later that she'd meant to say the *other*, main, car park. I sat there in my 'wrong' car park for an hour, on the grass, with my rucksack containing a packed lunch; and walking boots; and shorts and a sun hat; but nobody came. In the end I went for a walk by myself; and I saw a fence that needed mending but to be honest I don't currently have the requisite fence-mending skills at my disposal.

Truck out into the wild, wild brush not far from the exit to the southbound A3. After five minutes' rugged country lane-grinding we park up and set out towards some downland with rucksacks containing lunch, a strange wire metal grid-type construction, a giant pile of wildflower manuals (my blood runs slightly cold when I spy the wildflower manuals); and Merlin the dog.

'Is Merlin a girl or a boy?' I ask to break the ice, and it turns out he's a boy. So far I think I'm doing really well, really ruggedy, although the others don't include me much in their conversation, but that's fine – I've a lot of countryside information to learn and sometimes it pays just to listen. Today's task is to undertake a 'site survey'. To undertake the site survey, we have arrived at the site, and Zed has thrown the wire metal grid up the hill a few yards, where it lands on some grass and flowers.

'That's that then,' she says, and we sit down around the grid and unload the wildflower manuals. Zed hands me a clipboard headed 'Butser Hill Monitoring – NVC Quadrat Sheet', that lists the names of eighty-eight different types of plant in Latin. *Phyteuma orbiculare*, for example. There are no pictures. I am handed a pencil. There's obviously been some huge kind of misunderstanding, but I'm too nervous to say anything so instead I decide to bluff it. I take the clipboard and nod knowingly at the long list of plants in Latin and chew at the end of the pencil thoughtfully.

'I'm ready,' I say, followed by something along the lines of: 'Come on, let's nail these plants and be done with it. *Amo, amas, amat, amamus, amatis, amant. Caecilius est pater.*'*

Fortunately it soon emerges that the other guys don't know all that much about wildflowers either. (Actually the other volunteer David does, but he's too polite to rub our noses in it – most of the time.) We nail the first couple of plants within the grid – some daisies and a clover – but are soon arguing over what kind of wort, apparently, some long spindly thing is. The manuals all come out, and technical leaf specs are earnestly conjugated for a quarter of an hour. I take this

* I love, you (singular) love, he loves, we love, you (plural) love, they love. Caecilius is the father.

opportunity to have a nice little fuzzy daydream about butterflies.

'What do you think, Seb?' interrupts Zed in her khaki South Down Ranger shirt with chunky elbow patches.

'Cabbage white,' I eventually reply. 'Or white admiral cabbage.'

'Dan?'

'Actually it's a species of buttercup.'

The buttercup is controversially plucked from the ground and we all gasp.

'Please excuse my Victorian identification technique,' says Dan, sniffing the buttercup. 'Mmm, lovely.'

The buttercup's passed round. Mmm, lovely. Another train passes by in the valley below. We watch the train. We eat lunch. The sun continues to shine. Merlin comes and lies down right in the middle of the grid.

'Oh, Merlin!'

'We're not doing very well here, are we?' says Dan.

'I'm not sure,' I reply.

'I'm losing the will to live, to be honest,' says Zed. 'Usually things are more exciting than this. Usually it's things more like riverbanks, hedges, bonfires . . .'

'Yes, quite, bonfires.'

After lunch we look up a few more plants in the wildflower manuals before agreeing that we've all probably just about had enough of this now. We head wearily back to the Tonka Truck.

As she drives us the short distance back to the car park, Zed turns to me. 'So, did you enjoy today?'

'Yes, it was interesting. I just wish I hadn't sat on that thistle.'

'Would you like me to email you the details of our next task?'

'Yes, I'll be there. So long as I go to the right car park!'

Everybody laughs, including Merlin, and as I drive home I decide that I would really *really* like to be a full-time – I mean paid – Park Ranger, except in the winter, or when it's raining. But I'll tell you this for free:* Latin or no Latin, examining wildflowers

---

* Cover price excepted.

simply does not compensate for a vice-filled life. It merely comple-ments it. And that's just not good enough.

Appleby House, Staines
9.30 a.m.

Percentage of UK homeless that are male: 80–90%
Percentage of UK rough sleepers aged between 18 and 25: 25%

As I scan down the page, I notice there's a new face on today's High Risk register. His name is the Shadow. Just the Shadow.

'But it says to the side here that his real name is Jeremy, right?'

'*Never* refer to the Shadow by his real name of Jeremy,' says Kate. 'The Shadow is particularly dangerous.' In the column next to his name are listed all the unpleasant things the Shadow is liable to do. I read down the list and shiver.*

'We recently had to ban the Shadow from the premises, but it's been a while now and he's come back again and nobody's men-tioned the previous incident, so we're all giving it another try. It's down to the Shadow now to keep his behaviour in check.'

For my benefit, the previous incident is described in gore-splat-tered detail. I listen to it and shiver with delight.

'So if it's looking like there's any potential for *any trouble whatso-ever* involving the Shadow, then you must call the police immedi-ately – that's 999.'

'Emergency!'

'Right. The Shadow is also extremely paranoid, hyper-sensitive and suspicious, so I think it would be wise for you to be introduced to him as soon as he arrives, so that he doesn't mistake you for a secret government agent, or a cipher for the forces of darkness and evil.'

'So it's as bad as that?'

'I'm afraid so.'

Poor the Shadow.

★   ★   ★

---

* Stalking, knifing, paranoid psychosis involving knives and stalking, littering, body odour, halitosis, voting Conservative.

Before the Shadow's grand entrance, I'm urged to go to the day room and play pool with somebody, anybody. Project worker Tristan pushes me through the swing doors, and to the first person I see – a short person – I mumble: 'Would you like to play pool?'

'Yeah, all right,' mumbles Badger, and we shake hands. Badger's in his sixties and wizened, with greasy shoulder-length hair and tattooed hands. A drinker and – I learn later – an expert on the Sumerian and Assyrian civilizations. He plays pool from the hip, whereas I'm more of a Terry Griffiths kind of player: a thinker; a bore. Badger steadily annihilates me and then goes to sit down on a chair. I stand there for a short while and then decide to leave the day room, swinging my arms all carefree and natural.

As I push through the battered double doors, a short, incongruous-looking chap with tufts of black hair poking out from underneath a navy waterproof rain hat enters the building hauling a large black rucksack behind him – looking like a rambler at the end of his tether, basically.

Tristan sidles over and discreetly gestures towards him. 'The Shadow,' he mouths.

The Shadow creeps up the corridor, fixing me with a terrified, feral stare. Tristan quickly explains who I am. I smile and hold out my hand. The Shadow looks me slowly up and down.

'So you're staff then, and not one of us?'

I'm *appalled* that the Shadow might have mistaken me for an inmate, but wisely don't show this.

'Right,' I reply breezily; too breezily, for the Shadow double-takes.

'You're sure?'

'Sure. I'm staff. A volunteer even. Hello. It's nice to meet you.' I nearly add that I've heard a lot about him, but fortunately I just shut the fuck up.

'Nice to meet you too. I wonder. Do you like *Sesame Street*?'

'*Sesame Street*?'

'I said do you like *Sesame Street*?'

'Well, I . . . suppose I . . . do. *Sesame Street*. Yes.'

'I love *Sesame Street*, and I've seen *every episode*.'

'So do . . . so . . . do I. Love it, I mean – not seen every episode. I've only seen . . . not all that many really. But still.'

And he stands there and stares into my eyes for a further thirty seconds or so before finally taking his leave and heading down towards the day room.

'He likes you,' says Tristan.

'Oh, I like him too. I appreciate that sort of . . . thoroughness.'

'Do you really like *Sesame Street*?'

'Not really. All that bloody counting.'

'You *lied* to the Shadow?'

'I liked it when I was a kid though, I promise! I really quite liked it!'

For the rest of the day, I notice the Shadow shyly smiling at me. Later, he even shows me his most prized possession – a miniature stuffed Big Bird toy.

'What do you think?' he asks.

'Looks pretty accurate to me, Shadow.'

'Yes! And look . . .' He holds up the toy and does Big Bird's voice, covering his mouth with his free hand. 'Hi! I'm Big Bird. Who are you?'

'Hi, Big Bird. I'm Seb.'

'Hi, Seb! Will you be Big Bird's friend?'

'I guess.'

'Great! I think we'll be really great friends!'

'Yes, so do I.'

'Who's your favourite *Sesame Street* character?'

'Ooh, good question. I'd say probably Big Bird.'

'Good choice!'

Big Bird and I continue to converse like this.

'You know what?' I accost Kate. 'I do like the Shadow. In fact I find it hard to believe that such a nice guy can do all those bad things. I really think he's just kind of misunderstood. All he seems to care about is *Sesame Street*. How can that be dangerous? Big Bird is a fundamentally benign individual.'

Kate reminds me that the Shadow recently obliquely threatened to stalk her; and indeed that he subsequently 'just happened' to have been on her standing-room-only bus home to Weybridge, despite the Shadow having no reason to be in Weybridge, and in spite of his allegedly debilitating fear of crowds – of standing-room-only buses, for example.

'So what did you do?'

'He realized I'd seen him, and got off the bus. If it happens again, I'm calling the police, Big Bird or no Big Bird.'

'What about the Cookie Monster?'

'Shut up.'

Turkey for lunch, but without any trimmings, because Leanne feels nothing but contempt for poncey shite such as 'trimmings'. Fucking *la-de-da*. Murmurs abound regarding the turkey's pleasantness; and because of these scurrilous rumours, the queue is sixty people deep. Leanne stands in the kitchen glowering through the hatch with her arms folded and Radio One blaring out behind her. It doesn't take long for the food to disappear completely.

'Another day, another job done,' she says, hurling an industrial urn towards an industrial sink, making a large industrial clang. One of the admin ladies from upstairs comes down and hands me her dirty plate. My reputation obviously continues to coalesce.

'Thanks for that, Leanne,' says the admin lady. 'That was really . . . That really was . . . That really filled a hole.'

Leanne stands glowering with her arms folded, then throws a ladle towards where the urn landed; 1980s 'industrial' music used to sound exactly like this kitchen. Throwing myself into the unnecessarily loud spirit of things, I slam the dishwasher door as hard as I can and smile up at Leanne as the klang reverberates around the kitchen. She smiles back and tosses her grill tray crashing into the sink. This is a bit like that pottery scene in *Ghost*. In comradely reverie, I begin to wonder whether I might actually get offered a real job here soon; that would be great!

Or would it?*

Winchester Hospital Radio
Royal Hampshire County Hospital
Number of current hospital radio volunteers (UK): 4,205
Current holder of the Station of the Year Award in the National Hospital Radio
Awards 2007: Hospital Radio Perth

What you often get when you've asked a patient if they'd like to choose a song for us to play is: 'Well, I'd love to make a request, but you won't have it.'

But now I've learned to see through this initially impressive stalling tactic. 'Oh really? Try me.'

He looks up, sprawled plump and naked but for sagging pyjama bottoms, wheezing with wires coming out of his chest. I've learned never to look away. Looking away suggests distaste. Success is fixed eye contact – no matter what's going on with the body below – and smiling. In the very worst cases, the smiling can be visibly desperate, but patients always seem to appreciate the effort nonetheless. It enables both patient and disc jockey to retain fleeting elements of civil normality, even when we're doing something as meaningless as bantering about what records they'd like us to play.

'Something by the Beatles.'

'I thought you said you thought we wouldn't have it.'

'Oh, well, you wouldn't have had *that*, so I'm going with the Beatles. But none of that stupid Indian music they did on drugs. What a complete load of bollocks.' His monitor begins to bleep alarmingly.

'Stay calm.'

'Have you got, say, "Strawberry Fields Forever"?'

'I suspect that might have been a drug one.'

'Really? OK, how about "Day Tripper"?'

'Oh, drugs.'

* Superheroic counselling member of staff (unqualified), yes; kitchen assistant (qualified), perhaps less so.

'Well, how about "I Want to Hold your Bloody Hand" then?'

'You've got it.* And would you like this dedicated to anybody?'

'Yeah, to the nurses.'

Many requests are 'to the nurses'; the nurses seem to like it that way. Other popular dedications are:

'To everyone who's feeling down tonight.'

'To cheer everybody up.'

'For my wife/husband. Who is dead unfortunately.'

'Just for me.'

'Who the bloody hell am I supposed to dedicate it to, no one I know will be listening, will they? I'm in hospital, for Christ's sake.'

This last one's particularly popular; though we decline ever to broadcast it. Instead we say the patient's name followed by, '. . . who is one of [for example] Daniel O'Donnell's biggest fans.'

They don't complain because by the time it comes on they're quite possibly unconscious.

Tonight Ian and I collect an all-time record-breaking twenty-three requests for this evening's *The Sound Remedy* show. We swagger back to the studio like Dave Lee Travis and Mike Read after a hard day's kicking footballs into a mildly sunburned Roadshow crowd in Leamington Spa city centre. We are met in the record library by a tall, thin, unattractive young man whom Anna introduces as Jimmy.

'Jimmy is one of our star DJs,' says Anna, and Jimmy curls his lip at me like Elvis. 'You're going to be presenting tonight's *Sound Remedy* together.'

Jimmy looks like a nerdy, emaciated Shaggy from *Scooby Doo*; he has a strangely aloof bearing and regards me with contempt.

'Come on, let's go,' he grunts, grabbing the outside broadcast suitcase. As I follow him along the endless corridors up to the ward, he tells me he's not just a star DJ here, but also at a number of other hospitals and campuses (student radio – the same as this only more Bon Jovi). Jimmy says he's also a production assistant at a few *real*

---

* Though, it turns out later, we haven't. Ahem.

local radio stations. Basically, Jimmy's spreading his bets – perfecting his spiel on hospital and student radio until the call comes for him to be sucked up into the glamorous vortex of BBC Radio Solent. Happy-go-lucky volunteers such as myself are a distraction from the real job at hand (practising his links), and our relative ineptitude is a major pain in his arse.

Ten minutes later we're all set up on the ward right next to the nurses' station. It's seven o'clock and time for the show to begin. Jimmy is instantly transformed; a whole new persona emerges – let's call it Top Jimmy. Gone are his hollow cheeks, overbite and social inelegance; in their place stands a ruthlessly professional, oleaginous Smashey and Nicey (both of them, embodied within a singular torso). He ad-libs, he freestyles, he jokes, he joshes; his voice rises, it falls, it soothes, it caresses. Top Jimmy makes Simon Bates sound like John Cooper Clarke. It brings my ears out in hives.

'Crikey, Jimmy, you've done this before!' I exclaim as tonight's first request (Celine Dion's theme from *Titanic* again) flounders through our cans.

Top Jimmy manages to ripple with pleasure and sneer both at the same time. 'I've done hundreds of shows. Hundreds.'

'You sound incredibly professional.'

'Yeah, well.'

'Would you mind terribly if I read out tonight's Brain Tickler?'

'You *what?*'

Before we can negotiate further, it's the end of the record. Top Jimmy's eyes flash, he ups-mic and virtually whispers, 'The quite wonderful Celine Dion there, and "My Heart Will Go On" from that *classic* movie, *Titanic*. Coming up on Winchester Radio after the news, we've got blah blah blah blah . . .'

He can't even bring himself to say the word 'hospital'.

Despite Top Jimmy's cadaverous vibes, the fact remains that in several respects he's way ahead of the game; the only peril being that this is a dangerous game to be playing in regard to the development of one's karma. The harsh truth is that when this book is published, and Top Jimmy has achieved his dream of a slot on Ocean FM* or Power FM† or some other Vacant Nefarious Bilge FM,** then I *know* how keen I'll be to get on to his show to publicize myself and this book, kissing his raw haunted arse and laughing along with his ten-gallon gags in a crass attempt to ingratiate myself with his cult cabal of students, pensioners and pernickety drive-timers. And I'll be thankful. And he'll wield his power like a rusty broadsword, and we'll both understand that Alan Partridge has won again. Because of all this, I find Top Jimmy hugely fascinating, and end up staring intently at him throughout his astonishingly smooth and deftly ad-libbed broadcast. He catches my eye and wrinkles his forehead angrily. Poor Top Jimmy. Poor everybody.

Appleby House, Staines
9.30 a.m.

Billy's out of prison today. He struts, beaming, up the path wearing a very shiny suit.

'My lawyer bought me it. Six hundred notes!'††

You'll never see a more clichéd vision of a crim than Billy: polished head, flat broken nose, punched teeth, bull terrier eyes, comedy swagger – he looks totally brilliant; especially in the tight, £600 suit. Lots of the regulars are pleased to see him; a small crowd gathers around and he laps up the attention. Unfortunately, however, Billy's a bad influence on a few of our service users: Darren, for example. Darren's a sweet lad – polite, respectful and good-natured*** – but, as soon as Billy's through the door, Darren's eyes are ablaze and he's running in circles around him like a puppy in a box of condoms. Billy is just as excited. He heads for the day room. All that's missing is the donkey.†††

---

* Local.
† Local.
** Local.
†† In fact it was donated to him by Appleby for his original court case. Nobody mentions this though.
*** And a damaged, homeless alcoholic, natch.
††† It's a bible joke. You know – when Jesus rode into Jerusalem?

'Billy's certainly pretty popular!' I say to Tristan, who, it seems to me, is regarding all this rather cynically.

'Billy is a drug dealer. This might be one of the reasons why everybody's so pleased to see him. Or it might be because he's such a nice guy. Who knows?'

Tristan maintains a close eye on proceedings, because if anyone's caught dealing they're thrown out, and Billy knows this of course, and remains alert; *covert*. He struts back out into the corridor and glides past me, winking. The thought occurs that actually I could do with a little weed top-up, but I'm not certain this would be sending out quite the right message. Thus I eventually decide not to wink back at Billy, who is now nowhere to be seen anyway. Good work, everybody.

Later, on an errand to buy a ticket at the train station for someone who needs to make a court appearance, I spot Billy and Darren standing beside a fence in the station car park, gleefully necking a large pile of cans of super-strength lager. I wave to them but they ignore me. I hear them chuckling and burping and swearing. On my way back, they've vanished, and I never see either of them ever again. A week later Tristan tells me Billy's gone to London and Darren's now in prison. The Shadow's still here though – apparently he mostly sleeps in a shed that he broke into on somebody's allotment on the outskirts of the city, with his hoard of *Sesame Street* comics and his knife. He has managed to stay off Kate's bus for the time being.

An old and yellowed sheet of A4 is pinned to the noticeboard in the day room. Typed doggedly out upon it is the following:

A warm welcome to all at the door
Please don't bring drugs any more
Put your bag in the cupboard
Like old Mother Hubbard
Enter the time and your name in the book
Before you go through and have a look
Your mates will be there, and Leanne the cook

Having a game of darts or pool
Or a cup of tea or coffee for fuel
Use the shower if you like
See the staff, share a smile with Mike*
Everyone here, not all of them you like

See what's for lunch and rub your tum
Take your plate and say, yum yum
Always a queue, lots of banter
Is there any pud, shame there's no Fanta
Now it's time to have a smoke
Every day, there's another bloke
Staff we thank, and that's no joke!

L. Moseley
(with as much permission as is feasible)

Winchester Hospital Radio
Royal Hampshire County Hospital

Winner of the Male Presenter of the Year Award in the National Hospital Radio Awards 2007: John Murray (Victoria Radio Network)
Runners-up: Gerard Conway (Hillingdon Hospital Radio), Mike Taylor (Radio General), Iain Hart (Valley Park Radio), Dave Lockyer (Valley Park Radio)

I'm comin' right atcha live from Freshfield Ward, sidekicking Top Jimmy on the mic and he's freestyling, spittin' down the birthdays list, makin' it sound improvised and unscripted (although it isn't in the slightest) – if it's your birthday today, ladeez and gents, then you're in esteemed showbiz company: Bob Monkhouse; Alanis Morissette; *Edward Woodward*. All right.

A pyjama-clad pensioner shuffles past wheeling his IV stand alongside, on his way to the bathroom.

'Careful now, Mr Jones,' warns a nurse.

Top Jimmy glares; damn nurse is messin' with his flavour-flow. He

---

* I'm guessing Mike's an ex-member of staff; either that or a drug dealer.

takes a deep breath and gets right back on to the birthdays. Pat Boone.

A few requests later, Jimmy's mutterin' down the mic to Dave the producer when another nurse comes over to where we're standing in the doorway, holding our sheaves of requests, being important. She hands me five £1 coins; I regard her quizzically.

'It's not from me,' the nurse says.

'It's not?'

'No. It's a donation.'

I look at Jimmy. He is ignoring her.

'A donation from who?' I ask.

'That lady over there.'

I look over to the bed she's pointing at and see a grey-haired lady pensioner in a nightie sitting up in her bed with her headphones on – she gives me a thumbs-up.

'A donation for who?'

'For your hospital radio. She says years ago she used to do hospital radio herself, and she knows it's always short of funding so she says this is a small donation towards your station.'

'That's so sweet and kind!' I return the smiling pensioner's thumbs-up; indeed I wedge the mic between my thighs and give her a double thumbs-up with twiddles.

Top Jimmy continues to ignore the nurse. She leaves.

'Jimmy, can we accept donations?'

'No idea. Ask the producer.'

'I think we should go over and thank her.'

'No can do. I've got a show to present here, *mate.*'

In the end I go over alone, and have a nice chat with the lady – called Margaret – and she tells me she's been enjoying the show, and that she has a request in tonight herself: *The Pearl Fishers'* chorus (another request we get every night).

Back over with Top Jimmy, he's in full flight like a swan; like Concorde; like congealed Brylcreem slicking down the barber's plughole. He's Frank Bough doing the Streets, with Frank Bough winning on a knockout in the first ten seconds. I'm really rather shocked at his coldly contemptuous attitude towards the elderly patient and her donation. Surely moments of – especially fiscal – connection are what this whole set-up's about, right? Unfortunately in my self-righteous disgust, when the time comes for me to read out tonight's Brain Tickler (which Top Jimmy has reluctantly allowed me the honour of), I read out the question closely followed by the answer. I realize what I've done immediately.

'I'm sorry about that, ladies and gentlemen,' I announce. 'That was the answer there for you too, so not much of a tickler tonight, I'm afraid. Oopsy daisy.'

Top Jimmy is making frantic *cut, cut*-type gestures with his hand by his throat. I stop talking. A record eventually comes on. I hear a tired sigh through my headphones.

On our way back down to the studio after 9 p.m., Top Jimmy tells me he used to have his own show, but it was axed, and that he's still bitter about it. As is everybody else who had their show axed too.

'This is why there's nobody left at Winchester Hospital Radio – everybody walked out after they changed things around; after they axed everybody's shows and replaced them all with this new format – this once-a-day requests show. *This* is why they're so desperate to recruit volunteers now, since the exodus.' Top Jimmy is spitting this out with bitter relish. 'This is why they'll even have people like you broadcasting now.'

He realizes quite how rude that sounded and tries to paper over it but heck, I tell him, he's right: if they're relying on people like me to get things done, then something must be amiss, surely?

'Exactly,' agrees Top Jimmy. And then realizes that he's been rude again but at the same time realizes that he doesn't care – he's going to be a DJ on Ocean FM soon, so screw you, basically. And screw the patients too. His show used to be fantastic – everyone used to love it – someone wrote him a letter once telling him so; he appears to have memorized it and he quotes it at length as we stride purposefully down the corridors.

Step Six

The Southampton and Winchester Visitors Group
Southampton Library Café
UK applications for asylum received 2005/6: 22,750
Percentage of initial decisions granting asylum of the above: 15%

I am sitting at a blond wood table facing a thirty-something black man who is smiling broadly at me. His name is Appolinaire. I smile broadly back before remembering his circumstances and belatedly imbuing my grin with an expression of profound sympathy and as much sorrow as my eyes can muster. This all-new expression is atrocious; we are both embarrassed by it.

'Would you like a *cup of coffee?*'

'Yes please, why not,' Appo replies. He speaks with a heavy African accent but his English is good and I understand him perfectly. We stand to queue for coffees.

'How about *something to eat?*' I gesture expansively at the couple of cakes on display.

'Yes, why not.' He reaches for a muffin and places it on our tray. I spy a cupful of bright lollies.

'Lolly?'

'I'm sorry?'

'*Lolly*, look?'

'All right then.'

I pay for our goodies and we return to the table to resume our smiling – through the food and drink, which gets a bit messy.

Appo is from the Democratic Republic of Congo (a country that due to the stripping of its resources by shady foreign institutions barely qualifies as a bona fide republic; and as for democratic, you're having a laugh). He was born, lived and worked as a mechanic in its capital Kinshasa. Then in January 2001 there was an attempted coup and the

Congolese President Laurent-Désiré Kabila was assassinated; and the authorities believed a group of Lebanese men were responsible. Their investigations led them – via the getaway car they were believed to have driven – to the garage Appo happened to have been working in at the time. Appo was arrested and taken to the city's notorious prison where he was subjected to intense questioning regarding the assassination and subsequent whereabouts of the Lebanese men. Appo didn't know anything – he was just a mechanic. He was tortured. He remained in prison for five months, until one day a fellow inmate and former businessman recognized Appo from having had his car fixed in his garage; he offered to help Appo escape. Appo escaped.

He stayed for a few days in a prearranged secret location and then flew to Kenya and from there on to Heathrow Airport, where he claimed asylum. (He'd have preferred to have ended up somewhere like France, or Belgium – the DRC's original colonizers – whose language he actually speaks, but, hell, he wasn't in a position to be choosy.) While waiting to hear whether his claim had been successful, he was temporarily placed in Southampton, where he has remained ever since.

'What did you make of Southampton?'

Appo smiles – his nature is one of sanguine good humour and he laughs easily, using the top of his throat.

'Southampton was all right. But *cold*. When I was first here I had to wear five jumpers. Four trousers! Gloves, lots of gloves, lots of socks. But it is better than Portsmouth.'

I nod solemnly. Like 85 per cent of applicants, Appo's claim for asylum in the UK – due to a lack of evidence of torture and/or ill-treatment – was unsuccessful. Usually at this stage failed asylum seekers are forcibly repatriated, but the DRC (along with, at the time of writing, Zimbabwe, Afghanistan and Iraq) is one of the handful of countries deemed by the government to be too dangerous to return people to. Thus Appo settled down to begin his long period as a ghostly non-entity: a failed asylum seeker unable to be sent back to his home country but unable to work or claim any social security or benefits in this country either. Stuck. In limbo. Quite literally, a ghost in the machine; fallen between the cracks. Appo is officially destitute – he has been left to fend for himself somehow. The only way he's able to survive (or at least avoid the needs-must lure of criminality) is through a weekly subsistence payment from the organization I am now volunteering for, the Southampton and Winchester Visitors Group.

I am getting involved in this because I wanted to do something to help the plight of asylum seekers in this country. Because of their relentless demonization by the right-wing media, these people – who we used to refer to with the infinitely more sympathetic word 'refugees' – are having a tougher time than ever before on our shores; our alien shores; shores that ought to be providing them with safety, hope and perhaps even a new life free of persecution (simply *asylum*, you know?), and not resentment, opprobrium, or even violence which, to our collective shame, has sadly now become the norm rather than the exception. This isn't humanitarian any more, it's political. The SWVG began as a small band of volunteers visiting newly arrived asylum seekers in Winchester Prison in 2001, and then, after the Home Office dispersed a load of asylum seekers to the nearby city of Southampton, has since grown exponentially. It's now a formidable, well-oiled and nationally recognized organization, and its ranks include yours truly.

The SWVG gives Appo £20 per week and pays for an insalubrious bedsit in a run-down corner of the city. Since 2002 he's lived in eight different locations.

'So what do you do with your days?' I ask Appo as he bites into his muffin.

He shrugs, laughs, answers, 'Not much.'

I find it increasingly difficult to know what to say; indeed I can't think of anything appropriate or helpful or pertinent, so I offer another half-arsed Frank Spencer smile.

He shrugs once more. 'At least I am alive, and I have my health.' He laughs yet again and gurgles and it's infectious.

'How's the muffin?'

'It's all right.' He's wearing two jumpers today, and it's the height of summer.

The Southampton and Winchester Visitors Group
Southampton Library Café

Number of dead in Second Congo War (1998–2003): 4 million
Estimated number of daily dead in 2004 (the year after the war was supposed to have ended): 1,000

Appo had a bike – donated by the group – but it was either stolen or he lost it, it's unclear. We're sitting in the café; we've drunk our coffees and are now sucking lollies smiling at one another. A brilliant idea suddenly occurs to me.

'Hey, you can have my bike!'

'Really?' Appo's lolly stick protrudes at a cynical angle; and vibrates there slightly.

'Yes! I've been meaning to get a new bike for ages, and my old one's just sitting doing nothing propped up against the wall in our front garden. I'll take it along for a quick service and then stick it in the car and bring it down here. It's a great idea! Why didn't I think of that before?'

Appo removes the lolly and says, 'Thank you very much.'

'Hey, that's *my pleasure.*'

For the rest of the visit I stare out of the window in blissful do-goody reverie. Appo does too, politely.

A few days later I wheel my rusting old bicycle down to the bicycle shop. I stand with it at the counter and the man comes out.

'Hello. I'd like you to service my bike here, please.'

The man crouches down and gives it an inspection.

'You want my advice? Get a new bike.'

'But . . .'

'This bike is completely . . . How can I put this . . .?'

'But . . .'

This is skilled punctuation.

'A disaster.'

'Are you sure? It's not that old – it has, like, twenty gears or something.'

'Has it been left out in the rain?'

'A little.'

'How long?'

'Maybe a year or two.'

'I would never recommend that anybody ride this bike. As much as a bike can ever be, this vehicle is a death-trap.'

He takes one of the brake cables between thumb and forefinger and pulls lightly. It snaps.

'Oh.'

'You see? To fix this bike, you'd need to . . .'*

'Which would cost?'

'About £200.'

We look forlornly at the bike.

'Can I leave it with you then?'

'You mean dump it on us? No. Take it away with you. Now.'

I wheel the bike home and have a bit of a crisis.

Several days later I see Appo; we sit with our lollies and I think I'm getting away with it but then he suddenly asks about the bike.

'Ah, so you haven't forgotten.'

He shakes his head; and in the spotlight Nazi glare of his kind eyes, I panic.

'Right, well, I've taken it in for a service and they say it'll be ready next week. I'll bring it with me next week – yes! – next week you'll have a new bike!'

Appo smiles. We part.

The Southampton and Winchester Visitors Group
Southampton Library Café

My lie goes like this: 'Oh, well, I called the repair shop and they said, you know, it needs quite a lot of work and it'll take maybe another week or so to . . . finish. So next week. Definitely.'

Appo sucks delicately upon his lolly; looks pensive.

---

* He lists about thirty things: chain, spokes, gears, saddle, whatever else there is.

Rock School
Winnall Primary School, Winchester
Kiss records sold (worldwide): 80 million (approx.)
Kiss records that are actually any good:
somewhere between 1 and 2

Well, I saw the film with Jack Black and the television series featuring Gene Simmons, and they make it look so easy, so rewarding, this teaching kids rock chops malarkey, that I felt relaxed and confident as I made my way to the interview – a necessary precaution, so I was told over the phone, since we're dealing with children here, and they can't be taught by just anybody, apparently. But what about Gene Simmons? I wouldn't want anybody I know being taught anything at all by that man except, perhaps, that funky little fill in 'Detroit Rock City'.

Inside the interview room, I am faced with a panel of six interviewers, two of whom are under twelve.* I shake all their hands wishing I'd shaved, and am beckoned to sit. I see that everybody has a photocopy of my original application form, on which I had written – at the bottom of the section headed *Why do you want to do this?*: 'I believe in the liberating and transformative Power of Rock.'

I note that a few of the interviewers have underlined this section in red pen/crayon; clearly it was their favourite bit. The interview goes well to begin with, as I regale everybody with details of my various Rock Skills, but soon reaches crisis point when one of the children puts a stop to my intricate reverie and instead butts in to ask: 'Mr Hunter, do you like children?'

'Not only do I love children (which in reality, I don't), but I also . . . *have my own baby.*' (Eat my shorts, Jack Black and especially Gene Simmons.)

They appear nonplussed and so I say it again, with feeling: 'I have my own baby and his name . . . is Reuben!'

'Yes, but have you *worked* with children before?'

---

* To be honest, for this interview, I had been expecting just an electric guitar and some chicks.

'I used to be a dinner lady at upper-class educational establishment Winchester College.' (This is unfortunately true.)

They stare, looking vaguely horrified, but don't appear to have a follow-up.

When I stand to leave at the end of the interview, I knock a full glass of water all over one of the rock teachers. I expect this is why a week or so later I receive a call telling me that my services aren't required, as they doubt my motivation, but that I can come along to 'observe' the rock school in progress if I want. And I want, since I believe in the transformative, liberational Power of Rock; any time, any place, anywhere. It's a shame about the children, but hey. Maybe they should have respected Reuben a little more. Maybe *I* should respect Reuben a little more by not going to these sorts of interviews. Who knows? This is a particularly bitter footnote to have to swallow.*

The Southampton and Winchester Visitors Group
Southampton Library Café
Natural Congolese resources: cobalt, copper, niobium, tantalum, petroleum, diamonds, gold, silver, zinc, manganese, tin, uranium, coal, hydropower, timber
Percentage of Congolese population subsisting on less than 50 US cents (25p) per day: 80%

We sip at our coffee. Appo nibbles a muffin. There's a calm kind of a silence; a pregnant silence really, to be fair.

Eventually Appo says, 'The bike?'

'It's outside.'

'Outside here? Now?' He looks incredulous.

'It's locked up with the other bikes, outside the library here, yeah.'

'Can I see it?'

'Sure.'

We amble out to where the bikes are all chained up. Halfway down the row is an old, silver mountain bike, for teens. Appo appraises it.

---

* They never phoned me back to invite me to observe.

119

'It's small.'

'You're small. But I can put the saddle up; or down; or however you like.'

'You used to ride this small bike?'

'I did, but you know a long time ago, but *anyway*. Here, let me unlock it.' I unlock my own security chain, which I've thrown in due to a surfeit of guilt. 'Would you like to have a ride on it?'

Appo nods; mounts; cycles round in a circle, around the fountain outside the library. It appears to work; its brakes too. I'm relieved. I daren't tell him that up until two hours ago, this bike belonged to a Winchester teenager called Ollie, and that even now as Appo tentatively circles the fountain, Ollie has no idea that his bike belongs to somebody else.

The night before I'd been out drinking with my old friend, and Ollie's father, Johnny, explaining my spineless dilemma, when he came very much to my aid with a comment about his son's dissatisfaction with his current bicycle and desire for an upgrade.

'So maybe you could give this guy Ollie's old one.'

'Does it work?'

'Yeah, pretty much.'

'Is it a death-trap?'

'It's just a little out of date.'

'That's perfect. I'll come and collect it in the morning.'

So I took advantage of the number of pints my friend Johnny had drunk and drove around to his house in the morning after he'd gone to work. Ollie's mother only took about half an hour's convincing.

'This is such a *good thing* you're doing,' I repeated over and over as I lifted the bicycle on to the back seat of my car. 'A wonderful, honourable thing.'

She waved me away uncertainly.

'So you like it?' I ask Appo, as he squeals loudly to a stop before me.

'Yes!'

'Great. I'll see you next week.'

The Southampton and Winchester Visitors Group
Southampton Library Café

I have offered to teach Appo how to play the guitar.

'I just need to get a guitar from somewhere,' I tell him.

'I would really like to learn; very much.'

'Don't worry, I'll find one.'

'Thank you.'

I put my lolly stick in the ashtray and wonder whether or not my friend Johnny has a guitar too. I text him. He texts me back, telling me to fuck off.

The Southampton and Winchester Visitors Group
Southampton Library Café

Appo and I are sitting cross-legged in the park opposite the library. It's a warm summer's day. We're sucking hard on our lollies which, as regulars, the café now lets us have for free. Since I had no luck getting hold of a second-hand guitar, I've decided to lend Appo mine. I teach him E minor; I teach him A minor; I teach him D minor; the sad chords, for his sad set of circumstances. He strums them incompetently; the vibe is undeniably one of heavy and oppressive sadness. It hits me right away that I'm going to be a terrible teacher.

'I would like to sing as well,' Appo says.

'You *can* sing.'

'You can teach me to sing songs?'

'Yes.' I try to think of some songs Appo might know. 'Do you know the Beatles? You must know the Beatles, right?'

Appo thinks for a while and then says no.

As a stopgap, I teach him C.

'The Beatles were great, man. The Beatles are the UK's most famous group ever. You must have heard of Paul McCartney, surely?'

Appo shakes his head and says no again.

Meanwhile I rack my brains trying to get even vaguely beyond Youssou N'Dour. And fail.

'Youssou N'Dour?' I say.

'Oh, Youssou N'Dour.'

'Shall I teach you some Youssou N'Dour songs?'

'No, thank you.'

Phew.*

The Southampton and Winchester Visitors Group
Southampton Library Café

Percentage of Congolese population thought killed under Belgian King Leopold II's 'Free State' exploitation programme (1885–1908): 50%

Source of the uranium in the atom bombs dropped on Hiroshima and Nagasaki in 1945: the Belgian Congo (Democratic Republic of Congo)

I receive an email from fellow SWVG volunteer Christine informing me that she'd received an email tip-off from somebody suggesting there might be a new way of securing Right to Remain in the UK for Appo: claiming the right to family life under Article Eight of the Human Rights Act 1998, on a form provided by the Home Office called SET (O). Appo's 'family life' means a son, named Joy,† who is eighteen months old, and whom he had with a fellow Congolese asylum seeker he met in Southampton called Marie. Appo has just learned that Marie's case has been successful – there was video evidence of her opposition to the government, thus legitimate fear of persecution upon return – and she, and Joy, have been granted official Refugee Status. Marie and Joy live in temporary accommodation (permanent council housing accommodation pending) in Portsmouth, and Appo takes the bus down to see them as often as he can.

The plan is to argue that Appo has the right to live with his family; a family for whom it would be unsafe to return to their country of origin, as has already been proved and determined by the government of the United Kingdom. Kind of. Two-thirds so

---

* Although on the way home I remember 'Seven Seconds'.

† Yes, the name causes a lot of gender confusion.

far. It's down to me to square the circle; to complete their family chain. As you can probably see, readers, I'm in way over my head.

Apparently you can download a copy of this Human Rights claim form from the Home Office's website. So I download it, and it's as frightening as you might imagine. Its subclauses have page-long subclauses of their own. There aren't any pictures. I quickly minimize that and instead look up the Human Rights Act and that's even more frightening still. I warily scan down the Articles; the first one reads like this:

1. Everyone's right to life shall be protected by law. No one shall be deprived of his life intentionally save in the execution of a sentence of a court following his conviction of a crime for which this penalty is provided by law.

2. Deprecation of life shall not be regarded as inflicted in contra-vention of this Article when it results from the use of force which is no more than absolutely necessary:

> *(a) in defence of any person from unlawful violence*
> *(b) in order to effect a lawful arrest or to prevent the escape of a person lawfully detained*
> *(c) in action lawfully taken for the purpose of quelling a riot or insurrection*

I begin to feel rather bitter and resentful towards the kind vol-unteer who sent the email suggesting this might be the way for-ward.

Article Three is easier to digest: *Nobody shall be subjected to torture or to inhuman or degrading treatment or punishment.*

Article Four regards Slavery.

Article Five concerns Liberty and Security.

Article Six, the Right to a Fair Trial.

Article Seven: No Punishment Without Law, unless you've literally just stuffed a wad of twenties into the dominatrix's leather hood.

These Articles are all absolutely fair enough, but the one I need is number Eight: Right to Respect for Private and Family Life. It states that: *Everyone has the right to respect for his private and family life, his home and his correspondence.* * †

So it sounds pretty straightforward: just print out this Home Office form, write in all Appo's (and Marie's and Joy's) details and then state that he's claiming under Article Eight. I feel suddenly powerful, and just, and useful for a change. Who needs lawyers and shit like that when you've got a thrusting rapier brain like mine (devoted to the cause of justice)? It's a rhetorical question.

Winchester Hospital Radio
Royal Hampshire County Hospital

Anna, station kommandant, sits me down in the station's meeting room. She stares down at some papers; she appears slightly uncomfortable. I can tell she's gearing up to tell me something bad and I brace myself.

'Seb, just a small thing.'

'Go for it.'

'It was just, the other day, when you were up on the ward presenting.'

'Is it because I fucked up the Brain Tickler again?'

'No, but that statement is *illustrative* of the problem.'

I stare at Anna blankly.

'It's to do with your language.'

'Oh no, did I swear on air? I'm so sorry if I did. I don't remember swearing on air, but I might've after the Brain Tickler debacle,

---

* Oh, and also: *There shall be no interference by a public authority with the exercise of this right except such as is in accordance with the law and is necessary in a democratic society in the interests of national security, public safety or the economic well-being of the country, for the prevention of disorder or crime, for the protection of health or morals, or for the protection of the rights and freedoms of others.* I just copied and pasted this – I have absolutely no idea what any of it means.

† Article Ten, by the way, is Freedom of Expression; which might concern, for example, the freedom to reproduce articles of human rights law in a facetious manner without being Taken to Task somewhere within Article One. And Article Nine is Freedom of Thought, so don't even think about it.

but I was confused, but really didn't mean to ...'

'No, it wasn't that, this wasn't on air, but you did use the word ...' Anna lowers her voice. 'The word "shit", down the microphone, to Dave and me, when you were on the ward. I mean, it's not a disaster, because the word wasn't actually broadcast, but we really can't be heard, by nurses or patients, to be using that sort of language when we're up on the wards in our professional capacity. Do you understand?'

'Yes, of course, and I'm extremely sorry.'

'And you also said "shag".'

'I *did*?'

'Yes, you were joking about "shagging the nurses". And as you know, I like a bit of banter, but just don't use words like . . . that. Please. Not up on the wards. Just in case. I'm sorry to be a nag.'

'That's OK, I understand. It's sexist, isn't it? Sexist and nursist both together.'

'And if you could try a little harder to get the Brain Tickler right? Try not to read out the answer directly after you've read out the question.'

'Yes, of course.'

'We've all done it – but just not as much as you do it.'

'OK.'

'That's all. You can go now. Why not start pulling out tonight's requests in the record library?'

'OK. I'm so sorry about the shit and the shagging.'

'In the *record library*.'

And I'd thought I was such a natural broadcaster.

The Southampton and Winchester Visitors Group
Southampton Library Café
Number of languages spoken within the Democratic Republic of Congo: 242
Congolese appearances at the FIFA World Cup: 1 (as Zaire)

I was hasty with the lawyer comment; tipsy with noble Human Rights Act rhetoric. I could do with a lawyer right now. Instead,

I'm with Christine, SWVG's chief headmistress: a hepcat elderly lady with a sharp black bob, who's trying to help me through all this. I sit on her sofa as we drink tea and read through the Human Rights Act a few times, as you do.

'Well, we don't want torture,' says Christine, flicking through. 'Or slavery.'

'The email mentioned Article Eight and the right to family life, so I just wanted to double-check with you that I was doing this right. To be honest, I've never really had to use the Human Rights Act in my, ah, correspondence and all, thus far in my life. And I'm worried that if I mess it up, the consequences might be kind of horrific, you know? Deportation . . .'

'Torture (Article Three) . . .'

' . . . and so on. I'd feel pretty terrible if Appo got deported just because I'd messed up filling in some form.'

Christine suggests I write a letter to go with the application, in which I put down Appo's family circumstances in clinical yet moving, plangent prose; a little like those signs on pub doors that urge you to leave without punching the locals. Christine doesn't actually put it like this, but still, I think I have a feel for the appropriate tone.

'I haven't actually done an application like this myself; this approach is new to me,' she says. 'So we'll see how it goes.'

Lucky Appo, such pros on his case.

A few days later I see Appo and I tell him about this new avenue. He's understandably delighted; and excited. A religious man, he utters some positive-sounding oaths to good fortune – either that or he's ecclesiastically cursing me for being inadequately up to speed on the various Human Rights Act 1998 articles. Which would be fair enough. We're dashing with the lollies today, waving them through the air like Parisian cigarettes, and my conscience feels as clean and light as a little baby duckling feather floating down through the trees. Please don't ask what the duckling was doing up the tree in the first place.

The Southampton and Winchester Visitors Group
Southampton Library Café

The Home Office has replied with gnomic silence regarding Appo's application; instead it sends a request for £335, to process it. I neglected to mention earlier that to apply for Right to Remain in the UK with SET (O), you have to include a cheque to the government for £335. Certain categories (e.g. domestic violence, torture) are exempt from the fee; we had all thought Appo – being a destitute asylum seeker and all – was exempt from the fee too, but it turns out he's not. And even if we were to stump up the cash, that doesn't increase his chances of success: if he is turned down, the Home Office gets to keep the £335. Which is nice for it. Especially when to somebody like Appo, £335 is a truly gargantuan sum of money. How does the Home Office think destitute asylum seekers are going to be able to lay their hands on that sort of cash? And for a speculative application such as this? It's blackmail and roulette, all rolled into one, without the fun. I really ought to have been a rapper. There's still time.

I invite Appo round to our place for dinner. He accepts, getting a lift to Winchester with another SWVG visitor. He arrives bang on time, grinning from ear to ear.

'Hello!'

'Hello!'

'Come in!'

'Thank you so much!'

Everything we say this evening is followed by an exclamation mark! Which is hard work after a while! Not to mention incredibly patronizing!

When we discussed what exactly we were going to cook tonight, Faye and I had considered something involving okra, before realizing that not only did neither of us know how to cook it, but we weren't even sure exactly what it was.

'Is it a fish?'

'It's like a yam, surely.'

Instead, we cooked salmon; in special yam sauce. Appo left most of it, and who can blame him? My wife is a terrible cook. And I've been busy in the living room speaking with exclamation marks!

The evening is great fun, and the conversation never runs dry. Appo is excellent company and, despite his interminable predicament, still infectiously good-humoured. We offer him a bed for the night, but he says he'd rather catch the last train home, and I give him the fare.

The next time I see him, in the library café, he thanks me profusely.

'And you know what else?' offers Appo delightedly.

'What else?'

'I could not buy my train ticket at the station because the machine was broken, and then no one checked my ticket at the other end. I travelled home completely for free!'

His face suddenly falls.

'And I will give you your money back, of course.'

'God, no, keep it!'

This is strictly against SWVG rules, but if you don't tell 'em, I won't either. As for the fraud perpetrated against South West Trains: you can just sue me.*

Appleby House, Staines
9.30 a.m.

Average time between the triggers that lead to homelessness and when homelessness finally occurs: 9 years
The average amount of time it takes for the newly homeless to 'acclimatize' to rough sleeping, after which it becomes much more difficult for them to move back into conventional society: 4 weeks

Charlie, clearly drunk at the door, is refused entry. Everybody's sad about this, as Charlie's a great old guy, old hand, old lag – drunken old bastard, basically, whom everybody's fond of, except when he's pissed.

'What came first: the chicken or the egg?' says Kate. 'Do their lives fall apart, and so they then turn to alcohol? Or do they turn to

* Or rather: sue Appo. I have his address if you require it.

alcohol, and then their lives fall apart?'

'It's probably a bit of both. The vicious circle.'

Today, for the first time, the fundamental monochromatic under-current of melancholia in this place hits me hard. The sweet, sweet nectar of joyous self-righteousness (the novelty) has finally trickled away down Leanne's industrial sink: all I can see is the pain in every-body's eyes; the defeat; the hopelessness. But what can the staff do? What are they supposed to do when presented with the daily reali-ties of these off-kilter by-products of society? Give 'em a cup of tea; let 'em have a bath; allow Leanne to feed them; call social services on the telephone; give 'em some advice. Don't judge: this is what has happened to them; this is where they are; they don't need a lecture; they're *fully aware*. Kate tells me about half the visitors to Appleby House used to have jobs, houses, cars, wives, children. But then the booze (and still the booze) and now this (where's the booze?).

'None of them is ever going to be able to return to what they had in their old lives, are they? This isn't far from the end of the line for them. And it's heartbreaking. What's next for them?'

'Well, Leanne says there's pudding.'

And hearing Leanne say the word 'pudding' is like hearing a BMW driver saying, 'I never drive in bus lanes.' It plain does not become her.

But there's pudding all the same – ice cream that's actually just chilled margarine with some sugar mixed in. Stick *that* up your jacksie, *Masterchef*.

The Southampton and Winchester Visitors Group
Southampton Library Café
Congolese life expectancy (male): 54 years
British life expectancy (male): 76 years

After making a bunch of phone calls and eventually getting through to an unhelpfully aggressive Australian on an immigration advice line, I've reluctantly decided to ditch Appo's SET (O) Home Office application. The adviser angrily advised me that actually I'd been *mis*advised; indeed it would probably be a complete waste of time and, most importantly, £335, were we to proceed along these lines. He said it was much more likely that the government would just keep our money and reject the application.

I don't tell Appo this when I see him. He asks about it but I lie and tell him things are still under way – I can't face giving him the bad news.

Afterwards I feel like shit; strategic white lies are a dangerous road to go down. I don't know what to do next. Christine emails saying things are never easy when it comes to asylum seeker cases; she suggests getting in touch with Appo's old lawyer, Michelle, and asking her whether we couldn't somehow apply some other way under Human Rights law. I call Michelle and arrange a meeting, and the following week Appo and I show up at her cramped Southampton offices. She ushers us into her minuscule working space, where we haltingly attempt to explain the situation.

Michelle is great – young and earnest and switched-on. She thinks Appo stands a good chance of a new Home Office appeal under Human Rights right to family life (his partner Marie and baby son Joy), and she says she'll get on the case straight away.

'The bad news, however,' says Michelle, 'is that it's extremely common for appeals such as this to take at least a year to be processed by the Home Office. You could be in for an awfully long wait. The good news, though, is that they can't deport you while you've got a live claim going on. You'll be safe in the UK for the duration of the appeal. That said, this still means that you won't be able to work or claim any benefits.'

Appo seems pleased. This is progress, at least. And he's now in the hands of a professional (through Legal Aid), rather than me (ham-fisted, making-it-up-as-I-go-along aid).

'What are Appo's chances of success?' I ask Michelle as we get up to leave. She frowns and rubs her eyes. It doesn't look like she ever gets much of a break – her working day appears relentless.

'I prefer not to talk about odds. But I do consider Appolinaire's chances to be sufficient for me to take on the case.'

I wish I could talk like that sometimes – like people talk on television – though the dark circles under Michelle's eyes suggest such steely expertise comes at a price.* Appo and I repair to a café; a café without lollipops.

'On it goes,' he says. 'On it goes for ever. All I want is to work – to pay my taxes to the government – but I'm not able. And all these many Polish people, they come and they can work; it's not fair. And now they are letting Bulgaria, Romania do the same, but us – nothing! I don't even want to be here in this country!'

Appo says he's heard rumours that the Home Secretary might be about to grant an amnesty to all illegal aliens. He said this is the current word on the street, and that people are getting excited. I daren't tell him that in the current, hysterical climate around immigration, that's about as likely as the various Congolese militias giving up their arms for the sake of their beleaguered population.

'It's not going to happen,' I say.

'I know,' he says, and laughs.

The Southampton and Winchester Visitors Group
Southampton Library Café

As we sit and drink our coffee, I tell Appo that I have some bad news.

'The Southampton and Winchester Visitors Group has decided to kick you out of your paid-for Southampton bedsit.'

'Oh! Oh no! Oh no, no, no, no!'

'I'm afraid yes.'

Deep down, though, Appo knew this was on the cards. Because his partner Marie (plus baby Joy) has achieved Refugee Status, she's been given a flat, and because the SWVG is ultra-short of funds, they'd said to Appo that if and hopefully *when* this ever happened, he'd – naturally – move in with his family. The only problem is that Marie and Joy's local authority is Portsmouth – twenty-odd miles south-east down the road from Southampton.

* But I suspect not a particularly great salary.

'All my friends are in Southampton,' moans Appo. 'I know nobody in Portsmouth.'

'Except for Marie and Joy.'

'Except for Marie and Joy, yes.'

'It'll be great – you'll all be living as a family together at last! In, erm, Portsmouth.'

'Yes.' Appo sighs and looks out of the window.

'I just need to make a few phone calls to the Portsmouth housing authority people to make sure you can legally, you know, legally be there too. But I'm sure it's just a formality – I can't imagine why anybody would mind.'

'OK then.'

'So you have to be out of your Southampton bedsit in two weeks' time.'

'OK then.'

'To stride boldly onwards into your exciting new family life!'

'In Portsmouth.'

'In Portsmouth, yes.'

Our lollies are sour-tasting. There is a distinct absence of duckling feathers.

Independent Custody Visitor
▆▆▆▆▆▆Police Authority
▆▆▆▆▆▆ ★

Non self-inflicted custody deaths in England and Wales (2005): 93
Self-inflicted custody deaths in England and Wales (2005): 67

If you've seen the film *In the Name of the Father*, you'll be aware of the sort of thing that goes on every day in Britain's police cells, even

★ The Police Authority in question demanded access to this manuscript pre-publication, and I duly submitted it. They subsequently stated that the identification of the Police Authority in question contravened the confidentiality agreement I signed when agreeing to become an ICV. They also requested that I make all place names anonymous, and remove 'some of the more personal details to avoid embarrassment'. Thus I have either fictionalized names and places, or in some cases blacked out the text entirely.

for the most innocuous of alleged 'infractions'. I'm here to put a stop to all that sort of thing. First, though, I must endure the humiliating tedium of an interview.

'Hello?'

'Mr Hunter?' A stern lady's voice. Probably a pissed-up litter picker, phoning to bully me.

'Yes?'

'Helen here, from the ■■■■ Police Authority.'

Oh fuck, I think.

'Oh, God,' I say.

'Yes, well, you were supposed to be here for your interview for Independent Custody Visiting about fifteen minutes ago. Had you forgotten?'

'Oh, God!'

'Had you forgotten, Mr Hunter?'

'Oh, God, yes I had! It's because I have a *baby*. And the baby has been really *sick*,* and I'm just all over the place because of this ... illness.† I'm so sorry. I'll be with you in twenty minutes. Don't forget the ill baby thing though, right?'

'Hmm.'

'I'll run.'

'Hmm.'

And I leave Reuben sitting on the floor on his own.

Soon enough I'm sitting comfortably in the Police Authority building being grilled like cheese on toast by Custody Visitor Panel Convenor Graham and Authority Scheme Administrator Joan, but actually they're both lovely and explain everything fantastically well and are sympathetic about Reuben's terrible conjunctivitis that's so bad it's beginning to resemble leprosy. Yes, *leprosy*. They explain that Independent Custody Visitors visit police stations in pairs. And drop in completely unannounced, hoping – or at least prepared – to catch the

---

* He had conjunctivitis.

† A week ago.

pigs mid-assault on some poor, confused jaywalking granny (for example, my mother), to whose rescue we will have ridden; although a cup of tea would be nice first, Sergeant, ooh, yes please, I'm sure she did deserve it, yes indeed, Sarge, we all like a nice bourbon biccie; be quiet, Mother, and stop bleeding all over the lino.

Just as we're wrapping things up, Graham (sixty-something, wearing a mischievous expression and an Argyll jumper) says: 'Let me just ask one final thing. Do you have a strong stomach?'

'Erm.'*

'Because you get to see some strange things in the cells. And some very strange people. For example, there was one visitor – and he won't let me forget it – I took him out when he was quite new, and one bloke there in custody, well, he was staging a *dirty protest*. His you-know-what was all over the walls, and–'

'His what?'

'His *you-know-what*. You know what.'

'What?'

'Faecal matter.'

'*Oh.*'

'So his, this, *matter* was all over the floor and the bed and everywhere, and it stank something rotten, and this poor visitor, who was, like I say, new and eager, well, he just took two steps back. Three steps back. And then he said, *I think I'll let you handle this one, Graham.* So there we are. This is the sort of thing we can be faced with. Not very nice. As well as, of course, drunks and people with serious mental health problems, and people who can't speak a word of English, and so on.'

Frankly, this sounded suspiciously like the Appleby House dinner queue. Not that I'm equating Leanne's cooking to a dirty protest. No, sir. No, *madame.*

I got the job. It turns out they were understaffed and didn't really care who they got so long as it was somebody with a car.

Reuben had fallen over.

*See Chapter Three of my previous, superb, book *Rock Me Amadeus: When Ignorance Meets High Art, Things Can Get Messy.*

Appleby House, Staines
9.30 a.m.
Percentage of UK homeless over 60: 6%
Argentinians killed during Falklands War: 649

Today, for the first time since I've been here, the sun is shining, and this lifts everything and everybody: windows are opened and some of the heavy dead air that sits and moulds in this place begins to dissipate gradually. Which is nice because a few of these people do tend to whiff a bit; especially the Shadow, whose own aroma is a sickly blend of intense body odour and liberal dousings of aftershave. His is such a unique scent, I feel sure it's imprinted on my olfactory circuit board for ever – that if I ever bump into the Shadow again, his heady BO/Brut double whammy will trigger gigantic, horrific waves of Proustian recognition: *the Sesame Street theme tune.*

The Shadow is on edge today; he's annoyed by the volume of the radio in the kitchen. For Leanne, the volume of her radio is a point of absolute, confrontational principle – and woe betide anybody foolish enough to complain, since her stock response to complaints is to wrench the dial up even further. But now the Shadow is on edge, and nobody – not even Leanne – wants the Shadow in the building and on edge. The Shadow fingers Big Bird nervously, and is ushered into the Quiet Room, where I am already sitting, attempting to have a conversation about the Falklands War with a tall, rather elderly and bedraggled, bearded gentleman. I am having this conversation because a few minutes ago Tristan ordered me to go into the Quiet Room and have a conversation with the tall, rather elderly and bedraggled, bearded man, who Tristan said could do with a chat, and whose name is Tosh.

'I've got the Victoria Cross, the George Cross, all the crosses,' Tosh says, counting them out on his grubby fingers.

'Tosh, congratulations.'

'And now I'm just waiting for the call to go back.'

'Back?'

'To the Falklands.'

'To do what exactly?'

'Fight them bloody Argies.'

'What, again?'

'That's right. They're all just sitting there waiting to invade the Falklands – again! They are! And you know that Prince Andrew? Saved his life I did – last time we was there. And you know that Princess Anne? Saved her life too. Not in the Falklands though, this was in London. With the IRA and that? Great big bullet they was using – this big.' Tosh holds his palms a foot apart. 'Rip through anything, a bullet like that. Boosh. Thwack. Errrrrk. All over the place. Not pretty.'

'Princess Anne?'

'That's right. I've got all the crosses.'

Tosh stares beatifically at the wall.

'And now you're on standby to go out there all over again?'

'Right. The Falklands, the Gulf, wherever they want to send me, I don't mind really. Now that I'm not drinking, see? Guess how many pints I used to drink every day?'

'I don't know. Three? Four?'

'Seventeen. Seventeen pints, every day. But not any more. Maybe one pint every few weeks or so.' Tosh waves a finger disapprovingly. 'But no more than that. I'll not go back to all that.'

'I'm glad to hear it. My own father died through alcohol-related illness.'

'That's what can happen.'

'Yes, it can.'

'Right, well, I'm not doing that, not any more. Can't do that if I'm in the Falklands, can I? Well, you can a bit, but *I'm* not going to.'

And to be fair, Tosh doesn't smell of alcohol. He smells of roll-ups instead. The Shadow sits smiling at us. He's reading a *Sesame Street* comic book.

'Do you want to come and read it with Big Bird and me?' he quietly asks.

'I'd love to, Shadow, but I'm busy here with Tosh, look.'

'I don't mind,' says Tosh.

'No, *no*. Tell me more about how you rescued Big Bird. I mean Princess Anne. Or tell me about aircraft carriers. Go on. Quickly.'

'Aircraft carriers – now you're talking!'

Independent Custody Visitor
▇▇▇▇ Police Authority
▇▇▇▇▇

Number of UK police complaints, 2005/6: 26,268
Most common complaint from the above:
neglect or failure in duty

Before we get started in the cells, we must first attend a training day. Talk about patronizing. This involves a day down at ??? ???? – a huge Ministry of Defence military training complex; virtually a city in itself. Phalanxes of squaddies glare at me angrily (I have long hair) as I attempt to locate our training building and then, after I've found *that*, the actual conference room where we're to be briefed.

'You're late,' says Joan.

'I got lost.'

'Take a seat.'

We've all been at these kinds of days, right? Complete strangers sitting around a large table; pens, paper, coffee and lime cordial all lavishly laid on. At my place on the table sits a huge ICV training manual; and if a manual has ever possessed the power to glower, this manual was glowering harder than a Spaghetti Western box-set. There is a whiteboard; a laptop with PowerPoint all ready to go. Zero natural ventilation. Fluorescent lighting. Says Joan: 'I'd like each of you to turn to whoever's sitting on your left, and just have a little chat for five minutes. Then I'll go around the table and I'd like you to introduce that person to the group.'*

---

* Norman lives in Hull though he is originally from Penzance. He worked for thirty years in banking, retiring in 1992. Norman has been an Independent Custody Visitor for twelve years. He is also the chair of various employment tri-bunals and has been a high-ranking Freemason for thirty-three years. Norman also drives vintage motorbikes and is a keen cultivator of super-sized marrows. Norman considers his penis size to be 'medium'.

So you see.

Also present is a police chief inspector called Steve. Steve stands and talks about the law. We make notes. Norman then stands and talks about the Custody Visiting Process, aided by a PowerPoint presentation he designed himself. The text (Norman has used the Impact font) 'slides' in from the left. His text features a 'shadow' effect. Often, he impatiently hits the 'next slide' button two or three times and then even more impatiently has to scroll back several slides.

At lunchtime we are led across a multitude of parade grounds into a giant mess hall, where hundreds of squaddies and police cadets and officers and commandos and SAS and Double-O agents and that are collectively noshing at extremely long tables. They stare at us. I fight the urge to bolt; it would be futile anyway, as they'd catch me within thirty seconds and then play a kind of 'weird-rules' football with my severed head. Over lunch, I am unwittingly sitting directly opposite Chief Inspector Steve. We utter not one single word to one another. Heads down, we eat pie and chips. The women eat salad.

When the training day resumes, I learn something scary: you can now be arrested merely on the grounds that a policeman wants to arrest you. They used to have to provide a specific and legal reason to make an arrest (suspicion of shoplifting; being black), but not any more. Take a piss in the park, get arrested by some over-zealous, embittered copper (if such a thing were ever to exist), and back at the station they can (and will) take your fingerprints, a sample of your DNA, and even a footprint impression, just in case you're the Yeti. After they've let you go (without charge or caution), they keep your fingerprints and your DNA and your footprint *for ever*. This is all new legislation and, like Chief Inspector Steve says, the government has kept pretty damn quiet about it. Understandably, since it seems to me that what this boils down to is that we're now living in a police state.*

The time has come for the inevitable 'role-play' section of the day. We're led down to some cells which, fortunately for us, are empty

---

* Right, kids?

of naughty squaddies on ABH charges for the time being. An experienced Custody Visitor with a penchant for amateur dramatics is to
be our 'prisoner'; he assumes a different identity for each nervy pair
who enter clutching clipboards and cue cards.

When my partner Gavin and I enter the cell for our role-play, the
actor is standing on a small table at the far end of the cell, waving
his arms around in the air, saying, 'I'm flying! I'm a bird, watch me
fly! Wooooooooooo.'

I cough, and glance down at my cue card. 'Good afternoon, sir.
We are Independent Custody Visitors, and we were wondering if
you might give us just five minutes of your time to ask a few questions relating to your welfare in custody.'

'Woooo! I'm a bird, look, I'm flying. Wooooo.' He steps down
from the table and dances around the cell waving his arms.

My partner and I exchange glances.

'OK, sir, erm, have you been given access to a solicitor at all?'

'Wheeeee! Woooooo! Look! In the corner, behind you, a cat!
Come here, little kitty! Meeeeow! Come on kitty-cat, come to
Daddy.'

'May we ask, sir, have you had or been offered a meal at any point
since you've been in custody?'

'Look at the little kitty-cat, just down there! Isn't he sweet?' The
prisoner shuffles towards us.

This actor is *brilliant*.

'Erm, may we ask, sir, have you been given . . . Oof!'

The prisoner has attacked us. He has his hand around my throat
and is pushing me up against the cell wall. It's just like you get in
The Bill. I attempt to shout, 'Sarge!', but the prisoner has a tight
hold of my thorax. With his other hand, he has Gavin by the throat.
I have to say, it is all very convincing, although getting a little
unnecessary now, to be fair. With our heads still rammed up against
the wall, Gavin and I squint at one another.

'Erm,' I croak.

'Help!' my partner squeaks.

Our 'scene' is terminated.

Outside, my partner and I are frowned upon by the group.
'Now,' says Joan. 'What did Sebastian and Gavin do wrong there?'
'Where do we start?' offers somebody.
Factions.

Back in the hot and stuffy conference room, the training continues. As the afternoon agonizingly progresses, I feel a strange and powerful emotion rising within. At first, I assume it's either fact-fatigue or terminal boredom but, somewhat incredibly, it isn't. It's something way more unfamiliar than either of those – those I'd recognize, facts excepted. I let this weird sensation rattle around for a while. I let it inflate and grow while I fiddle with my selection of Biros and try to put my finger on what exactly it is. And then, at some point in between the Health and Safety Q&A and another whiteboard brainstorm, I suddenly recognize this nascent metaphysical prang.
It's power.
Power. Bubbling, hot, steaming, molten *power*. I'm going to be able to lord it over an entire police station!
'Oi, you there, Constable! Open this door immediately. And go and stand over there – quick march, double bloody pronto. Or else!'
My head lolls deliriously as I mentally humiliate every last officer in the station. A heady cocktail of adrenaline, serotonin and testosterone overwhelms me, and I begin to grin inanely at Chief Inspector Steve on the other side of the conference table. I can't help myself. Chief Inspector Steve looks frightened. As well he should.
I am not sure this awesome Castle Greyskull-grade power has much potential to improve me as a person. It feels too good to be having any positive effect upon my morality synapses. But then good kings (Solomon, Wenceslas, Alfred, Charles III,* Lord Alan Sugar) managed to marry power with responsibility (and good deeds), right? Must power corrupt? To quote that great philosopher Harry Shearer: 'If absolute power corrupts absolutely, does absolute powerlessness make you pure?' I make a mental note to ask a few of

* Ha ha ha ha ha ha ha ha ha ha ha.

the guys at Appleby House about this chewy conundrum next time I'm there.

Throughout the remainder of the training day I keep expecting the Custody Visitor actor to come over and apologize for his earlier unnecessarily prolonged attack on us in the cells, but he doesn't. My neck, where he grabbed it, is sore. I am considering suing him and Chief Inspector Steve both. And Gavin for not helping me. And some squaddies chosen at random. But I hold my fire for the time being, and instead decide to take my revenge in a few weeks' time, *inside the police station.*

The Southampton and Winchester Visitors Group
Portsmouth Library Café

You might have noticed that the library café in the heading above has switched cities. This is because Appo has now moved out of his Southampton bedsit and into – well, *onto* really – a friend's floor in Portsmouth. Marie and Joy's new, permanent council accommodation has been delayed by six months, and they have been housed in temporary council accommodation while they wait. But it would appear that Appo's not allowed to stay there with them; the council has expressly banned him from doing so. And since the SWVG has stopped paying for his accommodation in Southampton, this has turned into a bit of a fuck-up, to be honest. One minute Appo was happy there in his bedsit, the next he's in an unfamiliar city living with some bloke he barely knows.

'I'm sorry about this,' I offer, as we sit drinking tepid coffee in the considerably more depressing environs of Portsmouth library's third-floor café, where the waitress was quite openly and unapologetically resentful about having to serve a black man. I merely received a sneer, but Appo got the full-on distasteful expression of disgust.

'Don't worry,' I tell Appo. 'You won't be on your friend's floor for long, I promise. I'll speak to the housing people and get them to change their minds. This whole situation is ridiculous; for God's sake, Marie and Joy are in this great big city-centre flat and you, the child's own *father*, aren't allowed to stay there with them? It's absurd!'

Appo stares morosely into his coffee cup.

'This time next week, we'll have you in there with them. No more council workers coming round and turfing you out at seven o'clock in the morning.'

'I was asleep.'

'I know.'

'With my own family.'

'I know.'

'And they came and banged on the door and told me to *get out* of there.'

'I know.'

'Out of my family's apartment? Why is there a problem with this? I don't understand.'

'I know. I mean, I don't know. It's bullshit. But don't worry. I'll sort it.'

The waitress lumbers over and snatches away both our coffee cups even though Appo clearly hasn't finished.

'She is not so friendly,' chuckles Appo, wiping his mouth.

And once more I can only admire Appo's relentless ability to keep on chucklin' in these sorts of situations, five long years down the line.

Appleby House, Staines
9.30 a.m.

Percentage of UK rough sleepers who have been either
in prison or on remand: 50%
Percentage of those released from UK prisons who report having
nowhere to stay: 33%

One constant presence at Appleby House – filth and despair notwithstanding – is a short, hyperactive young man named Kevin. Kevin is seventeen, though he looks much younger (this helps when it comes to looking innocent while shoplifting), and he dresses in low-spec Chav Chic – baggy tracky-bottoms, baggy branded T, baggy tracky-top, baggy branded baseball cap, all set off by wristfuls of cheap, gold-plated jewellery. His gaunt frame writhes around within this get-up as he busies himself performing his daily ritual as Appleby House's own irritating wasp-in-residence.

Kevin's role in an average day's proceedings is to buzz around everywhere, winding everybody up, which eventually – inevitably – leads to somebody or other* attempting to swat him. By this I mean punch him in the face or lamp him with a pool cue.

But I like Kevin. In fact, secretly, pretty much everybody does deep down. He's cute, and funny, and is – if you'll excuse the cliché – *a good kid at heart.* You can just tell. He's like a hyperactive, criminal puppy. Bless. But of course he's troubled, and has fallen in with a bad crowd (the Appleby crowd), and has had a turbulent family life and basically can't be trusted; he needs guidance.

Always one of the first to arrive in the morning, Kevin comes swinging up the corridor, whining: 'Have I got any post?'

'It hasn't arrived yet, Kevin.'

Five minutes later, he bursts through the day room doors – pursued by shouting – and buzzes around the staff's legs, whining: 'Have I got any post?'

'The post hasn't arrived yet, Kevin.'

Kevin tuts, jogs down to the toilets and back again, smirking and flicking the walls as he goes; and back again; and through the day room doors to goad whoever's trying to play ping-pong. And back again.

'Have I got any post?'

'It hasn't arrived yet, Kevin.'

'*Tsk.* Why not?'

'Have I got any post?'

'No.'

---

* Usually a tired, elderly alcoholic trying to have a quiet game of pool. That's if anyone'll give me a game. Thanks again.

'What d'you mean, no? I'm expecting a letter, innit.'

'Well, it hasn't come today. Who's this letter supposed to be from?'

'Someone, innit. Have I got any post or what?'

'Maybe it'll come tomorrow.'

'*Tsk,* it's meant to be coming today, innit. You sure I haven't got any post?'

Kevin skitters off back towards the day room, avoiding several swung punches along the way: and this is Kevin's day-to-day.

We have a special guest visitor in the House today. His name is Alan. Alan is a representative of the Wildlife Trust, and he is wearing all green, like a volunteer ranger, only not as cool. Alan is standing in the corridor talking to a few members of staff about the forthcoming Big Move. Appleby House is moving a quarter of a mile down the road to brand-new, specially built premises that some say – at a distance of roughly thirty yards from the police station – is roughly thirty yards too close to the police station. But it's happening nonetheless, in about a year. Indeed it would have happened already were it not for the protected bats that are apparently in residence in the building due to be demolished to make way for the spanking-new Appleby House. The bats have delayed the move by – I'm told – a whole *year*. It's nice to know where the authorities' priorities lie, don't you think?

Anyway, Alan is here to rustle up a bunch of volunteers to come down and take some active interest in the Wildlife Trust-owned nature reserve that backs on to the new premises. He's trying to persuade some of our clients to participate in a 'nature walk' around the reserve this morning. The Appleby House staff think this is extremely amusing, especially after it soon becomes clear that Alan isn't wholly aware of the exact sociological make-up of our client group. He talks fervently about nature, and about the fact that he has somehow attained the funding to support his venture. Indeed there is so much funding rattling about* that Alan is accompanied today by a consul-

---

* Not in the direction of the House, I must add.

tant, Joyce, who stands alongside him carrying a bag full of sketch pads and disposable cameras, for those who want to join the nature walk to draw a duck, or take a photograph of a swan, should they feel inspired. Joyce looks nervous. Who can blame her? Her bag of valuable cameras and notebooks are about to be stolen.

An hour or so later, after much delusional canvassing, Alan and Joyce have two volunteers for the nature walk: Kevin, and Kevin's dodgy mate, Garry.

'I'll push you in the fucking river, you annoying little twat,' quips Garry good-naturedly to Kevin as we stand around waiting to embark.

I say 'we', because Kate just came over and asked whether I'd like to go along too, and that it would be *so helpful* if I could, as she *really couldn't* spare any full-time staff, so I'd be just *perfect*.

'It might be rather *muddy* in the nature reserve,' says Alan, who is unable to say anything without sounding monumentally patronizing, and who's trying *so* hard to disguise his heartbreak at the paucity of volunteers. 'Because today, you see, everybody, outside, it has been *raining*.'

'No, *I'll* chuck *you* in the river, you fucking wanker,' says Kevin to Garry.

And so off we set. Out of the front doors – which Tristan kindly unlocks, grinning – and down towards the nature reserve. Along the way, Kevin and Garry repeatedly push one another into the oncoming traffic.

'Whoa now,' says Alan, fingering the special emergency safety rope thing that dangles from his utility belt. Drivers beep, yell, swerve. '*Whoa* now.'

I strike up a conversation with Joyce. It turns out that she's come all the way down from the Peak District, just for this.

'*Just for this?*' I cry. 'You've come all the way down from the north of England just for this nature reserve walk here today in Staines with me and Kevin and Garry?'

'That's right,' she says.

She talks about what exactly her consultancy firm does, but it makes no sense to me; I'm not familiar with the sorts of phrases she's using, e.g. 'outsourcing', and 'rationalizing the business model' and then, worriedly, 'those two are going to get run over in a minute'.

Joyce is due to head back to the Peak District this afternoon, after the nature walk. Perhaps this illustrates why people are occasionally cynical about consultants. I don't know.

We arrive at the nature reserve, and Garry immediately grabs hold of Kevin and drags him towards the river's edge.

'You dare. No! Fuck off! Fuck off!' They scuffle.

A pair of strolling pensioners pass us along the path and I smile at them in greeting, but they don't smile back.

'Fuck the fuck off!'

'Now then,' says Alan, fingering his emergency rope.

Joyce fingers the sketch books and cameras in her holdall.

Garry fingers Kevin's tracky-jacket.

'I'm afraid you're going to get mud on your shoes, as it's a little muddy since rainfall has been somewhat higher than the seasonal norm,' says Alan. 'Mind out for the puddles!'

We cross a bridge, which Garry threatens to throw Kevin off.

'Oh look,' says Alan, raising his binoculars. 'A moorhen.'

Garry has thrown Kevin's lighter into the river.

'Get that back, you wanker!'

'Fucking make me, dickhead.'

'Get it back now or you're dead.'

Joyce looks through the binoculars. 'You're right, Alan, it *is* a moorhen.'

Garry and Kevin take turns to see who can spit furthest from the bridge.

And then in a blink of a wagtail's eye, lush strings blare out from the heavens and everything turns Spielberg. Kevin and Garry suddenly pick up on something Alan has said about swans – probably that old chestnut about them being able to break a grown man's arm.

'Yeah, but if some dickhead came too close to me I'd break his arm and all.'

'Yeah,' says Garry, and then threatens to break Kevin's arm, 'for practice'.

Macho statements duly out of the way, Kevin proceeds to talk, succinctly and engagingly, about swans as we walk. He tells us about their mating cycles, the number of eggs they typically lay, and a little about the black swan, most commonly found in the Antipodes. Even more amazingly, Garry also then chips in with his own swan ephemera. The swearing has stopped, as has the riverside scuffling. We're all just strolling down the muddy paths, talking offhandedly about nature. Well, the other guys are – I'm just listening. I didn't know any of this stuff, and I'm a genuine outdoorsy, yomping-kinda-dude. The guys then spot what looks to me like a crow.

'Blackbird, look,' says Garry.

'Male blackbird,' adds Kevin. 'Female blackbirds have brown plumage and a brown beak. So do the young ones. It's only the full-grown males that are black, ain't it, Garry?'

'Yep. Full-grown males also have yellow rings round their eyes,' adds Garry. 'Like that one.'

'Right,' says Kevin. 'And yellow beaks.'

Alan is rather lost for words. I think we all are. Joyce fingers her bag of sketch books. The conversation switches to voles and water rats; then to various ducks; and then on to grassland and fence-maintenance (to be fair, this is because Alan has started up talking again, and the guys are back to trying to push each other into the water).

'How do you know all that stuff about birds and that, Kevin?' I ask.

He shrugs. 'My stepdad I suppose. And I used to walk my dog round here, and you get to know stuff. I like it, nature and stuff. That's why I came on this walk, innit. S'nice. Why d'you think I fucking came on it? To hang out with you? *Not.*'

'Nature is important,' Garry admonishes me. 'I used to live in a tent just over there,' he adds, pointing to some grassy marshland.

'Was that with Ferret?' asks Kevin.

'Yeah.'

'Ferret nicked my bike, the bastard.'

'*You're* the bastard.'

Alan fingers his safety rope. Apologizes for the mud. Twenty minutes later, we've completed the trail circuit and pause in the spring sunlight to reflect. Kevin and Garry stand and spit. Alan, Joyce and I stare vacantly at their spit fizzing in the mud.

'Do you Wildlife Trust guys have anything to do with Park Rangers?' I ask Alan.

'No, we do not,' he says, anger rising in his voice. It turns out that the Wildlife Trust and Park Rangers are like countryside 'rivals' – in fact they openly resent one another.

'We manage *entire sites*, like here, and other great big, demanding sites like these,' says Alan. 'Unlike Park Rangers, who just go out and do a bit here and a bit there. Sometimes even on private land.'

The horror. I decide not to tell Alan I am a senior-ranking Park Ranger, just about. We walk back to Appleby House for lunch in silence (Leanne's cooking has that effect – it's morale-sapping). Garry pushes Kevin into three lampposts, a man in a wheelchair and a mother with a buggy.

After lunch, Joyce boards her train back home to the Peak District; Kevin heads back to his room in a council-run apartment block for troubled kids; and Garry, who is currently sleeping rough, heads back out on to the streets. Kevin tells me Ferret is living in a van in Reading, and that he still wants his fucking bike back.

Independent Custody Visitor
Camberwick Green* Police Station
Camberwick Green

Even though I have forgotten all my training, fortunately I can still feel the self-righteous power flooding through my creaking arteries; which is fortunate, since it's pouring down with rain and I'm getting soaked through standing waiting for my partner outside the police station. *They'll* pay for this*, I think, as freezing cold rivulets

---

* I have made the location of this police station anonymous.

148

trickle off my pretty nose. Soon my partner's vehicle rolls up and we shake hands. His name is Stan; he's in his fifties and chirpy.

'Your first time, eh?' says Stan. 'I'll have to try to remember how to do this properly then!' he jokes. At least I think he jokes.

We enter the police station, and the first thing I see is Kevin, from Appleby House, arguing with a policeman through a hatch.

Kevin turns, and eyes us suspiciously. 'What are you doing here? Are you some fucking copper's mate or what?'

I stand there, dripping, and reply, 'Erm, this isn't what you might think. You see, Kevin, I'm an Independent Custody Visitor, which means–'

'Custardy what? I hate custard. Ha-ha-ha.'

'Oh, ha-ha-ha.'

'Ha-ha-ha.'

'Ha-ha.'

Fortunately the policeman through the hatch then forcibly re-engages Kevin in conversation, and it's now Stan's turn to eye me, and then Kevin, with suspicion.

'Stan, it's a long story. But seeing as this . . . young gentleman's not actually in custody, my knowing him doesn't constitute any breaking of any rules, right?'

'Er, I suppose, right.'

So we wait for Kevin to finish whining at the coppers. He has a good whine. Some law he's broken. And when he finally leaves – goodbye, Kevin, no, not if I see you first – we introduce ourselves to the duty sergeant, who phones through to the custody suite† to warn of our arrival.

'He's not supposed to do that,' mutters Stan. 'He's supposed to take us through immediately.'

'Should we make a note that he did?'

'A mental note.'

'All right.' I make a mental note. And then, later, a note in my notebook, and then, later still, typing it out here like this. So far, the

---

* The police (inside the station).
† The all-new, politically correct way of saying 'cells'.

duty sergeant's having a nightmare – he can't seem to do anything right. Frankly the only thing stopping me from typing out his home address is the confidentiality agreement I signed.

The duty sergeant leads us through a number of steel doors to the custody suite, which reminds me of a slightly more sturdy version of the set on *Prisoner Cell Block H*, only without any lesbians anywhere to be seen, and more's the pity. Instead, here's the custody sergeant, sitting behind a big desk, wearing large epaulettes. He looks quite spectacularly unfriendly.

'Custody Visitors, eh? Just what we bloody need,' he announces with a sneer.

Stan and I chuckle nervously.

Behind the custody sergeant stands a plainclothes policeman wearing a leather jacket, iron-grey flat-top, Ben Sherman shirt, and an expression like contemptuous thunder. Stan and I glance at one another – we had not been expecting a reception like this. At the training day we'd been told – over and over again – that Custody Visitors and police were all supposed to be working together in harmonious tandem. There isn't much harmony here today; instead, there is dissonance and atonalism, and I'm feeling considerably less powerful all of a sudden. In fact I feel somewhat faint. And small. And *guilty*. God damn, it took all of twenty seconds to reduce me to this. I'm just about to raise my arms in surrender, when Stan bravely cuts in.

'So can we take a look at your cells then please?'

The policemen both sigh. Actually it's more like snarling. The custody sergeant glances reluctantly at a computer screen. For ages. We stand and wait, clutching our folders.* I start quietly to whistle the theme tune to *Juliet Bravo*. And then, after further protests that they're way too busy for this sort of thing (they are?), and further general unhelpfulness, we are eventually led down to the cell block where, due to aforementioned confidentiality agreement, some of the following has had to be blacked-out.

* Tight.

At the first cell, ██████ ████████████
████████████████████████████. ███████████████.
████████████

██

'Quite,' says Stan.

████████████████████, I reply, and everybody laughs.

'Seb, you're really brilliant.'

████████.

'Oh, my God!'

'Run!'

'But where?'

Suddenly, ████████████████

'Is he dead?'

'I'm afraid so.'

████████████████████, exhausted.

Out in the corridor, the custody sergeant is nowhere to be seen, so we close the cell door ourselves and then just kind of stand around for a while, admiring the steely decor. Stan wipes the blood off his folder with the sleeve of his Marks and Spencer cardie.

'It'll wash out,' he says. 'It usually does.'

█████████████████████, but the tourniquet is insufficient.

Cell number two is a similar situation. ████████████████

██

██

██

██

██ not funny any more,' says Bob.

I angrily disagree.

██

██

██

██

██

██

██████ lazy.

'All done?' asks the custody sergeant.

'Writing books is a piece of piss!' cries the detainee★ through the bloodstained grille, ████████████████████████████

██

██

██

██ for God's sake.

'Oh, all right then.'

'Following that exciting incident, in which my colleague Seb performed in a selfless and heroic fashion, we'd now like to inspect

★ The all-new, politically correct way of saying 'prisoner'.

the kitchen area, the exercise yard and the bathroom, please,' says Stan, writing on our report form.

'Bathroom! Pffft! Here, Sarge, he's calling it the *bathroom*. La-de-bloody-da!'

'Pffft. You mean the *shitter*.'

'Right, the, erm, the "shitter".'

We check the shitter. It's fine. In the kitchen, we inspect piles and piles of ready-meals. Twenty-seven of them are out of date.

'Oh, sorry, *sorry*,' snaps the custody sergeant when we mention this, ostentatiously sweeping them all off the shelf and on to the floor.

'You don't have to be like that,' says Stan. 'We're just reporting what we see. We're only doing our job.'

'And I'm doing mine,' replies the policeman, loudly throwing the out-of-date ready-meals into a bin.

We check the exercise area: a fifteen-by-ten-foot concrete-walled rectangle covered by a heavy metal grille – the most depressing area of this planet I have yet to stumble across.* After inspecting this (all was in order), it's pretty much time for us to go. We've had *such* a lovely time, thanks, Officers, see you again soon!

Out at Stan's car, we raise eyebrows at one another.

'Well. I've never had one like that before,' says Stan. 'They're usually, you know, nice. Friendly.'

'Maybe it was me.'

'Yes, maybe it was you.'

'I could have made them angry somehow.'

'You could have made them angry somehow. Anyway. Did you enjoy it?'

'Not really.'

'No, I'm not surprised. Goodbye then.'

'Goodbye.'

Stan drives off and I'm standing alone outside the police station in the rain again. Whether or not this particular volunteering

---

* I've only ever seen Fratton Park on the television.

activity is helping me to become a better person is a moot point – indeed probably a point best left for a debate on television's popular, book-sales-boosting *Richard & Judy*. Oh, go on. Just ten minutes!★

★ Seriously, although not very rewarding from a 'making-friends' point of view, this volunteering activity definitely feels worthwhile – like I'm providing a useful service to the, erm, incarcerated community (a community-in-need, if ever there was one). And, in ensuring the welfare of those cellbound, I am ensuring that the day you absentmindedly sink a few too many down the pub one sunny afternoon and then plough drunkenly into a group of Portuguese exchange students on a zebra crossing in your car on the way home, the duty sergeant in charge of your own custody suite is less likely to wander in and kick the shit out of you. Unless you're particularly unlucky and he happens to be Portuguese. So I'm going to carry on doing it.

Step Seven

Police Community Support Officer
Near Winchester Police Station

Crimes (UK), 2005/6: 11 million (approx.)
Percentage of UK population that has been the victim of some type of crime,
2005/6: 23%

I am in the pub with my dashing, temporarily out-of-work actor friend Owen, describing the various Good Works I've been involved in recently, when he raises a theatrical hand to stop me, stares off into the middle distance (through an open window) and then mysteriously announces: 'I have seen the future of volunteering.'

'Where is the future of it? And, more importantly, will it help me become a yet better person? I'm immeasurably improved already, you see, certainly kind of *broader* in my heart and general outlook than I used to be, except perhaps towards the police. But I also feel I have a kind of "celestial momentum" now, and that–'

'Aha, police, exactly!' he interrupted. 'Law and order.'

I paused. 'Do you mean vigilante groups? Because I'm not sure the–'

'No, I'd say vigilante groups were more . . . vindictive really, but they can be useful – they have their place; that's for when your citizens are really, thoroughly fed up.'

'With the state of the pavements.'

'Well, perhaps. But by law and order, I was specifically referring to those volunteer Police Community Support Officers, one of whom I just saw walking past the window over there and I must say looked very smart indeed.'

I have often wondered why people would want to do something like this: if you want to be a policeman, be a policeman; and get paid for it, for Christ's sake; whereas if you merely feel a burning desire to wander self-consciously through your locale while children (and adults) laugh openly at you, then the Winchester Litter Pickers are still waiting for your call.

'Why would anyone want to do that? I mean really.'

'Status.'

'You mean ego.'

'Conscience.'

'Solipsism.'

'Sense of duty.'

'Self-righteousness.'

'Kindness.'

'Fury.'

'What's the matter with you?'

'Sorry. Where do I sign?'

But wouldn't you know, as I am already gainfully employed as an Independent Custody Visitor, I am sadly – cataclysmically – ineligible to become a volunteer copper as *there is a clear conflict of interest.* Hooray!*

'Tell me more about these vigilante groups,' I say to Owen.

'These days they disguise their true motives beneath shifty cloaks of suburban respectability, a little like the Ku Klux Klan and the Republican Party in America. Nowadays, vigilante groups prefer to refer to themselves as "Neighbourhood Watch".'

'Oh, them.'

'Give it a go?'

'Well, I could put a sticker in my window or something.'

'"Paranoid Reactionary Lives Here".'

'Well, yeah, exactly. It feels like a regressive metaphysical gesture. There's a big difference between helping the community and walling the whole thing off. Let's go and play our year-delayed gig at the Thursday Club in Botley instead. Let's go and . . . *make a positive difference.*'

'Let me go, rock 'n' roll.'

---

* I have also subsequently learned that they're not actually volunteers after all – they get paid. Not much, but some. Thus I absolutely 100% cannot become one. Dance among the daisies!

Step Seven

The Southampton and Winchester Visitors Group
Portsmouth Library Café

It takes a short while to get our favourite obese, aproned waitress's attention, and to be fair she is a whole three yards away from us behind the counter, and there's nobody else here in the library café so she's probably busy meditating or something. Appo coughs.

'Yes, what do you want?' she says, peering at us with distaste.

'Appo, would you like a sandwich?'

'Yes, please.'

'No food after 2.30 p.m! Can't you read!'

Perhaps we're not that hungry after all; instead we order some delicious, refreshing drinks.

'And I suppose you want glasses with your drinks. Extra for me to wash up in other words?'

'Oh yes,' we both reply. 'Glasses most definitely.'

She bangs them down on the tray so hard they nearly break.

'So how's your friend's floor?'

Appo shrugs. 'It's OK.'

'Bearable at least?'

Appo shrugs. 'It's OK. Did you speak with the housing people? What do they say? Can I move in with Marie and Joy?'

Since I last saw Appo, I've made approximately thirty phone calls on his behalf. I won't bore you with the grim, Groundhog Day details; suffice to say that the bottom line appears to be that Appo can't even *exist* in the eyes of Housing Benefit unless he has a National Insurance number; but as a failed asylum seeker he's expressly banned from being in possession of a National Insurance number because this would allow him to work and claim benefits, neither of which Appo is allowed to do. Even if Appo were to hopefully and speculatively apply for an *emergency* NI number, he would have to have an address, which, at the moment, he doesn't.

Every which way I turn, I end up back in the same place: getting ratty with somebody I spoke to half an hour ago in a giant *please-hold-while-I-transfer-you* loop, in which every new person I encounter must have the entire situation explained anew which, alone, takes a good five to ten minutes.

Because Appo's situation is relatively unique, he doesn't fit conveniently into a tick box on computer screens; and since nobody is prepared to stand up and take personal responsibility for his situation, it's simpler just to put me on hold and pass me on to somebody else in a different department. Thus the merry-go-round continues.

'Seb? I just ask: can I move in with Marie and Joy?' Appo repeats his question.

'Right. Well. I've made some phone calls.'

'Yes?'

'And I'm feeling . . .'

Appo is looking at me imploringly.

'I'm feeling quite positive. We're not there . . . yet. But we will be soon. Don't worry!'

'OK then. Thank you. If you say so, I am not worried.'

'Well, that's right. Leave it to me. I'll sort this out.'

'I have faith in Lord Jesus Christ. Lord Jesus Christ, and Seb!'

Jesus Christ.

Before we part, Appo says, 'Have you heard about an amnesty?'

'An amnesty?' I smile. 'No.'

'I've heard there might be a new amnesty for everyone who has been in the country for five years or over.'

'Which would include you.'

'Yes, it would include me!'

'I haven't heard about any such amnesty.'

'OK, all right. I thought you might have heard about this.' He clucks.

'Not yet.'

'All right.'

And we chuckle.

Appleby House, Staines
9.30 a.m.

Percentage of UK homeless addicted to drugs and/or alcohol: 81%
(heroin comes first; then alcohol)
UK rough sleepers' average life expectancy: 42

A man I don't recognize stands at the door, engaged in lively conversation with Tristan. The man is short, round, white-bearded, and clothed in a style I can only describe as 'dirty-hippy-tramp chic' – he looks like a mystical Eastern guru who went missing on the outskirts of Ulan Bator in 1971. He looks fantastic. I go over to introduce myself.

His name is Zorbad; his overloaded shopping trolley is parked up outside the front door. Tristan has asked to have a look inside a few of the many old tobacco tins Zorbad keeps about his person; not because he wants to, but as routine, in case of drugs or knives or, by the look of this dude, a genie. Inside the tins are stubs of old pencils, an old compass, multi-hued thread, roll-up butts – lots of junk shop crap, basically.

'These are great, Zorbad!' I exclaim. 'These are genuine, mysterious Boxes of Delights, aren't they?'

'Don't be stupid, they're just full of old shit,' replies Zorbad.

Like you, his expression implies.

Zorbad is wearing a mass of long, looping necklaces. He looks like Santa Claus after a nine-year peyote bender. I notice, at the bottom of one of the larger tobacco boxes, a tattered copy of the Flann O'Brien novel *At Swim-Two-Birds*.

'Ah, Flann O'Brien!' I exclaim.

'You know Flann O'Brien?' Zorbad's voice is full of suspicion.

'Well, yeah, I've read *The Third Policeman*★ and *The Poor Mouth*.'†

'So tell me – what is the last line of *The Third Policeman*?'

'The last line? Erm. I can't remember.'

'You *can't remember*? For God's sake, man, do you know *anything*?'

★ True.

† Untrue. I had merely remembered The Poor Mouth, and was trying to appear better-read than I actually was. To a tramp I met thirty seconds ago.

I feel this is a little harsh.

'Is it something about a bicycle?'

'*Something about a bicycle* indeed. Jesus H Christ, and he says he's a fan of Irish literature! Come on then now. *Snap snap.* Name me three other Great Irish Writers. *Snap snap.*'

'Erm. James Joyce. Samuel Beckett. Spike, erm, Milligan.'

'Good *God*, man. What about *Yeats*? This man' – Zorbad thrusts a grubby finger towards me – 'is technically a moron!'

Tristan gravely nods his head in agreement.

I notice however that Tristan's not exactly being forthcoming about his own knowledge and appreciation of Irish literature. It also occurs to me that Zorbad hasn't actually *quoted* these 'famous' final lines from *The Third Policeman*, but just as I am about to round thus upon him, Zorbad strides away up the corridor and pushes grandly through into the day room, where he is greeted by braying (actually everybody's entrance into the day room is greeted by braying). The doors swing shut behind him.

'Zorbad,' says Tristan. 'An eccentric.'

Half an hour later, I am carrying a pile of dirty plates past the entrance to the dining room.

'Excuse me there, young man!' calls Zorbad. He gestures for me to come and sit down next to him, and so I put down the plates and do as he says.

'I'm sorry I was a little brusque with you earlier,' he says. 'As an esteemed citizen of the Emerald Isle, I am sensitive to the particulars of our culture, and in particular to their being taken in vain by an impertinent Englishman.'

'But all I said was–'

Zorbad holds up a hand to stop me. And with the other hand, he passes me a book. It's blue and dirty. 'I want you to have this. As a fellow man of letters, I believe you might learn a lot from it. God knows you need to.'

'Thanks.'

'That's no problem, my young friend. As a gentleman of the

road, this is something that I like to do for those I meet along the way – give them books. Like this cracking little one here that I'm letting you borrow in order for you to look a little less stupid.'

'Yes, OK already.'

The book is *The Fall of the British Monarchies*.

'Now, I'm off to the seaside this afternoon, to Worthing, for a spot of sun, sea and the drinking of booze. When I get back, in a few weeks' time, I'll test you on the contents of this book. All right?'

'Zorbad, this is so kind, I couldn't possibly accept.'

'I know it's kind. Shut up and just read it. I'll test you when I get back.'

'Right.'

That morning, as I walked through the small park that lies on my way to the House from Staines Station, I had noticed a small tent. It had been erected in the far corner, and was discreetly festooned with laundry. This struck me as unusual, since the park is in the middle of town, and doesn't – or at least shouldn't really – attract tents and laundry. It should attract dog-walkers and reactionary old people. It turns out this was Zorbad, and his malodorous marquee.

'I had no trouble. Indeed, everybody has been thoroughly courteous. No police; no kids; no aggro. Once people confer with me, and realize that I'm a decent man who treats everybody he meets with respect,* then they leave me be, and I leave them be. You see?'

He makes a Zen-type gesture with both hands. Far out, Zorbad.

'Apart from foreigners. I can't be doing with bloody foreigners.'

I take *The Fall of the British Monarchies* home and wonder how I might be able to wash it. But in the end I don't – I browse it holding it by the edges. I read some controversial opinions regarding King Charles I and some things about the Scots. Then I close the book, wash my hands, and put it by the front door to await Zorbad's return from the beach. I decide to take my chances with my history O-level and avoidance.

* For example, aggressively grilling them on modernist Irish literature moments after being introduced.

Appleby House, Staines
9.30 a.m.

Today I am instructed to help Tosh – the heavily decorated, Prince Andrew-saving Falklands veteran from earlier – in the garden, which hasn't been touched since the previous summer. When I say garden, what I mean is a large, rectangular, butt-strewn strip of bitumen off to the side of the day room, with a few shrubs around the edges and a filthy plastic table surrounded by even filthier once-white plastic chairs.

'Bit of vinegar will get those chairs clean,' says Tosh. 'Vinegar's like magic. Work wonders, vinegar will.'

'Tosh is a professional gardener, by trade,' says Tristan.

'I thought he was a navy man?'

'You never really know, do you? But Tosh has brought two pairs of secateurs in with him today, and some gloves, so he must at least have some sort of horticultural experience.'

'Yes, he must have.'

So Tosh gets to work clearing a bunch of brambles, while I sweep the yard. It's another bright sunny day, so every now and again people come out to sit in the sun and smoke roll-ups and take the piss out of Tosh and me for doing some/any work. You'd never catch *them* doing any of this 'work' business, they repeat over and over. But after half an hour or so, their banter begins to falter a little, you can see a few twinges of guilt kicking in, and so one or two of the older guys get up and start to pitch in and help us out. Russell helps clear the butts; Terry lugs some old planks of wood; and Kevin comes flying through the door pursued by Garry, and almost gets lamped by both Russell and Terry. In fact it is Garry himself who ends up lamping him, and we hear the cheers through the closed door.

This is my favourite day here so far. Tosh – who I often see now just wandering around aimlessly in the town centre (I always try to catch his eye to say hello but he seems away with the fairies) – and I are a team, and we smile at one another as we work up a sweat. Russell and Terry smile too; we're all a little sheepish about this, I don't know why. Such innocent, simple pleasure, I suppose. It's not very tough; and in Appleby House, toughness is a given – mandatory for survival. Things get so emotional (in my own, deluded mind) that I feel myself tumbling into Lawrentian reverie.*

'Why don't we *burn* all our accumulated rubbish here?' I exclaim to Tosh, standing before a large pile of vegetative detritus. 'You know, start a bonfire! Better that than sticking it all in the bin, right?'

Russell and Terry think this is a great idea, and both instantly produce their cigarette lighters, but Tosh is more responsible.

'We should probably check first,' he says, and so we check, and Tristan tells me not to be so stupid.

'Just light it anyway,' whispers Terry.

'I'd better not.'

'Go on, just light it!'

'Go on!'

Oh dear, look what I've started. I end up having to 'guard' the pile of garden debris from various rogue pyromaniacs, more and more of whom now appear through the back door brandishing their Clippers, as the bonfire rumours spread like, um, wildfire.

In the end, I put it all in the bin, under armed guard – i.e. Leanne standing nearby holding a ladle. Tosh comes out and pours vinegar all over the plastic table and chairs, but apart from everything smelling of vinegar, nothing happens.

The Thursday Club, Botley, Hampshire
Thursday
Botley official website: www.botley.com
Car parks in Botley: 5

'As it's been some time since I was last here,† I expect a few of the old ladies might have died in the meantime,' I solemnly inform

---

* Bloody hell, readers; I've mentioned Flann O'Brien and D.H. Lawrence in this chapter! Book me a seat on Late Night Review already, why don'tcha?

† Over a year. Blame the baby.

Owen in the car on the sun-kissed highway to Botley – the legendary B3354.

'Shall we dedicate our performance to the deceased?'

'Well, I suppose we could, although wouldn't that be a bit of a downer? They might not particularly want to be reminded of those most recently fallen from their midst. Let's just dedicate it to . . . Botley instead. Just Botley. The town or village or whatever it is, of Botley.'

'Just Botley. In honour of it.'

'Yes.'

I suspect the reason for this piss-poor level of pre-gig banter was because we were both actually rather nervous, though neither of us was prepared to admit as much.

'Are *you* nervous?'

'Oh no! Are you?'

'Ha! Nervous! Don't be ridiculous! I've never been more, like, *chilled-out* in my life, ever.'

Like that, you see? Admitting to nerves at the prospect of playing forty-five minutes worth of improvised music and poetry in front of fifteen to twenty either half or fully asleep OAPs would have been majorly humiliating; thus we brazen it out with increasingly cocksure, Gene Simmons-esque braggadocio.

It wasn't originally going to be improvised music and poetry of course; it was supposed to have been a jolly old piano and guitar sing-along ('We'll Meet Again', 'The White Cliffs of Dover', 'Roll Out the Barrel', 'We All Live in a Botley Submarine'). However, due to our brief window of rehearsal time (half an hour) – which was entirely due to Owen claiming to have 'frankly better things to do with my life' – we have decided on a last-minute change of plan. A change of plan that, we are hoping, requires zero amount of preparation.

When I informed Rosemary over the telephone about this change of tack, there had been a long and rather stern silence, followed by a weary and resigned 'all right then, whatever you like'-type comment. One suspects the Thursday Club can't really afford to be all that choosy about the ents, especially when one notes that one of their 'favourites' is my mother reading poetry to them. According to my mother. So you see, Owen and I plan to take this poetry-reading thing one step beyond – into brave new worlds of improvised inspiration and something else. Delight maybe. Delirium.*

'So long as all the ladies don't fall asleep, then I'll feel we'll have succeeded,' I say. 'To see all their delighted expressions lit up before us, well . . . It brings a tear to my eye just thinking about it. It will definitely have been worth it, for that. An elderly lady's warm, contented smile will be its own reward, and even–'

'My train leaves at seven o'clock.'

'I don't care what time your train leaves at!'

In Botley, we park behind the village hall and unpack the gear – the poetry book and my electric guitar, amplifier, series of effects and violin bow.

'Jesus Christ,' says Owen. 'What the hell are you planning on inflicting on everybody with this little lot?'

'Atmospheric soundscapes,' I reply, unwinding my multi-socketed adaptor lead, lining up and plugging in the effects, and tightening and applying a liberal coating of rosin to the bow. And then doing some stretches.

'They'll love it. I'll make 'em go all dreamy and wistful, and then when you hit 'em with some Wilfred Owen and that – *kaboom* – they'll be in the palm of our hands. Weeping with pleasure, and emotion.'

'Weeping is about right.'

'Let's not have a falling-out right before we play. Just this once.'

Botley village hall is like the village hall in *Dad's Army*: quaint and boxy with a high stage up at one end, whose vast woollen curtains weigh and smell roughly the same as a blue whale. Owen and I greet the ladies as they arrive and seat themselves in their regular horseshoe shape at fold-up, Formica tables. There is a distinct sense of anticipation in the air.† Rosemary sidles over to where we're nervously

---

* Doldrums.

† For their imminent cup of tea.

standing, behind another Formica table, not actually on the stage, but in front of it. (I'm not sure why, probably modesty, or terror.)★

'Are you ready?' she asks. 'Shall I introduce you?'

We nod.

And this is how she introduces us, verbatim, as I recorded the whole thing with a professional recording device: 'Right. We have with us this afternoon . . . Seb, who you've met before . . .'

'Hello again!' I cry.

there is some unimpressed muttering at this point

' . . . Heather's son, who is an author of note, he asked me to say. Ha-ha. And his friend, his long-time friend, Owen. Owen is an actor, and is late of the National Theatre . . .'

ripple of applause

' . . . but is at the moment having rather a long rest.'

'Thank you, yes,' says Owen.

'So. I don't know what they're going to do, but I await it with great interest. Thank you, lads, off you go.'

'We're just going to do some nice music with some poetry. As simple as that,' I announce. 'Are you ready? Are you *ready*?'

Everybody seems to be ready. I count our audience; they are fifteen strong. Four are already asleep. So eleven conscious.

'I would like to dedicate this performance to the town of Botley,' says Owen. 'And shall I just go and shut that door?'

'Yes please, if you wouldn't mind.'

'Righto, hang on.'

Whatever the word slightly below 'smattering' is, that's the level of applause that greets this introductory dedication. Oh well. Let's effing well rock anyway!

I begin. My improvised atmospheric soundscapes fast begin to shimmer and evoke vast oceanic sunsets and desolate snowy peaks, etc. Owen comes in with a dramatic poem, read in a very actorly voice. So far, so bloody marvellous. Except that two minutes and twenty sec-

---

★ Not that kind of terror, American reader(s).

onds in, Rosemary clumps over to where I'm standing throwing dramatic shapes with the violin bow, and tells me to turn it down please, as several ladies have already complained that they can't hear the poetry. I nod and turn it down; then as she's walking back to her table, covertly turn it back up again. I mean come on. Effects I am utilizing during this performance include: analogue delay, reverse digital gigadelay, analogue reverb, wah-wah, ring modulation and some quivering, pulsating tremolo. The racket I'm whipping up basically makes My Bloody Valentine sound like George motherfucking Formby. I'm kicking some serious, sonic-cathedrals-of-sound butt here, readers.

Owen finishes his poem, flicks briefly through his volume of poetry, and then begins another, this time I think a little light T.S. Eliot. But who really cares? The throbbing, rainbow shards of bowed guitar cast a vast, swelling hallucinatory shadow over the whole of Botley and neighbouring Hedge End as I summon forth the ghost of Ayler, the spirit of Hendrix and the searing bloody soul of Takashi Mizutani at his most blissed-out and bulldozing. Oh, God, here comes Rosemary again.

'It's too loud!' she screeches. 'You'll have to turn it down! Nobody can hear anything! Look at them!'

I gaze out at the Fifteen – the Conscious Eleven – and note that Rosemary may have a point, as six or seven have both hands desperately pressed over their ears. Thus I reluctantly concede, and ease off on the old volume a little, lifting my foot off the swirling gas just long enough for the ladies to come back down to earth for the merest fleeting few seconds before . . . *Wham!*

With Rosemary's back turned once more, off I blast into the further reaches of the ionosphere, my red-hot bow mapping reverb-drenched cosmic ley lines between the constellations; fusing whole stars into a lysergic maelstrom of psychedelic incantation. With my guitar I summon forth the spirits of the recently deceased members of the Thursday Club, and make synapse-shredding sweet love to their glowing irradiated souls on a blazing array of multi-hued, deep-pile astral planes. Yeah, baby! We are one. We are together. We are all the stars in heaven above.

And here comes Rosemary for a third time, oh dear.

'Seb, I'm sorry but the ladies can't hear *anything* with all this noise going on. You'll have to turn it right down, I absolutely insist.'

Sulkily, I turn my amp down to beneath even one on the dial. You can barely hear it at all. Suddenly I can hear Owen, talking. Reading a poem. Ah yes, poems, of course. The ladies slowly remove their hands from the side of their heads and tentatively begin to smile. At Owen, who wanders among the ladies sitting at the tables, lonely as a cloud with his frilly white shirt open to the waist, the great big flouncing ponce.

Proceedings continue boringly like this for another thirty minutes or so, with me leaning against the stage, strumming the occasional, barely audible chord, and Owen shamelessly reading popular poems that appear to be going down sickeningly well.

Some time later, Owen arrives at the end of another overlong poem, and the ladies deliver him a prolonged and enthusiastic volley of arthritic applause. Owen looks over at me and winks triumphantly. I scowl back, pointing at the clock on the far wall, which shows we've overrun by at least double our allotted time.

'The End,' I attempt to announce.

But instead Owen raises an arm and portentously blurts out: '*The Rime of the Ancient Mariner*!'

And then proceeds to read the whole of *The Rime of the Ancient Mariner*, which takes at least another fifteen minutes, and over which I play virtually nothing, two notes at most, two crappy, dissonant, discouraging notes which sadly have no effect whatsoever. When he finally finishes, the ladies are all in tearful raptures once again.

'Thank you, Owen, for a marvellous reading!' exclaims Rosemary, over the frenzied applause. 'And to Seb, too, for the interesting music.' The applause stops abruptly.

Bob comes over carrying a plate of biscuits. 'Would you like a biscuit?'

'Yes, I bloody would.'

I eat my biscuit while Owen busies himself bowing deeply, from the waist.

While I pack up my gear and lug it all back to the car, Owen takes impromptu requests from the floor. He does the famous bit from *Hamlet*. He does something from *Macbeth*. He does something else.

And then Betty pipes up hopefully: 'Can you read something from my little book?'

Owen strides over and chivalrously answers in the affirmative; leafs sensitively through Betty's poetry book (skilfully ignoring requests to read a few of her own poems) and proceeds to over-ham a wholly unnecessary 'Macavity – the sodding Mystery Cat', to squeals of decrepit delight and appreciation. Oh, Owen, you're so *brilliant* and bloody *smouldering*.

And there's no need to bore you with the ladies' post-show comments; suffice it to say that the general consensus was that my improvisations had owed something to *Live-Evil*-period Miles, a little to the Velvets' 'Sister Ray', and perhaps the merest soupçon to Christian Fennesz's *Endless Summer*, with a bit of Fred Frith and Lee Ranaldo (*circa* 1989) thrown in for good measure. So fuck you.

Appleby House, Staines
9.30 a.m.
Number of times more likely UK homeless are to suffer mental health issues: 8
Number of times more likely UK homeless are to suffer chronic chest and breathing problems: 3

In my absence (I'm only here one day a week), the Shadow, Kevin and Knuckles have been banned from the House; thus things are unnaturally quiet at Appleby today. A few days ago, the Shadow had a run-in with a female member of staff,[*] became agitated and fled to the lavatory. Staff, concerned, lurked outside in the corridor. Staff then heard sounds of breakage – it turned out the Shadow was

---

[*] 'You touched my arm!' 'I didn't touch your arm, I was just walking past.' 'YOU TOUCHED MY ARM.' 'Uh-oh.'

destroying the bathroom soap dispenser. The Shadow then emerged, transformed: crouched and feral, hissing, clawing the air with his hands. His hat had come off and tufts of black hair stood rigid on his head. This sounds pretty amusing to me, until I hear that he proceeded to threaten to slice aforementioned female member of staff's breasts off with a bread knife. The police were called. Tristan gingerly unlocked the front door and the Shadow kindly fled rather than getting down to any breast-slicing. The police soon apprehended him. At the time of writing, the Shadow is in a secure mental health unit, which is probably the best and safest place for him. (Kate tells me that she felt something might have been amiss when she noticed his Big Bird was in a different pocket from usual that morning.)

Kevin was banned from the house for annoying everybody with his mobile phone – i.e. playing loud dance music on it all morning, and waving it in people's faces. Kevin was also found to have a screwdriver about his person. When questioned about said screwdriver, Kevin's inevitably gleeful response (featuring groinal thrusts) was: 'It's to do some screwing, innit.' Which was reasonably ironic considering he'd just been acquitted of charges of forced sexual relations with a minor (who turns out to be his girlfriend). His mobile phone and screwdriver were duly confiscated, and now Kevin's not allowed back for two weeks. For the first couple of days, he lurks around outside the building.

(I'm not quite sure what happened with Knuckles; only that he has been banned for two months. So it was probably something quite bad.)

Today I'm posted in the day room. I stand in the day room. I am merely a presence – one hopes a calming presence. It's cold and smoky. I stand here for two hours. I get a headache. It is cold, and smoky, and I am miserable. An ex-boxer by the name of Graham approaches and asks if he can have a word, and I reply yes of course, let's go outside.

We stand in the drizzle, in our recently refurbished garden area, and Graham shuffles around a little and then says: 'I suffer from depression. And I'm worried that I might not make it through this time. It'll be all right though, won't it?'

I look at Graham. He is in a bad way: in his fifties; head shaved; very dirty; teeth missing; shaking hands almost blackened by nicotine; his face almost trembling with anxiety. His left eyelid twitches uncontrollably.

'Yeah, I'm sure it'll be all right. You've just got to try to . . . think positive. Get through today and you might feel on top of the world again tomorrow.'

'I'm worried I might not make it through this time. Is the nurse in today? I'd really like to speak to her.'

I tell Graham that unfortunately she's not, but that she'll be in tomorrow, if he can wait that long. You can wait that long, right? He looks down at the ground; chews his lip. I don't know what to say. I worry that saying the wrong thing might plunge Graham into yet deeper sloughs of despond.

'Been depressed for a while now then, have you?'

Graham nods.

'Oh dear.'

Graham nods.

'Oh dear. That's no good.'

Graham shakes his head. I wish I'd had some training on what to say to somebody in a situation such as this. I'm so terrified of saying the wrong thing, I'm too nervous to have just a normal conversation. Graham looks up; his eyes are black and huge.

'Sometimes I feel I can't go on. Sometimes I just want to . . .'

'Shall I go and, you know, *double-check* the nurse isn't in today?'

Graham nods.

Off I trot. Two minutes later I'm back.

'She definitely isn't, goddamn it. But hey – are you feeling any better about things?'

'No.'

We stand in the drizzle. Graham sucks at a nail-sized roll-up, squinting. His eye continues to twitch. I feel terrible for him.

'It's extremely possible that you'll feel a little bit better tomorrow morning.'

'I might.'

'And at least then you can talk to the nurse about it.'

'Yeah.'

'And it'll be lunchtime soon, eh?'

'Mmm.'

'And Leanne's cooking roast chicken.'

Graham exhales. We stand in the drizzle. The garden still smells of vinegar.

The kitchen stinks of slow-boiled gizzards and rank dishwasher steam.

The day room reeks of smoke and body odour.

The dining room hums with bleach and Marmite.

The Quiet Room is infused with the violent olfactory impact of six unwashed elderly men all crammed into a tight, narrow space.

In the bathroom I always hold my breath so I couldn't tell you how it smells.

Appleby House's heady rainbow of scents.

S. Hunter

(hell yeah permission)

The Southampton and Winchester Visitors Group
Portsmouth Library Café

The Democratic Republic of Congo has just witnessed its first multi-party elections since its independence in 1960. Appo and all his expatriated countrymen have, naturally, been following events extremely closely. The upshot is that the incumbent, Joseph Kabila, has been elected president with 45 per cent of the vote. His opponent, Jean-Pierre Bemba, made only 22 per cent. When the results were announced, supporters of the two opposing factions clashed on the streets of the capital Kinshasa, leaving up to 600 dead. When Bemba made comments regarding the potential threat of a renewed Congolese dictatorship, he was

accused of 'high treason' and eventually forced to leave the country. Now that President Kabila and his government can claim a
'democratic victory', the regime has been officially recognized
by the government of Great Britain. As a result, those who fled
or are fleeing the administration are now in great danger of being
repatriated. It's amazing what difference an 'election' can make,
isn't it?

Over cold coffee, Appo tells me about his pal (and fellow
Congolese, failed-asylum-seeking national), Pierre. Pierre was
woken in the middle of the night by immigration police, bundled
away (separated from his girlfriend) and stuck on a charter flight
packed full of similarly herded compatriots heading back to
Kinshasa. It was only thanks to last-minute intervention from,
among others, the Bishop of Winchester, that Pierre was taken off
the plane and spared repatriation. The remaining hundreds on
board were not so lucky. Reports detailing the treatment of these
forcibly returned exiles have not made pretty reading: the word
'persecution' makes a regular appearance; as do the words 'prison',
and 'torture'. The same kinds of words that, remarkably, used to
apply before the Democratic Republic became 'democratic'; the
kinds of words that had once meant the UK wouldn't send these
people back.

Dear readers, I have included this Congolese overview in order to
illustrate and contextualize Appo's situation, and to cover up for the
fact that, despite a further twenty to thirty phone calls to various
branches of Portsmouth social services, I have thus far utterly failed to
get Appo legally housed with his partner and child; he's still staying on
his mate's floor – still homeless – i.e. in a significantly worse-off state
than he was before he met me. I remind Appo of this, and he laughs.

'But, Seb, if you had not sorted out my new Home Office
appeal, then I might be on one of these planes also,' says Appo. 'It is
because of you that I am safe now, is that not right?'

And I suppose that's true. We smile at one another. Small mercies.

173

Appleby House, Staines
9.30 a.m.

Percentage of women in the UK who cite domestic violence as the key reason for their homelessness: 63%

Percentage of young homeless women who have experienced sexual abuse in childhood or adolescence: 40%

Appleby is unnaturally quiet again today, as the weather is so pleasant. Quiet, that is, except for Leanne's radio, which today regales us with music from hot young indie sensations the Arctic Monkeys.

'I really love the Arctic Monkeys,' says Leanne. 'They're my favourite band.'

'I didn't realize you were that young,' I reply.

She glares at me. 'Well, I am!'

Lunch today is 'sausages casserole'. It's utterly heinous. I have to stifle an urge to gag with every mouthful, and I'm sure I'm not the only one. To our service users, meals as bad as this must be perceived as yet further merciless punishment from the gods. Or the sausages' ingredients' revenge from beyond the abattoir. Their revenge is sweet. Raw. So far as I can bear to remember, it's the worst meal I have ever eaten.

With the absence of Kevin (still banned), the Shadow (sectioned), Knuckles (still banned), Billy (in London), Darren (in prison), Smasher (got a job!), Garry (temporarily banned), Badger (in court today), Charlie (drunk in the town centre), Graham (ditto) or Zorbad (still down by the seaside, apparently), all the most dominant personalities are absent, and a Zen-like calm settles upon Appleby House. Tosh is still here, though. He's wearing a pair of 1980s women's sunglasses. We discuss battleships and gardening. I do like it here. (I can actually feel my conscience becoming clearer by the hour.)

I have not, however, been offered a job yet. And with sales of my previous books being what they are,* I could do with the money right now, to be honest. This fundamental absence of remuneration is one of the potential 'downsides' of volunteering, albeit rather an obvious one, perhaps.

* Risible.

Step Seven

Independent Custody Visitor
Nutbush City Limits* Police Station
Nutbush

For my second custody visit, I have a new partner, called Big Dave. Big Dave and I shake hands outside the police station. Although he is the same as Stan, in that he's grey-haired, friendly and in his fifties, Big Dave is altogether more thrusting and confident and portly and tanned; he's just come back from a month's pharmaceuticals-selling in Israel. (I can't help but feel that Nutbush can only come as a massive disappointment to Big Dave after this.) It's interesting to see what kinds of people do this sort of thing. You wouldn't expect an Israeli pharmaceuticals-seller to spend his spare time checking on the welfare of prisoners in police stations, would you?† Who *would* you expect to be doing this? Reformed criminals? Old ladies? Reformed old lady criminals? Imelda Marcos, perhaps?

'Don't worry, I'm not selling the detainees drugs,' jokes Big Dave as we enter the station. 'Their wallets are confiscated at the booking-in stage, and this makes it impossible.'

This time, the policeman on the front desk is courteous and polite; he lets us go through to the custody suite immediately. And then, in the cells, the custody sergeant welcomes us cordially, without sarcasm or withering death-stares. His young colleague smiles warmly and answers all our questions without hesitation or resentment or heinous obfuscation. What's going on here? It's almost as if Nutbush Police Station has *nothing to hide*. But let's not get too carried away with ourselves – let's check the cells, from whence I can already hear deranged howling and metal bowls being ritualistically banged against cell doors in a frenzy of rage at their ready-meals' use-by dates. Ah, I can feel the power coming flooding back, readers! My chest's all puffed out and I'm holding a Biro!

Nutbush's custody suite is huge; certainly in comparison to

---

* I have made the location of this police station anonymous.
† Oh my god, maybe he's selling the detainees drugs!

Camberwick Green's. Whereas Camberwick Green is very much yer wobbly *Prisoner: Cell Block H* village amateur hour, Nutbush is more *Strangeways*; *Papillon*; and *Alcatraz*.

When we interview – chinwag with, really – the detainees, we ask permission to look at their custody record. This contains every detail pertaining to their arrest: the charging, coshing, cuffing, reading of rights, arrival at station, solicitor called, merciless beating etc., etc. As Custody Visitors, it's our job to scan this (computer print-out) document carefully, keeping an eye out for omissions (drinks, a meal, medication, their one telephone call) and/or inconsistencies (15.40 – detainee healthy; 15.45 – detainee missing two front teeth and drenched in blood). And so if anything seems out of place or dodgy-looking, we make a note and go to speak to the sergeant about it. The sergeant then roars with laughter. We also mention anything the detainee themselves might have mentioned to us, e.g. I'm not enjoying this withdrawal much; please may I have some heroin?*

As we have already demonstrated, under the confidentiality agreement I have signed, all dealings with detainees must remain resolutely top secret (which is a shame, as some of the transcripts of their offences make superbly entertaining reading). What I *can* tell you, however, is that cells – all cells (with people in them) – stink to high heaven. There are three reasons for this, I think.

- Detainees' shoes must remain neatly outside the cell at all times; this means socks or worse: bare feet.
- Cells have no windows and are stuffy even when empty.
- The detainee is often not the most hygienic person on earth in the first place. All of which exacerbates the overall olfactory impact into crimes against the nose that *must* be more serious than the original offences, readers, I mean *honestly*.

Today there are only two people in the cells, and very nice they are

---

* Big Dave taps at calculator.

too. And not only that, but they're also pretty darned happy with the way they've been treated, so we're happy too. Having investigated the shower, the exercise yard and the ready-meals, we inform the Nutbush police officers about their clean (old) bill of health and they're all happy too. It's like Haight Ashbury in here, man. Peace, love and appropriate adults.

'Are we all done, then?' I ask Big Dave, as we finish off our report form notes and accept a wad of used notes from the custody sergeant (it seems to be all sergeants, everywhere – where are the colonels and the majors?).

'All done. And I'm noting down here also that we've been "well-received". It's always nice when you can put that at the bottom of a report.'

'Well, haven't we just?'

The sergeants all stand there beaming at us from behind their nice desk.

Big Dave and I then leave the police station, shake hands and part, and I drive home in the belief that the television show *Heartbeat* is, in actual fact, a documentary.

The moral of today's episode: if you're going to get arrested, get arrested in Nutbush; and make sure you wash your feet first, and then the 0.5 per cent chance of your receiving a custody visit while you're there will be nicer for everybody. Until, that is, the pigs start taking your toenails out with pliers. I'm sorry but we can't help you there; you'd better just confess.

Etc.

Appleby House, Staines
9.30 a.m.

Other regulars at Appleby House are Olaf and Pavel, a pair of convivial middle-aged Bulgarians. Olaf and Pavel speak no English. It is believed that they paid several thousand euros each to get to the UK.* Nobody is sure, however, how they ended up in Staines of all

* Presumably nobody thought to tell them about Ryanair and EasyJet.

places, since there isn't much of a Bulgarian community here-
abouts. (The local Conservative Club is quite popular, but *Eastern
Europeans*? The bloody French are bad enough. Don't make my
liver spots rheumier.) Every day at eleven-ish, the pair stroll in clad
in regulation bloc-wear – stonewashed jeans and leather jackets –
smiling and waving at everybody, heading for the day room where
they play lots and lots of ping-pong. Occasionally I play ping-pong
with them. They seem like super-nice guys.

Olaf and Pavel are under the impression that since Bulgaria recently
joined the European Union, they are entitled to live and work here
with impunity. *I've got you dead in the sights of my blunderbuss, you
scoundrel.* Sadly, this doesn't actually seem to be the case (we think you
need to have been invited over by a prospective employer), and since
their tourist visas are due to expire in just a few weeks' time, nobody's
quite sure what's going to happen. They're currently homeless. I see
them around town on my way back and forth to the station all the
time. All Olaf and Pavel ever seem to do is wander around Staines town
centre, smiling at everybody. And then they wander up to Appleby for
a spot of lunch and ping-pong. Does this beat their previous lives in
Bulgaria? One certainly hopes so; although the food's obviously considerably worse. One wonders what will happen to them.*

So that's the Bulgarians. There's also a shy, almost mute young
Slovakian man who comes and sits in the corner of the Quiet
Room every now and then. Plus, today for one day only, we get a
pair of heavily pierced Czech heavy metal fans who are slowly
cycling across Europe on what they merrily describe as their 'grand
homeless tour'. One of the Czechs asks if I've got a drink. I tell him
no, sorry, but there's tea in an urn in the dining room. But, he snarls,
what use is that? The Slovakian, the Czechs and Bulgarians do not
intermingle; indeed, they pointedly ignore each other. It seems that
nobody's told any of these guys about the grand new tradition of
self-supporting Eurovision Eastern European bloc voting.

---

* Somebody eventually tells them there are some other Bulgarians, apparently,
in Newbury. So they go to Newbury and we never see or hear from them again.

Step Eight

Coconut Shy Assistant
Stanmore Primary School Summer Fête, Winchester
Most common prize at summer fete (UK): bottle of sherry
Average money raised at UK summer fête (for church roof fund, etc.):
£341.23

My friend Steve, a Status Quo-obsessed vocalist in a local pub rock band,* had heard about my admirable recent catalogue of Good Works, and suggested I come and help out on a coconut shy he runs annually at his kids' local primary school summer fete. Since we have our own baby now, I thought it was a great idea to while away valuable post-birth chores and nappy-changing time by agreeing to help out for the day. This'll be knowledge-investment for baby Reuben's future, right? And if anything was going to re-engage me with my local community, then surely this was it?

'We can always do with extra helpers for the fête,' says Steve, humming a lengthy snatch of 'Margarita Time' as usual. 'So long as they're not on the Sex Offenders Register, ha-ha!'

'Ha-ha! It's OK though, I'm not.'

'Ha-ha! All right, good, you can come.'

'Can I bring my camera?'

'Erm.'

First, we help out erecting the large tents under which the cakes, raffle tickets and general bazaar ephemera are to be traded by yonder grannies who aren't here yet because it's pissing down with rain. An early summer Saturday morning motley rabble of helpful dads (hi there) stand in their Gap fleeces and khakis (but please note not 'hi there' here), grapple furiously with tarps and poles and eyelets, and fast become drenched. There's unpleasant grunting; sodden huffs; filthy expletives.

* I mean, he's not *that* good a friend.

'Keep your voice down, Seb, this is a primary school playground,' warns Steve.

Eventually the tents are all erected but unfortunately they soon blow over in the wind and scud like billowing phantoms across the playing field, whereupon we all give chase; all terribly Benny Hill.

The grannies arrive with their tins of Quality Street and cheap bars of soap and huddle under the school building's eaves to complain about things generally.

Steve and I repair to the edge of the grass running track to set up the coconut shy.

'If this weather keeps up, nobody will come,' calls Steve over the whipping wind and lashing rain. We doggedly ram metal coconut holding-poles into the grass and set up a net behind them. Then I spot the large tray full of Tesco coconuts lying on the grass that's slowly filling up with rainwater.

'If no one comes, do you think we'll get to keep the coconuts?'

'What, you want a coconut? Just take one.'

'Can I really have one?'

Steve looks at me through the gale. 'Yes,' he says.

I excitedly put a coconut into my bag. What a result already. 'Roll up, roll up!'

An hour later, the rain begins to ease and a few solitary rays of sun pierce the purple storm clouds.

'There'll be a rush on now, just watch,' says Steve, and as if by magic, about a quarter of an hour later, a few waterproof-clad punters arrive with their miserable-looking children strung out in a sullen line behind them. They trudge around the edge of the field, pausing briefly to inspect each stall: there's a pin-the-tail-on-the-donkey, a tombola, us, and – this one's new to me – a stall with a table full of old crockery piled up on it. Of all the immeasurable delights on offer in the field here today, the family wanders blithely past all us traditionalists – the children sneering at our finely balanced coconuts – before settling *en masse* in front of the stall with the plates.

'What's that stall?' I ask Steve, peering through the drizzle.*

'You'll see.'

I watch the father hand over money. The stall-holder hands a large rubber mallet to each of the three children. I watch, horrified, as the children proceed to lay gleefully into the crockery: chinaware splinters noisily everywhere – smashes, crashes, explodes into dust. The kids all squeal with delight. The father and stall-holder stand and watch fondly with tickled, avuncular expressions while the little darlings wreak kindergarten revenge upon dinner-plate after cereal bowl after side-dish. After a few minutes of wanton destruction, the – by now visibly psychotically frenzied – children reluctantly lay down their arms and follow their father in a slow wander around the rest of the field, then leave the school premises and head back to their Sports Utility Vehicle.

'The plate-smashing stall,' muses Steve, scratching his chin. 'Always the most popular stall in the field.'

'Well, why don't you start your own rival plate-smashing stall if that's what the kids are into?'

'Yes, but who'd do the coconuts?'

'Well, nobody.'

Steve looks puzzled. We stand and watch the stall-holder replace the crockery debris with fresh plates and bowls and, sure enough, more kids are running across the field now, like sportswear *Railway Children*, to wallop it all to buggery. Put off by the rapidly growing queue, a couple of stragglers are momentarily distracted by our coconut shy.

'Here we go, look,' I whisper to Steve. 'They can't resist!'

'How much?' one of them enquires.

'Three throws for 50p, eight throws for £1.'†

They each hand over £1 and receive three wooden balls in return. They hurl them with so much blind violence that they all miss.

'Oooh, bad luck,' I exclaim, still clinging to the myth that primary

---

* I am running out of words for 'rain' and 'storm' and suchlike.

† Or something, I don't know.

school fêtes are one of the last bastions of innocent, cloudy lemon-ade, *Boy's Own* jolly japery, rather than an orgy of tartrazine-fuelled arbitrary violence and plate-smashing. I crouch down to the net to retrieve Kid A's wooden balls and then feel an unexpected whoosh past my left ear: Kid B's throwing his balls – at vicious velocity – while I'm still in the line of fire!

'Wait!' I cry, raising an arm to my face. 'Noooooooooo!'

His second throw gets me smack on the knuckle. Blinding agony. I collapse on to the grass and begin to writhe in pain. I hear Steve raise his voice at the youth, but the wooden balls keep coming.

'For God's sake, stop them!' I shriek, rolling through the wet grass, clutching my bloodied hand. '*Stop!*'

With his final ball, Kid B finally knocks off a coconut, which falls off its pole and on to my legs. His hands drop to his sides.

'Gis it,' he says.

'Look what you've done!' I cry, raising my hand so the blood begins to flow down my wrist.

The kid shrugs, and mutters something about wanting his coconut and me being a lady's parts. I stand, and sternly present the coconut. The kids walk off.

'Are you all right?' asks Steve.

'Can you *believe* that?'

'Kids, eh?' says Steve, who has two of them; daughters, though; I suspect that's different. My Little Pony; brushing hair all day; some skipping.

'When my son's older,' I bluster, 'I'm telling you now, he will *not* be anything like those two little bastards.'

Steve stands and surveys the fête, smirking.

'He'll be a decent, fine, upstanding little fellow.'

'Is your hand OK?'

'Just about. No thanks to your excellent supervision of proceed-ings.'

'I beg your pardon?'

'Nothing.'

The sun comes out and the field fills up. We even get a queue. Roughly 80 per cent of all the kids throw the wooden balls with frightening violence. As do their parents, when they insist on having a go too, which is often.

'There are other primary school fêtes in Winchester where people wouldn't throw the balls as hard as this,' muses Steve after we've been stripped of all our coconuts – even the one in my bag that some eagle-eyed whippersnapper somehow spotted although my bag was *zipped shut*.

Faye and baby Reuben arrive and cross the field towards us.

'Where are all your coconuts?' she asks.

'Gone. Pillaged.'

'And why is there blood all over your hand?'

Actually she didn't ask that; instead I scuttled up and thrust my knuckle in her face while whining and then, after a few moments' squinting, she uttered: 'Ah, diddums.'

I was glad there were no coconuts left for her.

Steve said that my help here today had been invaluable. At least I'm pretty sure that's what he said; I had trouble hearing him over the sound of smashing crockery away to our right. And if I learned one thing here today, it was that primary school fêtes aren't what they used to be. The fucking mayor wasn't even here.

The Southampton and Winchester Visitors Group
Portsmouth Library Café

'I have something for you,' I tell Appo, fumbling inside my rucksack while he frowns at me over his tepid coffee and a factory muffin. Meanwhile our respective infants Reuben and Joy tussle on the floor underneath the table. (Joy tolerates Reuben's playful-yet-relentless face-slapping with deft, stoic feints and uneasy laughter before Reuben attempts to steal Joy's biscuit, crawls away to attack the Coke machine, gets his hand stuck inside, and then starts to cry. And that's the first ten seconds.) Meanwhile I continue to fumble around inside my rucksack.

'I definitely have something for you,' I repeat.

'I am feeling like giving up on everything now,' says Appo glumly who, needless to add, is still sleeping on his friend's floor.

I pull out a large manila envelope triumphantly. 'Aha!'

Appo looks nonplussed.

'Open it!'

Appo opens it nonplussedly.★

'Read it!'

Appo reads the letter and peels an orange, credit card–sized piece of plastic incredulously off the bottom of the page. He sits and stares at it for some moments.

'Does this mean . . .?'

'Yes! It's a National Insurance card! Which means that, after all this time, you finally officially exist!'

Appo stares at it. Holds it up. Stares some more. Turns it around.

'I can't believe it. With this card, now I can work, I can claim benefit, I can do anything, isn't this right?'

'Yes, except you're not allowed to.'

'I know, I'm just saying.'

'Yes, well, you *could*, technically, but it wouldn't be very wise. If you got caught you'd probably be deported or something.'

'Yes, this is not so good.'

'No, not really. But this NI card means that you can now officially live with your family. If we go over to the housing office right now, we can give them the number on your card here, and you should be able to move in with Marie and Joy immediately.'

'Really?'

'That's what I've been led to believe, yes.'

'Wow!'

We extricate Reuben's hand from the Coke machine, dab at the blood with a napkin, gather up our gear and head over the civic square to the giant council office building, where we ascend to the housing department and queue for a chat with the man at the main

---

★ Is this a word? *No – Ed.*

desk. We ask him if it's now OK for Appo to move in with his family. The young chap disappears to check with his superior. He is gone for three or four minutes. The clock on the wall ticks loudly. Those queuing behind us begin to mutter impatiently. Reuben and Joy yammer and lunge at one another. Reuben slaps Joy. Joy slaps Reuben. It's like New Order's 'True Faith' video. Eventually the young man reappears. Retakes his seat. Hands the letter back to Appo.

'Yes, that's fine. You can move in whenever you like.'

'Thank you!' says Appo. And we all glide out.

Over at the railway station, we say our goodbyes.

'Appo, you know what this means though? It means that, now you're housed, the SWVG are going to stop giving you money. Their funds are really short, and they figure that now you're together as a family, Marie's money should be enough for all of you, at least for the time being. There are others that the SWVG consider more in need of money than you now – proper, destitute, failed asylum seekers. If your Home Office case is successful, which we hope and pray it will be, then of course you'll be able to work and everything with impunity; but in the meantime I'm afraid it's, kind of, goodbye from us.'

Even though I've informed Appo of this situation a number of times, he always manages to look convincingly shocked whenever I mention it.

'What! End of my money? Oh no!'

'Yes, I'm afraid so.'

'Oh well. I am so grateful for all your help.'

'That's fine, it was a total pleasure. I'm only sorry it took so long. Enjoy living with the guys!'

'I will, yes!'

'Goodbye then. I'll come down and see you in a few weeks. To see how you're getting on.'

'OK, goodbye.'

'Goodbye.'

Reuben and Joy have a clumsy – and largely accidental – farewell embrace, as only a pair of under-twos can.

'They are so friendly,' comments Appo, as beaming Reuben lands a final, flailing slap hard on Joy's cheek and he bursts into tears, followed by howling.

'Best friends.'

Bring on the duckling feathers, mothers 'n' fathers.

My house, Winchester

Appleby House's manager Brian phones.

'I felt I just ought to warn you. You heard that the Shadow was sectioned, and placed in a secure mental health facility?'

'Yes?'

'Well, unfortunately he's escaped. He loosened all the bolts in his cell window and then escaped out of it. And he stuffed his bed full of pillows to make the staff think he was still there under the covers.'

'Wow, just like in films!'

'I suppose so. But the reason for my phoning you like this is that he was last seen in southern Hampshire, indeed in Nether Wallop, not far from Winchester.'

'What! When was this?'

'About half an hour ago. So if you do happen to see him, call the police immediately.'

'Oh, God!'

'Although it's extremely unlikely, it's certainly possible that he's on his way to Winchester to find *you*, seeing as you made the unfortunate error of telling him where you lived.'

'Oh, God!'

'But that's just personal speculation.'

'Well, thanks for that.'

'Everybody must stay calm.'

'Oh, God!'

After five minutes of kind counselling and then reassuring goodbyes, I hang up, step to my front window and tentatively look out into the street. It appears normal, albeit slightly sinister. I narrow my eyes. Then I go round to the back of my house and step tentatively out into the back garden, where there is a man in a baseball hat, slowly walking towards me.

'Aaaaarrrrggghhhhh!'

But it's only our friendly Polish builder Remi, who's rebuilding a collapsed wall and has come to beg for – I don't know – another cup of coffee or something; his English isn't so good.

'Get back to work!' I shout. 'Back!' And so, finally, Remi retreats. (There is no sign of the Shadow for the remainder of the day.)

Appleby House, Staines
9.30 a.m.

First ever author of note to present a typewritten manuscript to a publisher:
Mark Twain (*Life on the Mississippi*)
Typical cost of 70cl bottle of sambuca (UK): £14.99

(No sign of the Shadow yet today.)

Tosh found an old typewriter at the local dump. A small crowd has gathered in the Quiet Room to assess it; it works fine – nobody understands why anyone would throw such a thing out. A few even get angry at the wastage. Some sheets of blank paper are sourced, then everybody patiently takes a turn tappety-tapping for five minutes. Thus a kind of impromptu 'writing group' forms. As I'm seventh in line for a go, my own tapped musings came directly after the following:

```
'Once uppon a time their was a typwriter'
'shiT SHIT shitshity shit shitsTainesss
issssshit Staines is SHit'
'qqqqqqqqqqwwwwwwweeeeeeeeeeeeerrrrrttttt-
tyyyyyyy7777777777'
' Martin. Cculver_MartinCulvvvr MArtin cUlver'
'Dogfukker11 u fuX doggZZ11!! Kevinu wankerr
///keviN FUXX DOGZZ ––tRUE garry woz her'
' qqq q'*
```

---

* FYI my own contribution was: 'I worship Satan.' 'Do you?' asked Tosh.

Following this initial warm-up session, the first thing the writing group discusses is the poor state of contemporary fiction. The consensus is that books with 'actual things happening' in them, 'like war and murders' are best; rather than 'the kind of boring wank that wins the Booker Prize and shit like that'.

'Who reads it?'

'No one!'

'Bollocks to it!'

'Fuck off!'

'Calm down, everybody.'

Novelizations of films also prove popular, though not art-house ones. As do Jeffrey Archer and Clive Cusser.* Then it emerges that two of those present are currently engaged in writing film scripts of their own.

'Really?' I ask, probably a little too disbelieving; thus in response I get one of the films' entire plot, throughout the extraordinary intricacies of which everybody wanders off, except for Tosh, who sits lovingly polishing his typewriter, nodding along. The plot is convoluted; owes much to *Die Hard* and the oeuvres of Chuck Norris and Sylvia Kristel.

Over coffee, Leanne reveals her gentler side by informing everybody present that she sleeps with a knife under her bed.

'In case, you know, *he* comes to visit.'

'What, me? That's not terribly romantic.'

'No, but I'd stab you if you tried it on. I would.' Leanne stares at me fiercely. 'But I mean the Shadow. Ever since he escaped I've been having these dreams. I've been waking up in the middle of the night with these cold sweats and that, so I bought a knife just in case.'

Leanne mimes a thrust and then a twist upwards; and then a twist downwards and on to general disembowelment. Then just as I was about to say that at least the Shadow wasn't heading for *their bloody house*, Kate pipes up: 'I'm the same. I can't go into my garden after

* *sic*

dark now. Because the Shadow's got a history of stalking and violence towards healthcare staff he considers "let him down", I've
found myself becoming scared of the dark. It's bizarre, I know, but
all the same . . .'.

Tristan says he's been feeling uneasy too. I'd had no idea the
Shadow's escape had caused quite so much collective unease. For
the sake of Appleby staff morale, I decide to keep schtum about the
severe possibility that the Shadow is, as we speak, waiting in the
shed at the bottom of my garden for me to come home so he can
slice my nipples off with his bread knife. But then I change my
mind and tell them anyway, to get attention, and they all laugh.

'You won't be laughing when next time I come in here, it's without nipples.'

'Yes, we will,' says Leanne. 'Annoying Mr No-Nipples. Ha-ha-ha.'

Later I type out two letters on behalf of Appleby visitors: one is a
reference for potential housing, and the other an apology-and-
mercy-plea regarding a recent drugs-related eviction. I'm delighted
to have been asked – the younger guys who use Appleby have until
recently maintained a withering distance from me, but, finally, they
seem to be accepting me. They even include me in (a bit of) their
banter. This involves telling me to fuck off a lot. Gawd bless the
little tykes. Sadly, Kevin takes this all too far and starts to tell me to
fuck off rather more excitably than the rest, and gets banned for the
rest of the day. Ha-ha-ha. *Bye, Kevin.*

'Piss off, you long-haired hippy wanker!'

'Come on, Kevin, that's enough, *out.*'

Me and the boys share a laugh – many brilliant laughs – at
Kevin's expense as he's ushered out of the building and the door's
locked behind him.

'I'm going to get totally mashed on sambuca this afternoon,'
boasts one of the lads, daring me to recommend otherwise.

And of course I don't; indeed my expression is politely egging him
on. Several more lads concur that getting right mullered on sambuca
sounds like a forward-thinking way to spend the afternoon. I think

it's probably time for me to go and load up the dishwasher.

'Yeah, go on – fuck off, you boring bastard!'

'Oh no, I'm not boring, I'm just going over here for a while.'

'Scared to come and get pissed! What a twat!'

'Arsehole!'

You really can't beat banter.

(Shed's clean.)

The Southampton and Winchester Visitors Group
Appo and Marie's temporary apartment, Portsmouth

(Unless I specifically mention it, you can just assume from now on that there have been no further sightings of the Shadow.)

A few months back, Appo had asked whether, when it came to time for his family to move from their temporary accommodation into their permanent home, I'd be able to give them a hand moving their stuff, with my car. I'd replied, sure, I'd be happy to. And so, a few weeks after I'd seen him last, he calls to say they have a date on which to move to their new council flat, in a week or so's time. No problemo, I reply – I'll be there.

'With your car?' stammers Appo.

'Yes, with my car.'

'Is it a big car?'

'Appo, you've been in my car several times. It's a very small car. You told me you didn't have too much stuff though, right?'

There was a pause. 'Right.'

'*Is* there a lot of stuff?'

'Maybe Marie's stuff.'

'Does Marie have a *lot* of stuff?'

'Some stuff, yes.'

'Like, for example?'

'I think, a sofa.'

'You *think* a sofa.'

Appo chuckles. 'Yes, a sofa. Oh yes!'

'Well, the sofa won't fit in my car, so I'll call David, who has a big

Volvo, and ask if he can help out. Would the sofa fit in a Volvo?'

'Oh yes!'

'Are you *sure*?'

Appo cackles. 'I don't know!' Forces himself to be serious for a moment. 'I think actually yes.' Resumes the cackle.

I call David anyway, a big SWVG cheese (or at least as big as we get), and he agrees to come and help move Appo's sofa.

It's a warm and sunny afternoon when, the following week, we drive down to Portsmouth in the Volvo. After we've found the right council block, we climb the grim, grey concrete stairs to meet a smiling Appo, Marie and baby Joy at their front door on the second floor.

'Let's have a look at this sofa then,' says David jovially, pushing through into the flat. 'Yep. That should fit, no problem.'

Appo stands, simpering at David's shoulder.

'There is also . . .' he says quietly.

'Also?'

'Also, yes . . .' We are led into the master bedroom, where there is a large double bed and a pair of side tables. Then into the kitchen, where there is a fridge and a cooker. In the lounge there's a large coffee table. Two large televisions. A stereo system with big speakers. Two armchairs. Numerous large suitcases. Boxes. Bags. Black bin-liners. Loads of toys. A bookcase. A bona fide large removal van's-worth of gear, basically.

'I was told just a sofa,' says David quietly.

'The sofa, yes?' replies Appo, pointing to the sofa.

'And I've got to be somewhere else in an hour.'

'Yes, so are we,' says Appo. 'At the new flat!'

And everybody laughs. Because otherwise it would have all kicked off. We make a start loading the Volvo with gear anyway, because what else, exactly, were we supposed to do? After much aimless yet hopeful driving around various Portsmouth suburbs, Appo actually *locates* his new flat (a mile away – third floor), and we get into some kind of removals rhythm. Soon, we've hauled a good seven or eight Volvo-fulls of possessions across town and up and into their new pad, which turns out to be a mere two minutes' walk from the world-famous ship-of-the-line, HMS *Victory*!

'Hey, Appo!' I exclaim as we struggle up yet more dirty, grey, communal concrete steps with one half of the double bed's iron frame. 'This new flat is fantastic! You'll be able to take Joy to see HMS *Victory* whenever you like! It's so near! Isn't that brilliant?'

Of course, Appo has absolutely no idea what I'm talking about. His time in the United Kingdom has been sadly lacking in opportunities to soak up our nation's proud naval history of killing (and being killed by) the French, the Spanish and all the rest.

Also possibly distracting might be the fact that their new flat is tiny and completely undecorated. Its previous white, English tenants had been so abysmally filthy that the council had to strip out all the carpeting and wallpaper, which they'd scrawled all over with pens and paint and God knows what else. You could still see some of this bizarre domestic graffiti on a few of the ceilings – outlandish swearing and drawings of penises. Apart from this, every room is completely bare. Appo and Marie have managed to pick up a few rolls of dirt-cheap carpet, which stand forlornly in the tiny hall, ready to roll.

But still. HMS *Victory* is just around the corner! Chin up!

'Kiss me, Hardy?' I call up the stairwell. 'Or, perhaps, kis*met*?'

Silence.

'Admiral Nelson, yeah? Did you have Admiral Nelson in Kinshasa?'

No response. We arrive breathless on the ammonia-reeking second-floor landing, and haul the bed frame along the forbidding concrete walkway outside their flat and up to their battered front door. After much heft and grunting, it just about fits into the stripped, bare-floorboarded bedroom.

'Somebody has drawn unpleasant things all over your ceiling, Appo, look.'

'I know. It was on the walls also, but we have painted all of those now.'

This explains why some of the walls look like they're bleeding silt, and why Appo's clothes are caked with what I now realize, with relief, isn't Joy's dried-on diarrhoea after all.

'Ah yes. Don't you have a brush?'

'Not yet!'

And we laugh and stand there for five minutes reading the ceiling* (despite the fact that both David and myself were supposed to be back home doing prearranged other stuff hours and hours ago. A friend in the hand is worth two in the bush or something, right?).

I'm hoping this is the beginning of a bright, new family life for Appo. Until we hear back from the Home Office regarding his Human Rights application, that is. And that could take at least two years. Just a minor shadow to be living under, then. Thank heavens for the morale-lifting vicinity of HMS *Victory*.

Cue the national anthem.

The Southampton and Winchester Visitors Group
Southampton Library Café

Christine (headmistress/fierce bob) phones.

'Seeing as we've now stopped funding Appo, and you've stopped seeing him . . .'

'Well, I . . .'

'*Officially* stopped seeing him, then, we were wondering, would you be prepared to take on a new client? We have a family from Zimbabwe who are desperate, and there's nobody else within the organization currently free to take them on.'

Cripes. Somewhat naïvely, perhaps, I'd never even considered the possibility of taking on somebody else. I don't know what I'd thought really. Perhaps I imagined that, post-Appo, my duty to 'these-sorts-of-people' was now done. What a pile of bullshit, I suddenly realize. Of *course* there are others in need; and of course I should take on another client. As a volunteer for the SWVG, surely this was what it was all about? Staying the course. The clients our organization take on can't work or claim benefits and

---

* It is my belief that the perpetrators are in genuine need of some sort of mental health counselling.

would otherwise quite possibly be destitute, so who the hell else was going to help them? It was a complete no-brainer. Any other decision would have exposed my motivation for being involved in the first place as utterly cynical – a situation I've tried hard to stay firmly on the right side of throughout all this volunteering.

'Yes, of course,' I tell Christine, who has been waiting patiently for my internal monologue to finish. 'I'm totally cool to take on somebody else.'

'Well, you did so much for Appo; now you can use all your new-found skills to help somebody else.'

'Yes! I suppose. If you'd call them skills. Anyway. Tell me about this family.'

They are the Kambias* – husband, wife and baby daughter. Mr and Mrs Kambia came over from Zimbabwe in 2002, with work permits, to continue their studies to become chemists. They subsequently unwittingly overran their permits, by which time it was too late either to apply for an extension or for new ones. And so they slipped into the realm of the illegal immigrant. Applying to the Home Office for Right to Remain, Mrs Kambia was successful; Mr Kambia wasn't. In need of money, Mr Kambia got an illegal job as a hospital porter. His employer became suspicious after one of his references didn't add up, and he was promptly unmasked as an evil, swan-munching† failed-asylum-seeking pox on the backside of society!

'I know it was bad, but we just didn't have any money at all – we were desperate,' Jo Kambia, a tall, handsome young man sporting tied-back braids, tells me over coffee in Southampton library café, the same place I'd first met Appo many months earlier. 'And I didn't even get to do any work. I was caught before I started. I've got to go to the police station this afternoon, so that they can read me the

---

* Names changed. Appo was totally cool about me writing about him. These guys' situation was a lot more sensitive and strained, thus I never really had the opportunity to ask them.
† This infamous 'asylum seekers eat the Queen's swans!' story was in fact a complete fabrication, made up by our kindly tabloid newspapers. As was the 'asylum seekers eat donkeys!' one too.

charges. I am very worried about this. About being sent home, away from my wife and daughter.'

Jo's wife Eva sits beside him, rocking their sleeping, six-month-old baby. Eva is silently weeping. I am extremely uncomfortable. This is completely different to my dealings with happy-go-lucky Appo, with the lollipops and the chuckling duckling. I feel completely out of my depth. I can't think of any reply to Jo's relentless catalogue of misfortune. To make matters worse, although his English isn't bad, I'm having a hard time understanding exactly what he's saying through his thick accent. The fact that I'm only picking up about a third of all the detail he's giving me makes me feel particularly useless.

'Well, I'll certainly do as much as I can,' I finally reply, hoping Jo can't read the fear in my eyes (fear that pales into insignificance beside their own), or the illegible notes I've been scrawling into my notebook.* 'I'll make a few phone calls and speak to a few people, and then we can talk through your options when I see you again next week. How does that sound?'

'It sounds pretty good. Thank you.'

We all shake hands. Eva is still silently crying. As now is their baby daughter. All three file slowly out of the café past the gift shop, visibly cowed by life; by the gravity of events. And they're both only about twenty-five years old. I watch them leave and scratch my head with my pen. Exhale. Welcome myself to the real world.†

Appleby House, Staines
Midday

I'm there when the call comes in. From the police.** All staff are ushered hurriedly into the office. As we file in and the door is pulled closed behind us, Kevin and his friends gather to taunt us.

'Scared, are ya!'

---

* e.g. 'Do something about all this.' And 'Sort everything out.' And, most of all, 'Phone Christine'.

† Not long after this - thanks to the collective efforts of the Group - the Kambias are rehoused under social security support – up in sunny Darlington.

** Sadly not those cuddly coppers down in Basingstoke.

'Oooh, Mummy.'

In fact they should be the ones who are scared, since with us all in the office, Leanne's temporarily in charge: expect ladle injuries all round. Inside the office, there is silence. We're all looking at Kate. Kate looks back at us, and raises her eyebrows.

'Well, I've just got off the phone to the police. And the news is that the Shadow has been found,' she says.

Please not in my shed, I think.

'He's dead, I'm afraid. He was found last night, in some bushes at the side of the A34, near Newbury. The police think he was hit by a car or, more likely, a lorry. His injuries suggest that he'd been run over, although nobody's reported hitting anybody, at least not yet. They think he might have walked out into the oncoming traffic, been knocked down and fatally injured, and then somehow crawled away into the bushes by the side of the road, where he eventually died. Apparently it was all a bit of a mess.'

'Christ. Like a dog or something.'

'The police aren't treating it as suspicious.'

'But it could have been a hit and run?'

'They say they think suicide's more likely. But it's early yet. They just called to let us know. And they wanted to know whether we knew anything about any next of kin anywhere.'

'And do we?'

'No.'

We all sit and digest this information. For the Appleby staff, unfortunately this sort of news isn't exactly uncommon.

'So that's that, then?'

'That's that.'

'Do we tell the other service users about this?'

'I think we'll only tell people if they ask. Most people here didn't like him – they were scared and intimidated by him – so we'll try to avoid any triumphant gloating.'

'OK.'

We filter out.

It's chips for lunch. Leanne even manages to mess those up – half of them end up burned. I didn't know you could burn chips. Nevertheless, they are all eaten: every last blackened witch's pinkie. Chips for lunch inspires a kind of collective joy. They're devoured with hearty, gay abandon and eight or nine large vats of NO FRILLS vinegar. You just can't beat chips. Chips!

'I hate chips,' says Kevin, sulking at the hatch, and Garry pushes him into the dining room door. Everybody cheers. Chips!

RIP the Shadow. I liked talking about *Sesame Street* with you.*

---

* Minor revisionism.

Step Nine

Wells for India
My mother's house, Winchester

Fraction of the world's poorest people who live in India:
one-third
Percentage of Rajasthan (NE India) children who suffer from malnutrition:
50%

Allow me to begin by explaining that Wells for India isn't actually based *in* my mother's house. I am here to ask my mother whether she has any suggestions about fundraising activities that I could participate in to raise money for – you guessed it! – the charity Wells for India, who I have recently been to visit.

I felt that maybe my various activities to date had been perhaps a tad parochial; that maybe the time was right to extend my gaze to distant lands, lands whose populations were denied the luxury of drop-in centres or £7 tongs or expensive Christmas puddings. These lands sounded mighty fine, yet in need of funds for progressive activity. Stand back, coming through.

Julia and Tania at Wells for India were very helpful and nice, and told me that I could do pretty much anything to raise money, within reason, and that I should get back to them when I've come up with an interesting idea. I don't really have much of an imagination, which is why I've asked my mother, only I already wish I hadn't bothered.

'But how can they be?' says my mother.

'How can what be?'

'How can they be for India?'

'Well, that's where they're needed.'

'I think it sounds rather cruel.'

'Providing poverty-stricken Indians with sustainable water supplies?'

'No, you've lost me now.'

'I've been lost for a while here, to be honest.'

'Let's start again from the beginning,' says my mother. 'Why, exactly, do they need all these whales in India?'

'OK, I have identified the source of the confusion. It's not whales, it's *wells*. As in wells that provide water; that children fall into, on the news.'

Oh, how we laughed.

'Right, let me think for a minute.'

My mother, she thunk.

'You could go around and visit all the strange families.'

'What?'

'Or, I don't know, visit all the churches.'

'What?'

'You did ask!'

And she's right. I really ought to have known better.

Later that day, I ask my wife if she's got any suggestions of her own.

'You could run a marathon,' she says.

'No.'

'Or a half a marathon.'

'Nope.'

'Or a ten-mile run or something like that.'

'*No*. I hate running! You know I hate running. Why do you keep going on about running when running is something I go out of my way specifically to avoid and have done my whole life?'

'Well, that's the reason. I think this should be something outside your comfort zone. Something strenuous. Something that people will feel happy sponsoring you doing. Otherwise you'll just have, like, a sponsored "listening to some music" session, for which nobody will sponsor you.'

'That's a great idea!'

'You see, exactly. Maybe you could run across the whole of the South Downs, with Reuben strapped to you.'

'May we have some more sensible suggestions?'

'But I like the idea of you running. It would be fun. And you could write about it!'

'Well, yes, of course I'm going to bloody *write* about it. What else do you think I'm going to do: keep it all to myself as my own little secret?'

'You mean like most people do, when they do things for charity?'

'Oh yeah, right. Please sponsor me. What for? Not telling – I'm too modest. But actually I do see your point. Which I'll counter by, get this, raising £1,000 for Wells for India.'

'Well, that would certainly go some way towards cancelling out any lingering cynicism your readers might feel.* You just need to work out how to do it.'

'But, darling,† that's why I asked you in the first place.'

'A half-marathon is only thirteen miles; come on, stop being so lazy.'

'Only!'

Etc.

I decided to search online for some inspiration. The Internet came up with the following fundraising ideas:

– Shave off all my hair. (I am too vain to do this. Also, as a long-haired, rock 'n' rollin' kinda guy, this is pretty much against my religion.)

– Baked beans bath. (I'm sorry but this idea is just too revolting. Also logistically unpalatable. What does one do, just fill up one's own bath with baked beans and then get in and invite people round to watch? Sounds a bit weird. Or should one go to one's local park and humiliate oneself in one of those old cowboy tubs? And how long would I have to lie there for: all *day*? It's the height of summer, readers – the aroma would be highly unpleasant. And then what would I do with all the

---

* Well, you bastards? *Does it?*
† Ha ha ha – as if.

baked beans afterwards? Give them to the homeless? Stick 'em all in a wheelbarrow and take 'em up to Leanne at Appleby House? I'm warming to this idea now.)

– Car boot sale. (I haven't got enough things that people would want to buy; plus this would also be extremely boring and would not deliver to you, my reading public, the high-octane thrills 'n' spills you have been used to on a page-by-page basis, e.g. the Stanmore Primary School Fête.)

– Abseiling. (I have a fear of heights.)

– Donkey Derby. (This is cruel, plus I don't know anyone with any donkeys.)

– Longest chain of paper clips; line of coins, etc. (With my limited authorial skills, this one would just be too much of a challenge to write interestingly about. Hard to believe, I know. Pardon?)

– Murder mystery evening. (Just unfettered, complete and utter knavery.)

– No-Work Day. (As a writer, most of my days are like this already.)

– Parachute jump. (See abseiling, only more so.)

– Throwing wet sponges at person in stocks. (I don't really fancy this one, especially after getting assaulted like that at the coconut shy.)

– Dry cornflakes / cream cracker eating competition. (I find it difficult to believe that people might want to give me – or rather Wells for India – £1,000 for just sitting around eating a load or cornflakes and/or crackers. Also, as with the baked beans, where would I do this exactly? In my garden? Under strict laboratory cream cracker conditions in Winchester Guildhall?)

– Coffee mornings. (See No-Work Day.)

– Face painting. (Unless I were just to paint Kiss faces on everyone, this idea doesn't interest me. And actually the painting-Kiss-faces-on-people idea is brilliant, were it not for the fact that Gene Simmons would undoubtedly sue me for ten times whatever I managed to raise which, let's face it,* wouldn't be very much.)

The fact gradually dawns that I might have no choice but to do something involving running after all. Running feels like the only fundraising activity I might be able to perform for which I wouldn't feel like a total arse asking people to sponsor me. It would be raw cash, legitimately earned. After a little extremely reluctant further online investigation, I learn that there's a marathon/half-marathon due to be run exactly fifty-four days from now, called the Great Clarendon Way, and which runs† from Salisbury to Winchester. The full twenty-six miles is too far – even as a non-runner, I know that's delusional and frankly unnatural. But the half-marathon? Thirteen miles (Broughton to Winchester instead)? Sounds like it might just be doable. I email two friends who I know run regularly, as I often poke fun at them about it.

My friend Paul replies thus: 'A half-marathon is running for two hours solid. If you are serious about this, try running for small distances at first: twenty minutes, thirty minutes, getting longer as you feel fitter. The first run will destroy you, and you will be sore for days. So remember to stretch before and after running. I would say that if you are regularly able to do an hour's running without difficulty, go for the race. Just remember that a half-marathon is the length of the Great North Run, in which a few folk die each year.'

I felt this had been going really positively right up until the dying part.

My other running friend Steve wrote: 'Eh?! A half-marathon in under two months' training for someone who doesn't run? You could do it but it will totally fuck you. Btw can do boozing on Thursday if that suits?'

A far more agreeable coda.

* Face it!
† Runs!

Twenty minutes sounded like a long time, so, highly attuned to the fear of death, I decide to start with just ten instead. Fully aware of the dread you must currently be feeling at the prospect of wading through pages and pages of boring detail regarding my rigorous training schedule, why don't we instead cut to a *Rocky*-esque literary montage[*] of my increasingly panicky attempts to get fit in time for the race (which I have officially entered now), and which will, I hope, act as a clever stylistic cloaking device for pages and pages of boring detail regarding my rigorous training schedule. Here we go. Begin motivational playlist. *And switch to italics to imply dynamism.*

'Eye of the Tiger'

Due to lack of professional running clothes,[†] I emerge for my first ten-minute jog wearing an old T-shirt saying *Finland*, a pair of swimming trunks, brown Marks & Spencer socks, and old brown trainers entirely unsuited to running. Faye thinks my stretching is 'hilarious'; Reuben even more so – indeed he laughs so hard he actually falls over. My first experience of speeding up whenever a woman comes into view occurs fifteen seconds after I leave the house, and then ten or so times after that, even for a really fat one waddling up a hill in a Sainsbury's uniform. Overall, the run goes well, although it's tiring accelerating past all these women, and I enjoy getting into some vague kind of 'zone'. Afterwards I am relieved my chest has not exploded.

'Simply the Best'

Feeling self-conscious about my trainers, I venture into one of those youths' sports shops and stand self-consciously by the trainer section but then flee when approached by a young man in a track suit asking if I'm 'All right there, mate?'

---

[*] William Burroughs meets Ron Pickering?
[†] i.e. vests, right?

Step Nine

'I believe I can Fly'

I email Julia at Wells for India to inform her of my decision to raise £1,000 on their behalf by running a half-marathon.

She replies: 'You have come up trumps and we very much hope you don't die. You are running for a very good cause, and we much appreciate it. Women in Rajasthan walk up to five miles per day fetching water; sometimes they have to do this more than once … If you would like a water pot on your head you are welcome to borrow one, but it may make things even more tricky holding it on as you run.'

Thanks, Julia. However this is particularly good news as it means I don't have to load up my brain with complicated Wells for India info in order to attract sponsors – I can just run, walk, crawl, collapse and then be airlifted to safety; after which I can simply hand over all the cash at a small ceremony, live on local radio, presented by Top Jimmy.

'Total Eclipse of the Heart'

The subsequent few, slightly longer runs begin to hurt more. My legs are OK; it's my chest that's malfunctioning. Also I seem to spit rather a lot when I run, which is somewhat unbecoming. On my fourth run (thirty minutes), the voices in my head begin in earnest. And not just quiet, muttering, unobtrusive ones either – these are full-blooded, Royal Shakespeare Company, Brian Blessed roars. They boom: ALL YOU HAVE TO DO IS STOP RUNNING, AND THIS AGONY WILL INSTANTLY VANISH! STOP! YES! RIGHT HERE, RIGHT NOW! JUST DO IT!* IT WILL FEEL ORGASMIC! AND WHO'LL KNOW? NO ONE! YOUR HEART REALLY WILL EXPLODE OTHERWISE. SERIOUSLY. YOU CAN FEEL IT, CAN'T YOU? I CAN. BRRRRR, THOSE ARE THE THIN BLACK FINGERS OF THE GRIM REAPER ON YOUR SHOULDER. YOU DON'T WANT TO DIE, DO YOU? HERE ON CHILBOLTON AVENUE? SO JUST STOP

---

* A nice, ironic subversion of the Nike catchphrase there by my schizophrenic subconscious and Mr Blessed.

RUNNING! IT'S SO EASY! AND IT'D BE SO BLIIIIII-
ISSSSSSFFFFFUUUUUULLLLLLLLLL.*

'I Will Survive'

My running friends Paul and Steve say that they are going to come
down and do the half-marathon with me. I am delighted, although
bang go all my brilliant 'loneliness of the long-distance runner'
gags. Trust me, they were pretty usable. Actually I might still deploy
them if those two bastards leave me behind, which they're already
saying they will.

'My Heart Will Go On'

I really must get some new trainers; these ones are shit. My stepfather has lent me a vest though. (Not *that* kind of vest, I wanted to
tell him.)

'Sex Action'

Here I am, running along again, through a rainy wood, panting.
Not much of a montage this, really, is it? Let's imagine the guys in
Chariots of Fire instead, with Vangelis's theme music. This is some
soundtrack now. Ragin' epic mash-up, let's have it.

'Chariots of Fire' (Danny Rampling remix)

When I was a child, I used to like Sebastian Coe because we had
the same first name. It was only later, after he revealed his true
colours by becoming a Tory MP, that I belatedly realized that actually Steve Ovett – Coe's bitter 1980s rival – was the dogged, work-
ing-class hero one really ought to have been egging on. It certainly
hadn't helped that Ovett was so pig-ugly, and that Coe had always
looked foppish and dashing and *middle class, like me*. I have, however,
always known that Tiger Timmy Henman was fundamentally unacceptable, so don't panic.

---

* It's at this point that I usually run into a tree.

'I am the One and Only'

YOU IMBECILIC LIGHTWEIGHT! cries Brian Blessed as I hit
yet another wall. You often hear about this 'wall', in running, but
I'd never realized that although obviously it's just a psychological
wall and not a real one, it feels just as painful to run into. I lurch
manfully through it; or rather stagger, stumble, claw and scrape.
Then I get an agonizing stitch in my groin. I've never called my
groin region my groin before. This now probably means I'm turning into a bone fide actual sportsperson! Turn up the volume.
Drink isotonic drinks.

'Man in the Mirror'

I buy a copy of *Runner's World* from my surprised local
newsagent. *Runner's World*! On the cover is an attractive young
lady in full make-up with large, bulging breasts, 'running' in very
tight shorts.* This isn't why I bought it, however; at least not the
only reason. I bought it because if you take your eye off this nice
lady for just a minute, it also boasts inside: RUN FASTER AND
LONGER. Yes, I would like to be able to run faster and longer;
this magazine is for me. And THE BEST NEW SHOES FOR
YOU. Yes, I do need new shoes; this magazine is for me. And 21
EVERYDAY SUPERFOODS FOR BETTER RUNNING. Tell
me what the superfoods are! This magazine is for me. One won-
ders, is there ever a time when *Runner's World* instead screams
from its cover: FAT PEOPLE GO SLOWER: PHOTOS
INSIDE; or OLD SHOES ARE BEST; or EAT WHATEVER
YOU LIKE, IT DOESN'T REALLY MATTER THAT MUCH
SO LONG AS IT'S IN MODERATION, YOU KNOW? JUST
CHILL OUT AND DON'T WASTE YOUR MONEY ON
ALL THIS CYNICAL AND CONSUMERIST CRAP WE'RE

---

* Is there no publication exempt from selling through sex? A few years ago
when I was buying classical music magazines for research purposes, they too featured cleavage and breasts prominently on their front covers. What next? Ann
Widdecombe in a bikini on the front of the *Spectator*? *Again*?

ALWAYS FORCING ON YOU – WE'RE ALL INSECURE
ENOUGH ALREADY AS IT IS.*

That Enigma song

I get a bad case of nipple rub. It's agony. I read, in *Runner's World*,
that apparently nipple rub can be cured by rubbing Vaseline on
to your nipples. This is all getting a bit stupid now. I buy some
Vaseline anyway. Smear some on to my nipples. Throughout the
whole of the subsequent run, all I can feel is the Vaseline rubbing around all slimy on my nipples underneath my stepfather's
vest. And, incredibly, this feels even more unpleasant than it
sounds.

'Candle in the Wind'

I can now manage to run without stopping or walking for a whole
hour! Funny, though, how the novelty of doing something new
soon wears off. For the first couple of weeks I'd really look forward
to going out for a run – it was new! And interesting! And made me
aware of parts of my body that I'd never known existed! For example my legs. But now, as the training has become routine, I have lost
all desire and motivation to go out in the wind and rain and pointing, laughing pedestrians. It's painful and mundane and I'm fed up
with hills, and nettles, and heartburn, and stitches, and sudden, terrifying muscular spasms, and slippery nipples, and being overtaken
by women runners and old ladies out walking their dogs and Brian
sodding Blessed's received pronunciation. Worst of all, running is
actually incredibly boring. Fortunately, the thought of letting the
guys over at Wells for India down is just too humiliating to con-
template, and so I persevere for the sake of the thousand
Huckleberry Hounds. That's rhyming slang. You get everything in
this book.

* You want to know what the superfoods are though, don't you? They're
pomegranate, cranberry, acai, goji, gac-chi, wild blueberry, mackerel, Müller
Vitality yoghurt, sardines and peach schnapps over ice, necked fast, about four or
five of them, halfway through the race. Then have a fight.

'Beth'

And for the icing on the cake, just as the excitement of running vanishes, the creaking old hunk of useless shite that is my body goes and exacerbates the situation. I go out for two innocent little boozy late nights in three days, followed by the inevitable hung-over junk food insatiability. Outrageously, the next time I go out for a run, I find that the lithe sex machine of a body I'd been cultivating has, overnight, been replaced by something more like a waddling lactic walrus. Suddenly I am a spluttering, hobbling heart attack waiting to happen. As I run, or rather stumble through the wet nettles and fall into ditches, I silently curse the *Runner's World* editorial team, because *nowhere* within its glossy and pedantic pages does it mention that it might be even *slightly* unwise to go on several irresponsible alcoholic benders during the course of one's training regime. Do they think we're psychic? We runners need to be told these things! And not just by our wives the day before we go on them. We ignore our wives; we have to, otherwise we wouldn't go on the benders. So, anyway. I have to run the walrus back into a cheetah, via the halfway handles of the baby seal. It takes a week. A week of more pain than all the previous weeks put together. (We are now on three weeks.) Readers, I was wrong about the peach schnapps.

Piano Sonata no. 14 in C-sharp Minor (Op. 27, No. 2)

Hungry for yoghurty-fitness bran bars. Not. I get heartburn when I run, whatever I eat.

Runner's World says: 'Rethinking your nutrition strategy will give you an extra edge when you stand on the marathon start line. It is no longer considered beneficial to undertake a depletion phase (where you eat less carbohydrate than usual) prior to carbohydrate loading, and this may even impair performance if carried out for an extended period.'

Concerned about my lack of nutrition strategy in general, I email Paul and Steve. *Should I have a nutrition strategy? And if so, what should it consist of?*

Paul: 'My strategy is to have a curry without the beer the night

before. Maybe have a double helping of rice, potatoes and naan as well. I think that's how it works. High carb? I hope this helps.'
Steve: 'You are a gaylord.'

'There's No One Quite Like Grandma'

The running porn is getting to me – I'm beginning to believe the hype. My latent consumerism can't help but inquisitively emerge from the righteous cocoon of my training psyche. You can get these trainers, right, that have sensors in the soles? These sensors work out your speed, distance travelled and even how many calories you're burning off as you run. This data is then automatically transferred to your portable mp3-playing device, relaying the information in a sexy woman's voice over the top of your music. Isn't that incredible? The only thing stopping me buying one is the tension that would doubtlessly result as my brain struggled to cope with the voices of this sexy woman *and* Brian Blessed battling it out for supremacy. Also it's pathetic. Talk about self-obsessed. Just run, for God's sake! Faster! And call me an ambulance.

'Green Door'

So begins my aggressive sponsorship campaign. I sign up to www.just-giving.com, enabling friends and acquaintances to donate money quickly and easily online. The site can cleverly send out an email to everybody in your email address book; thus 143 friends and acquaintances receive an electronic missive outlining my fundraising activities followed by a bullying plea for sponsorship. In the meantime, I have doubled my target – I'm now pushing for £2,000. This is because I realized I'd really like to raise some money for the Southampton and Winchester Visitors Group while I'm at it, seeing as they're always so skint. And, since I'd already promised to try to raise £1,000 for Wells for India, the logical step was just to try to raise the same amount for the SWVG. This maths is just about within my reach.

In reply to the initial 143-person mail-out, a risible three people pledge money straight away: Status Quo–obsessed rock vocalist and coconut-shy attendant Steve; my bearded Scottish Jesus-lookylikey pal Andrew; and Faye, my wife. I am outraged at this miserly initial response. But what can you do? There are two options really:

a) Feel despised/descend into self-pity.

and/or

b) Get the thumbscrews out.

After a day or two wallowing in option a), I begin in earnest to email people individually, a guilt-trip mechanism considerably more effective than the faceless exhortation of the group email. This approach yields immediate results, and over the course of a single afternoon I more than treble my previous total. Alongside the amount of money pledged, there is also a space for these friends and acquaintances to write encouraging messages to you, to egg you on and inspire you through your charitable labours. Here is a selection of some of the messages people have left me:

```
'Good luck, Seb. Cut your hair; it could save a
  lot of wind resistance when you run.'
'Get yer hair cut.'
'Nice beard.'*
'Who says the Scotch are tight?'†
'Win it for the kids, you brutal athletic
  beast.'
'Cut your hair, mister!'**
'I am breathless with admiration.'††
'Are you by any chance related to John the
  Baptist?'
```

and

```
'My donation seemed more generous in American
dollars.'
```

*I really shouldn't have used that old beard photo.
† This alongside a donation for £2. And yes, from a Scotsman.
** In the face of all these hair-related comments, perhaps I ought to have shaved it all off for charity after all?
†† This is my friend Owen mocking me.

Does Noel Edmonds suffer from this level of disrespect? Does Jimmy Savile? Did Roy Castle? Is that everyone?

'Shaddap You Face'

A few weeks back, I belatedly realized that I could listen to music while I ran, to make it less boring. Thus I began a system of trial and error, auditioning all different kinds (and pieces) of music in a search for the ultimate in audio-vascular transcendence. I publish the results here exclusively, despite much pressure from the *British Medical Journal*, *Runner's World* and the *Lancet*.

Good:
 - The first Agitation Free album, Malesch. Highly recommended, this one, especially the organ and drums track when the extra percussion bit kicks in. Made me run a teeny bit faster.
 - Bruckner's Ninth Symphony. Conducted by either Bernhard Haitink or Daniel Barenboim; both are acceptable, though Bazza's brass is brighter and has more oomph and pizzazz. That said, Haitink's lower-frequency plate tectonic shiftings-around are waaaay superior.
 - Johann Johannsson's IBM 1401: A User's Manual. Quite nice.
 - John Cage's Indeterminacy. Diverting.

Bad:
 - All techno. It's too artificial/synthetic-sounding for one's land-scraping biorhythms; also too tiring.
 - Drone, generally. A shame this, but it's just annoying.
 - Les Rallizes Dénudés's Heavier than a Death in the Family. Just terrible to run to – really dispiriting all round.

Sadly, this is as far as I've got, listening-while-running-wise. Rather than experiment any further, I'm tending just to stick with the Bruckner. It goes on long enough. And if you're thinking it sounds a bit weird – perhaps contrary – to listen to classical music while out pounding the fields and the streets, then you're clearly the sort of person who requires cheap motivational beats over the eternal sunset glory that is the unimpeachable epicness of horizon-defying classical music (see Bruckner). And I pity you, quite frankly.

'Tears in Heaven'

With just two weeks to go now until race day, I portentously announce to Faye that: 'I am now taking this so seriously that I am going to drink *not very much* alcohol in the week before the race. What do you think of that then, eh?'

She looks at me. 'I am deeply moved.'

'So Long Marianne'

A week before the race, Paul comes down to Winchester and we go out running together, in order for him to get a measure of the local terrain. He usually runs on Clapham Common, which is completely flat, and never for more than fifty minutes, thus my hill experience and longer run-times ought to make me the stronger contender in today's outing – the first time I have ever run alongside somebody, overtakers and dog-walkers aside. Paul's trainers cost £80. In the shop, they filmed him running on a treadmill and then watched it back on TV in slow motion, then ultra-scientifically moulded £80 worth of contemporary fabric around his feet.

'And how does it feel?' I splutter, as he immediately surges away.

'Great! It feels like I'm running on . . .'

'What was that?'

But he's fifty yards ahead already.

'This is the slowest I have ever run,' declares Paul when we are one kilometre from my house (we know this because Paul has a GPS machine strapped to his wrist, which he keeps on checking while he waits for me to catch up). 'Usually I run at double this speed.'

As this is by far the fastest *I* have ever run, I am sadly unable to reply, as I am too busy trying and failing to breathe. The hills don't seem to be troubling Paul quite as much as I'd anticipated.

'The tortoise and the hare,' I manage to wheeze at one point.

'Mmm, yes, you might be right,' he replies kindly, and then

shoots off again. In order for my analogy to bear fruit, I need him to stop and take quite a long nap in the scrubland alongside the path which, I notice, is full of litter. I fight the urge to text Hermione.

Afterwards, thirteen kilometres later, Paul tells me that although I'm not exactly Sebastian Coe, thank God, I did pretty well, all things considered, and that's enough caveats already, thank you.

'I think you'll be fine for next week. I like your dogged approach. Every time I stopped to wait for you, you just kept on coming, slow yet determined; grinding it out.'

'That's the furthest I've ever run by miles. I mean literally, by miles.'

'Me too actually,' says Paul.

'Really? You seem to be in really good shape.'

'It's these incredible trainers. And the physio session I had this morning, before I left London.'

'Physio session? *Before* you left London?'

'Although the six pints I had last night probably didn't help much.'

'Six pints!'

'Oh, or seven, or . . .'

'I feel particularly humiliated now, considering you still massively outran me.'

'But you still did brilliantly, especially since this is all new to you.'

'Although not as brilliantly as you.'

And despite the fact that our relationship is based upon relentless sarcasm and abuse, we went on being weirdly polite like this all evening. Running: it brings out the patronizing, *faux*-gentleman in one, what-what?

Joy Division medley

Just five days to go and I'm still £1,600 short of my total. I have clearly overreached myself to an embarrassing degree. I send out yet more begging, pleading emails to friends and now also to complete strangers. A few more people sign up. One writes: 'All right, all

214

right, I have just sponsored you. It didn't feel altruistic at all, I just felt like I'd been bullied.'

'Yes, but think of all those wells!' I wrote back.

But that was the end of the correspondence.

'Highway to Hell'

With only two days to go now until race day, I finally bite the bullet and enter a sports shop to buy a proper pair of running shoes. It had got to a point where I had been receiving serious warnings from friends about the damage I was doing to my feet/knees/entire body by running in my old brown unsuitable faithfuls, down boy. I have come to a specialist sports shop. No surly, pimpled youths here – instead tall men with sober wedge haircuts dispensing even more sober advice. First, I am ticked off about my brown shoes; indeed even a fellow customer trying on shoes sitting next to me adds a few disparaging comments of his own. The assistant makes me take my shoes off. They are hurled aside. He punches me in the face. I stand there, naked, ish, in my stockings, for all the world to see, publicly humiliated, my feet.

'Well, these are my feet,' I say.

'Your poor feet,' he replies, heading soberly off yonder to rummage through piles of shoeboxes. He returns with an eye-wateringly garish selection. I try some on. Some more. And some more. Finally a pair fit that aren't lime green and purple, only they're £70. Oh well, I buy them. I've thought quite long and hard about this but I just am not able to make this episode any wittier or more interesting. But then a rhino crashes through the plate-glass window and gores the female sales assistant at the till; there is blood and rhino slobber everywhere. She twitches impaled upon its crusty horn. Life's like that, and laughter is the best medicine.

Later that afternoon I go for a run in my new shoes and bounce, like Zebedee. Boing-boing-boing I go, up Cheriton Road. Bounce-bounce-bounce I go, along Dean Lane. Ping-ping-ping; we get the picture.

OK, so the half-marathon is the day after tomorrow. Time for a status check.

Plusses:
- A few days ago I ran for about eight miles and it was OK
- I have new and performance-enhancing footwear
- I think my chest will be able to manage
- I have plenty of raw, manly stamina*
- At the sports shop, I also bought a three-pack of nice furry white sports socks, like it's 1984

Minuses:
- There is a pretty much constant twinge/ache in my left hip/groin region
- Ditto left knee
- Ditto, after a while, my right knee too
- The arches of my feet got very sore today in these new shoes. There was new pressure somewhere. Perhaps in the arches of my feet.
- So far I have raised only a little over a quarter of my sponsorship target.

Let's get this over with.

'Rabbit'

In the chapter after next, though, to give us all a bit of a break. All the training above took place throughout the following section anyway, so the chronology is trustworthy, folks. Folks?

Where has everybody gone?

* Stupidity and delusion.

Step Ten

Famous Mongo residents: Ming the Merciless, Vultan, Prince Barin, Queen
Fria, Queen Undina, King Thun, Queen Desira, Gundar the Desert Hawk,
Gillmen, Lionmen, Hawkmen, Arborean Hunters. (This list was a little more
pertinent before I was forced to change it.)

Because I hadn't realized how far away from Winchester Mongo
actually is (■ miles), and as I couldn't be arsed to check, I am sitting
in my car on the outside carriageway of the A■, travelling at ninety
miles per hour. I have an appointment to meet my fellow ICV Bea
outside Mongo Police Station in ten minutes' time, and I'm thinking that if I maintain this sort of pace, I reckon I'm pretty much
going to make it on the dot, as well as permanently maim anybody
who gets in my way. As I career manically along, I ponder the irony
of being hauled up on charges of vehicular manslaughter at Mongo
Police Station while Bea waits outside, angrily checking her watch.
Ho-ho-ho, I chortle under my breath, speeding past what looks suspiciously like a police car parked up half hidden by a hedge on the
hard shoulder.

A minute or so later, I recognize the unmistakable sight of a
squad car looming in my rear-view mirror with lights ablaze. My
heart sinks. He's upon me a few seconds later, flashing his headlights
overtly. With a heavy heart (and conscience) and with my legs a-
tremble, I move over into the slow lane to look for a spot to pull
over. Being done for speeding on my way to a police station to
check that those in the cells (quite possibly having been done for

★ The location of this police station has been made anonymous.

217

speeding themselves) are being looked after OK, strikes me as deliciously ironic. I'll tell the arresting officer all about it, I think, I'm sure he'll find it hilarious! So hilarious they'll just let me go with an avuncular warning not to do it again. And I won't, Officer, I absolutely promise. Gawd bless the boys in blue, eh?

Hang on, where have they gone? The police car has disappeared. They're not behind me any more. I crane my neck around; they're nowhere to be seen. It suddenly strikes me that they didn't want to pull me over after all – they just wanted me to get out of their way because they had something important to attend to. Gawd bless the boys in blue! As a conciliatory gesture of goodwill, I decide that I'm going to be extra generous in my assessment of Mongo Police Station today. So long as Bea hasn't gone home already, of course.

I finally arrive, and here's Bea waiting outside with a face like thunder. She's actually smiling, but her face *really does* look like a thundercloud – purple, puffy and somewhat menacing.

'Hello, Bea, nice to meet you. I'm sorry I'm so late, my excuse is that–'

'I don't care! I've got to be somewhere at midday so let's go inside and get on with it. You can do the paperwork.'

'I, er, haven't got a sheet thingy.'

Bea passes me a sheet thingy. And a pen. Waits while I smooth down my hair with spit. And we go inside.

There's nobody in the cells.

'Nobody?' asks Bea.

'Not a sausage,' replies the sarge. 'Take a look for yourselves.'

We study the cells on the CCTV screen at the front desk. They're all empty.

'What do we do now?' I whisper to Bea, who continues to squint suspiciously at the television screen for prisoners – sorry, detainees – lurking in the corners or hiding under their bed.

'Nothing,' she says. 'We just write down that there's nobody here, and then leave.'

'So you mean I've driven all the way here for nothing?'

'Why is he whispering?' asks the sarge.

'Sorry, I'm just . . . it's confidential!'

'Actually you're in luck,' says the sarge. 'There's one coming in now. Want to stay and watch?' He presses a button on his desk, a door clunks and another policeman enters, accompanied by a ■■ wearing handcuffs and looking sheepish.

Bea tells me that observing the booking-in procedure is useful for getting a greater overview of the whole arrest-to-custody process. And that it's also quite entertaining.

'So long as they don't start shouting or breaking things.'

'OK, this sounds like pretty good fun!'

'And £1 says I'll have this ■■ booked-in in nine minutes precisely,' says the sarge, who is a spit for Mark Blundell, off ITV's Formula One television coverage.

'You're on,' says Bea, who I suspect might have met this sarge once or twice before, or been on holiday with him or something. They synchronize watches on their wager.

The ■■ has been arrested on suspicion of ■■■■■■■. He seems very relaxed about the whole thing; even about the fact he's just had a sample of his DNA taken, which as we now know will remain on central police records for ever and ever, even if he's found innocent, which I doubt; his guilt is apparent from the fact that he looks quite like Phil Mitchell off *EastEnders*. In order for all present to have their own televisual frame of reference, Bea resembles Wendy Craig in *Butterflies*, the arresting officer looks a bit like Tony Hancock, before he died, while I resemble my namesake Hunter from *Gladiators*, if he had fallen on hard times recently.

Bea and I stand behind the desk and watch the procedure. Bea was right: it is fascinating; and compelling. I study the young ■■'s body language. *Did he do it or didn't he? He clearly did it. Ah, he doesn't want a solicitor. Maybe he's innocent after all! Or maybe he's just stupid. Hmm, it's a real conundrum.* Interrupting this TV-obsessed reverie comes the loud and brutal ringing of my mobile telephone. The booking-in procedure pauses, and everybody looks at me. I have no choice but to answer. The sarge, Bea, the arresting officer and the ■ all just stand there watching me. I recognize the number – it is my son's nursery.

'Hang on a minute, this won't take too long. Hello, nursery?'

'Reuben's daddy?'

'Yes?'

'Reuben's nursery here.'

'Yes, I'd gathered that. What's the matter? Has something happened? Is Reuben OK?'

'How are you?'

I tell her that I'm absolutely fine thanks, but that I'm in a police station at the moment and can't really talk, and instantly regret it. Why would I be in a police station unless I'd done something that made me fundamentally unsuitable for parenthood? The woman on the other end of the line is silent. 'So, erm, Reuben's all right then, is he?'

'Well, I don't want you to be alarmed, but–'

'*Yes?*'

'Reuben has a small splinter in the top of his foot.'

'A splinter?'

'Yes. We've put a plaster over it, and then a bandage over his foot to keep it in place, but I'm phoning really to warn you in case when you came to pick him up later, you were worried by the big bandage on his foot. It's only a little splinter! We're just phoning to let you know, and to tell you not to worry.'

I look at the sarge, the arresting officer, Bea and the ■ who looks nothing like Phil Mitchell. They look back at me. I smile weakly.

'Well, thanks so much for letting me know. You're right – I'm not worried at all. Goodbye then.'

'Goodbye.'

'OK, thanks everyone, I'm done.'

'So where were we?' asks not Phil Mitchell.

'I was asking whether you considered yourself a white male of British origin,' says the sarge.

'And I said yes.'

'So it's the dietary question. Here we are. Do you have any specific dietary requirements?'

'No.'

'This is way over nine minutes,' I whisper to Bea. 'You've just made £1.'

Bea doesn't answer; she merely grips her folder and looks like she's grinding her teeth. This makes her look very unattractive.

Walk Your Talk, Buriton, Hampshire
9.20 a.m.
Cost of 'Lifestyle Lazer Range' 14KW patio heater: £285.00
Cost of second-hand woolly jumper:
£1.99 (Help the Aged); £4.99 (Oxfam)

Matt Kemp – Messiah Matt – and I are standing at a road junction in the small Hampshire village of Buriton, twiddling our thumbs. We met fifteen minutes ago and have been making slightly laboured small talk ever since. It's cloudy.

'So obviously this isn't an ideal start to your day,' I say.

'No, it's not ideal,' replies Matt. 'It would have been nice to set off, you know, when we were supposed to. This makes everything much ... harder. And it's hard enough in the first place if I'm honest with you.'

We are standing in Buriton waiting for his three bandmates to join us. Band-wise, Matt is the singer/guitarist/songwriter/group messiah; and the rest are:

Emlyn (not currently present) – bass and b.vox
Laura (also absent) – percussion and b.vox
Spanish Alex (ditto) – percussion

The band is called Nimomashtic, and their summer tour 2007 involves walking from their home town of Brighton to the Eden Project in Cornwall – that's 300 miles – playing gigs along the way and, most hardcore of all, *carrying all their equipment*. Even though they're essentially a folk band, this is still quite a lot of stuff for them to be hauling all the way from East Sussex to the distant south-western coast. They're doing all this in order to 'raise awareness of climate change'. Nimomashtic did the same thing last year, only they walked much further – 900 miles – with no tour bus or support vehicles and a bare minimum of supplies. Their instruments. A tent. Delusional idealism. Tellingly, however, the three other, currently absent, members of the band are a different three members of the band from the ones who went on last year's walk. Matt aside, none of last year's Nimomashtic has returned for a repeat prescription. This is an all-new line-up. Or at least it will be when they get here.

Matt and I stand and wait. It's still cloudy. I hum discreetly to myself.

'So tell me again,' says Matt. 'Why have you come to do this with us?'

'Well, I'm trying to improve myself through volunteering, and one thing I was keen to get involved in, somehow, was something involving climate change. I didn't know what, though. I considered going to Antarctica but appreciated that probably wasn't the most productive way forward, emissions-wise. So then I Googled 'climate change'* and somehow stumbled upon you guys and your inspired yet arguably hare-brained scheme. And then when I saw your route was due to pass through Winchester, I thought it might be *perfect* to come and join you crazy dudes for a day's walking, to help in your raising of awareness of climate change and so on. And so here I am.'

'Brilliant.'

'Yeah.'

---

* Presumably we call it climate change now instead of global warming because some people refused to accept it was really happening if their own localized environment wasn't rising in temperature on an almost daily basis. Calling it climate change acknowledges that weather, like stocks and shares, can go up as well as down – for example in the summer of 2007 (the summer of writing), when the Gulf Stream was suddenly redirected northwards and the United Kingdom drowned in the absence of its ultraviolet umbrella.

'And so have you?'

'Have I?'

'Improved yourself.'

'Ah. Well. It's like the President of China answered, some time in the 1950s, having been asked about the greater consequences of the French Revolution.'

'Oh? And what was that?'

'He said, "It's too soon to tell."'

'I see,' says Matt, peering up the hill for his bandmates.

'But in all seriousness, I would say yes, I have improved myself. Definitely. I am certainly more aware of my incredibly fortunate position in the overall worldly scheme of things; less twenty-first-century uptight and screw you. Zenner. What can I add that doesn't make this sound so glib? I mean, it's been working!'

'Congratulations.'

' . . . and celebrations.'

'What?'

'Oh, come on. *Cliff.*'

'Cliff?'

Matt peers up the hill for his bandmates.

Matt and I continue to stand there. Overhead clouds muster. Then Emlyn comes down the hill, covered in blood and chalk marks, carrying a wooden box covered in blood, and chalk marks.

'Emlyn, what happened! Where have you been?'

'The path I took down from where we were camping was extremely precarious. I had a few tumbles.' He dusts himself down, smears the blood.

'Where are the other two? We were supposed to be on the road half an hour ago.'

'Well, they said they're coming. But Laura doesn't want to walk to Winchester. She says she's going to take the bus instead.'

'Does this happen often?' I ask Matt quietly.

'Never!'

Matt, who looks like Michael Stipe's lanky kid brother, sighs and scratches his stubble. This is only the fourth day of the tour and they've covered barely fifty miles; this is not an ideal moment for the tour's first desertion – especially not with me along to record proceedings like this. It makes the whole enterprise look less professional.

'Are they following behind you?'

'I don't know. They said they were going to, but . . .'

We stare back up the hill Emlyn just descended.

'Can't you just call them?' I ask.

'They don't have mobiles,' Matt replies. 'And I don't have a mobile either.'

'I'm the only one with a mobile,' says Emlyn who, with his neat hair, check shirt and glasses looks and sounds much too normal to be doing this sort of thing. Like Matt, his backpack is gigantic, and Emlyn's electric bass is strapped precariously to the back of it. I pity whoever's got to carry the pyro.

'So just the one telephone between the four of you?'

'I know,' says Emlyn. 'It's not ideal.'

'We're trying to rid ourselves of the trappings of the modern world,' says Matt. 'Or at least I am.'

We stand there. The village comes to life around us. It's beginning to feel a little awkward.

'What's that wooden box with a hole in it for?' I ask.

'It's the *cajon*. Or Spanish box. It's basically our drumkit. Alex plays it. We all take turns carrying it.'

'As my own rucksack is very light,* would you like me to carry it?'

Emlyn hands it over immediately.

'The *cajon* doubles as a bin, a water-carrier, a food-carrier, a stool, a bird-box, a table . . .'

'And a toilet,' says Matt.

I put the *cajon* down.

'What does *cajon* mean in English?'

---

* Contents: one triple-decker sandwich; one cagoule; one packet BBQ Cheddars; one small bottle water; one prissy Marks & Spencer salad; one emergency flare gun plus six flare bullets.

'Box.'

'Ah, like *boîte*.'

'Except that's French.'

'Yes, so it is.'

We stand there. Yawn. Stretch. I wipe the blood off the *cajon* with some tissue. After twenty or so further minutes' waiting, Matt decides to head back up the hill to look for Laura and Spanish Alex. As he grumblingly disappears, Emlyn and I stand in the road in the village of Buriton and make friends. He tells me there was trouble in the ranks up at the free campsite last night, after Laura accused Matt of walking too fast and leaving her behind. Further complicating matters is the fact that Laura and Spanish Alex are a couple. This makes the two of them an *axis*. Also Spanish Alex isn't used to walking long distances. He has new boots, and terrible blisters.

'He was cutting the tops of his blisters off using scissors last night,' says Emlyn. 'And I think he's in quite a lot of pain this morning.'

'It sounds to me like you all need to . . . *pull together* somehow.'

'Yes, I really think we do. The problem is that Matt's done this before and it comes really naturally for him, but for the rest of us it's a bit of a learning curve. It's not that easy. This is quite a strenuous enterprise.'

We stand and wait. Soon Laura and Spanish Alex come trudging up the road towards us, but from a different direction to the one Matt's taken to find them. We shake hands. Laura has big beautiful eyes and Spanish Alex has long hair and a beard. There is a strong aroma of body odour.

'Where's the bus stop?' asks Laura.

'Right over there.'

'Thank God.'

We stand and wait, and Laura and Spanish Alex stand apart from the group, talking quietly between themselves. Emlyn and I are by now firm friends. Ten minutes later Matt comes back down the hill, and it's even more awkward – I've only just met them and already they're having a bardly barney. Minor accusations fly back and forth. I try looking away and whistling. After tempers have cooled slightly, Matt tries to give a unifying pep talk and, for the time being, things settle.

'Alex, are you going to take the bus to Winchester with Laura, or are you going to walk your talk* with us?'

'I am coming with you,' says Spanish Alex defiantly.

Matt and Emlyn brighten. Alex kisses Laura goodbye. She walks over to the bus stop, to wait alongside some pensioners who have been staring at us for some time now.

It's 10.30 a.m. Over an hour later than scheduled, Nimomashtic are finally ready to begin today's leg of the tour: from Buriton (over on the far side of the A3 from Petersfield) to Winchester, where they have a gig lined up at O'Neill's pub on the High Street at 8.30 p.m. I have put up posters and exhorted friends to come, and generally acted as their 'road manager' for this leg of the tour. I have also, somewhat naïvely, offered to put them all up for the night in my house.

'Otherwise we'll be sleeping in a hedge,' Matt had said over the phone. 'You're very kind.'

'Whatever I can do to help.'

'Do you really mean that?'

'Steady on, please!'

On the road, Matt wears a large, impressive straw hat. With the hat on he is instantly transformed into Messiah Matt – a character not dissimilar to Jesus only with added mung beans. Hat-off he's merely a personable hippy with a gentle Sussex lilt, but with the Hat of Destiny atop his stubbly dome his personality shifts dramatically. Meek Matt becomes a gnomic visionary: epic horizon-defier; man of purpose; the Mick Jagger of the miles; the meandering meditator; misty mountain-hopper; a magnetic personality under whose spell everybody mysteriously falls, myself included. We are Following the

* This is called the 'Walk Your Talk' Tour, actually.

Leader – especially since Matt walks the fastest. As we walk, we earnestly discuss individual environmental responsibility.

'Getting people to a point where they're forced even to *think* about whether they care about the environment is an achievement in itself,' says Matt. 'Often you find that people haven't even considered it. Which seems bizarre in this day and age, but you'd be surprised.'

'Do you face much cynicism along the way?'

'Not really. Mostly just ignorance. Although we like to convert people wherever possible. Not to preach so much as ask people to make a pledge. At our gigs. Their own personal pledge. It can be anything. Just do something, no matter how small. Because little ripples – they make waves.'

'Little ripples make waves,' repeats Emlyn alongside.

'Little ripples make waves. That's our mantra.'

'Like a catchphrase.'

'Exactly.'

'And some of the pledges people make are fantastic! It's inspiring! We had a bloke who had some old scrap land and he said he was going to plant an orchard on it!'

'Was that the really pissed bloke?' asks Emlyn.

'Yeah.'

I find myself passionately agreeing with everything they say, especially when Matt has his messiah hat on.

'So, Seb, how about you? What's your pledge going to be?'

'Well, we're already pretty green: we're thorough recyclers; our car is small and we use it as little as possible; our electricity is ethically sourced; we've cut right down on our flying; and I always turn off the tap whenever I brush my teeth. And Reuben's teeth. Or rather tooth.'

'Excellent.'

'So let me have a little think about what my pledge could be.'

'Do you use low-energy light bulbs?'

'Yes.'

'Right. Well, have a think.'

'Yeah. Hmm.'

'Hmm.'

Birds twitter.

We've been walking through rolling countryside – up on to the South Downs Way to be precise – for about half an hour when we pass a sign that says: *Winchester – 23 miles*. Nobody says anything for about five minutes, but then Spanish Alex suddenly blurts out: '*Twenty-three miles?* I thought you say it was twelve!'

'It can't be twenty-three miles,' says Matt, scratching his head. 'We checked on the map. It looked like it was about twelve. Max. If it really is twenty-three miles from here to Winchester, then I'm not even sure we'll make it in time for the gig tonight. Seb, do you think it's twenty-three miles to Winchester from where we are now?'

'Oh, I'm completely lost, I've no idea. But no. I don't.* Is it time for a sit down yet? This *cajon* is bloody heavy.'

'Would you like me to take it for a while?' offers Emlyn.

'No, that would be really un-manly.'

So onward.

From the top of Butser Hill you can see for miles in every direction – even, to the south, the Isle of Wight. The sea around it glistens dully. As we yomp down the chalk paths, Matt spies a young farm-hand lazily reclining on the back of a flatbed truck, pensively chewing corn. You never got this in Brentford.

'Excuse me!' he calls to the farmhand. 'Do you know how far it is to Winchester?'

'No,' replies the farmhand. 'But it's bloody miles.'

'Is it actually *twenty-three* miles, though?'

'I dunno. It's bloody miles.'

'Thank you for your guidance!'

'Whatever.'

---

* I said this for team morale.

We walk on.

'You've got to try to spread the joy,' says Matt. He talks about joy quite a lot, but then he is, I suppose, from Brighton.

'Would you call yourself a hippy, Matt?'

'I'm a mystery even to myself, to be honest.'

Spanish Alex is walking much slower than the rest of us. At a junction, we wait for him to catch up, and ten minutes later he shambles into view through the trees.

'Are you in much pain?' asks Matt as Alex shuffles towards us, pain etched all over his beardy face.

'Yes,' he replies. 'My feet, they hurt so much.'

'Alex, I have painkillers. Would you like a handful?' I ask.

'No.'

'*No?*'

Perhaps he rubs natural roadside worts on to his feet or something instead.

Onward.

Lunchtime comes and goes without us stopping. This is because the guys have no food – they ate all their supplies last night in a gluttonous paganistic feeding frenzy. They were planning to stop and pick up something in a village or in a pub but none has yet materialized. High on the Morestead Road, still on the South Downs Way, we pass a natural burial site on our left. My father is buried here and I kind of want to mention it but don't want to ruin the joy vibe. I mention it anyway. There is relatively joyless silence.

'However, happier news is that I have a sandwich and a salad and some crisps that I bought in a petrol station on the way over,* if you're all OK sharing that for lunch,' I say. 'It's, erm, chicken and bacon so not really very vegan or anything though, I'm afraid.'

'Oh, don't worry, we're not vegetarians,' says Emlyn. 'In fact

---

* My friend Johnny gave me a lift: a thirty-five mile round trip in his gas-guzzling people carrier, the irony of which he regaled me with throughout the journey's duration.

we've been eating rather a lot of roadkill.'

Matt chuckles. 'That's kind of you to offer, but we can't eat your lunch,' he says.

'Yes, but all for one and one for all, right? Come on, let's share!'

And so we sit on a small patch of grass at the side of the road and eat, ravenously. When we have finished and the unnecessary plastic packaging litters the ground, Matt jumps up holding a plastic pot and a trowel and says, 'OK, it's seed-planting time!'

As well as the walking and the playing of gigs, carrying equipment and raising awareness of climate change, Nimomashtic are also planting apple seeds all along their route. According to Matt, this is in tribute to the little-known American folk hero, Johnny Appleseed, who did the same thing back in the mid-nineteenth century, with a saucepan on his head.

'Have you ever heard of Johnny Appleseed?' asks Emlyn.

'No,' I reply.

'Funny that nobody's ever heard of him except for Matt.'

'He sounds like an interesting character. The saucepan on the head thing and all. Why did he do that, exactly?'

'No one knows.'

'I see.'

Matt returns from planting his apple seeds, grinning. They did the seed thing on last year's tour too. Matt guesstimates that if 40 per cent of the seeds he has planted catch (the average, apparently), then he and his colleagues have already planted well in excess of 1,800 apple trees.

'And just think how many apples that little lot will have provided for people to eat!' says Matt.

'Erm. Hang on. About . . .'

'Thousands! Little ripples make waves, you see?'

'Little ripples make waves,' says Emlyn.

'It's a legacy,' says Matt.

My back hurts a lot.

Onward.

★　★　★

We finally unearth a pub, in the small village of Warnford. Slumped in the beer garden out back (Emlyn is particularly sensitive to the possibly negative effect of four heavily kitted-up hippies bursting through an establishment's front door), we drink tea and load up with power snacks – nuts, raisins and chocolate. Alex then disappears inside the pub for twenty minutes. Nobody mentions this odd, prolonged absence; I guess they're used to giving one another time and space to get their individual heads together. Because, as Matt constantly has to remind everybody, the key to getting through this is all in your mind.

'That's where all battles are won and lost,' he says. 'You've got to try to get into the *zone*. Then you'll be able to walk as far as you want, no matter how much your feet might protest. This is what Laura has yet to realize. It doesn't matter how much her legs hurt – it's all in her head – she's got to get into the *zone* or she won't make it.'

'What's the furthest you've done in a single day?' I ask.

'Forty-five miles. Last year. The final push, home into Brighton. We were so desperate to get home, we took a decision, Ollie* and me, to walk through the night. We were tripping over roots, falling into hedges, it was chaos. Pitch black. But we made it. And then we sat on the beach in Brighton and watched the sun come up. It was incredible.'

Spanish Alex has still not come back. But he returns eventually, and off we creak. The nuts, raisins, chocolate and tea have worked their nutritional magic, and my legs, fifteen miles in, feel suddenly less leaden. This is probably because, inspired by Matt again, I'm finally in the zone.

'I think I'm in the zone!' I cry.

'Wicked,' replies Matt.

'I wish I was in this zone,' says Alex. 'I think my foot, it bleeds.'

We schlep on across the downland. Though the heavy cloud cover is ideal weather for walking – i.e. it's not too hot, not too cold – it's

---

* Last year's last man standing, Matt aside. They finished the tour as a duo.

not exactly good for the spirits when the world looks so muted and sullen and lifeless. Also, I despise this *cajon*. So I give it to Emlyn to carry. That was easy.

'Yesterday, Emlyn and I came up with an incredible plan for next year's tour,' says Matt.

'Are we telling people about this already?' Emlyn frowns.

'Well, the more people we tell, the more pressure we'll be under actually to deliver.'

'Spill the beans, guys. This could be a Seb Hunter world exclusive. At last!'

'Except that Matt's probably going to blog about it as soon as we find a computer,' says Emlyn. Accursed bloggers, always ruining things for the rest of us.

Matt takes a deep breath. 'We're going to walk from Brighton to Ben Nevis, pulling a patio heater behind us all the way.'

There is a silence.

'As a symbolic gesture?'

'Right.'

'You're not going to carry this patio heater all the way up the mountain though, are you?'

'Yes, of course.'

'And play gigs too?'

'Of course.'

'Whose idea was this?'

'Emlyn's.'

'Emlyn?'

'Yeah, but just think of the fantastic photo opportunity! Us at the top of Ben Nevis, standing next to a fuck-off great big patio heater. It'd be brilliant!'

'So you are going to go ahead with this frankly totally insane plan, you nutters?'

'Yes, I think so. The more I think about it, the more I realize it's just got to be done. It's our *destiny*.'

We walk on in respectful silence.

'Where are you going to get a patio heater from?'

'Well, my parents have got one,' says Matt. 'They just don't get it at all. I've told them over and over – a patio heater puts more carbon dioxide into the atmosphere than a car! You're using fossil fuels to heat the *outdoors*. It's crazy! But do they listen? No. I sometimes think it's a generational thing. They just don't get it. So I think I'll steal theirs.'

'Or we could nick one from a pub,' says Emlyn.

'We're thinking of doing the trip with a horse and cart. And then the horse can pull the patio heater on a trolley sort of device. Obviously, if we do that, we'll have to do a lot of research into horses. How to look after them and so on.'

'And will the horse come with you up the mountain?'

'That'll be the horse's decision.'

'Yes, of course. Well,' I suggest, 'this all sounds perfect for Laura – she can just sit on the cart all the way to Ben Nevis.'

'I don't think Laura will be coming.'

'Laura's basic problem is that she doesn't really like walking.'

'In fact she hates it.'

'Even with a cart?'

'I'd say even. But, Seb, this could be your pledge! To walk with us from Brighton to Ben Nevis! Why don't you come too? It would be fantastic. And then you could also officially catalogue the journey, in one of your books!'

'Does anyone have any other suggestions for pledges?'

'Come on – you know you want to!'

'Seriously. Emlyn. Other suggestions, quick.'

Onward.

Seven o'clock. We're still miles from Winchester. The light is going; things are getting rather gloomy.

'We'll have missed our sound check,' says Matt. 'But it shouldn't be a problem, so long as Laura's found the venue and explained why we're taking so long to get there. We're due on at eight thirty, so if we can make it for eight then I reckon we'll be OK.'

We enter a field full of cows.

'Careful,' says Matt.

'Careful? Of cows? Ha-ha!'

A cow is standing in the middle of our track. I slowly approach, assuming it'll lumber out of the way. It doesn't. I circumnavigate, making friendly mooing noises.

'Seb, do you realize these are steers? Young bulls? You're being very brave.'

I notice that I am now standing among a sizeable group of these steers. A number of them snort at me. The other guys have taken a more circuitous, diversionary route. I am literally stranded amid the bullshit.

'Be very careful,' Matt calls. 'Walk very slowly away to your left. Steers can be extremely dangerous.'

Heart thumping, I inch away from the herd, a number of whom are doing that comedy bull-aggressively-scrapes-hoof-on-ground thing. I make it to the gate and exhale.

'You could have told me they were steers, man!'

'I tried to, but you were there in among them already, making weird mooing noises.'

'I thought they were just *cows*.'

'You have to check for *udders*.'

As darkness descends and we push on towards Winchester, Matt announces that it's time to plant some more seeds. Because today has involved a considerably longer trek than usual, the seed-planting has been neglected somewhat. We down packs and instruments and Matt gets his pot* and trowel out.

'Is this legal?'

'I doubt it. Do you want to have a go?'

I tell him yes, I'd love to, and so the band select a spot for me, at the edge of a field over on the far side of a barbed-wire fence.

'Why does it have to be on the other side of the barbed-wire bloody fence? Why can't I just plant it where we're sitting? I'm *tired*.'

'It's the best spot. It won't get munched up by animals over there;

---

* Not *that* kind of pot.

now stop complaining and get over the fence.'

Over in the field I clear a few square inches of moss, and dig a small hole in the earth using Matt's trowel. I put five or six apple seeds into the hole and replace the soil on top. Pat it down. Pour over a little water from my drinking bottle. Blow it a kiss.

'Or you could piss on it instead,' calls Matt.

'No, it's fine.'

I clamber back over the barbed-wire fence. The guys all high-five me.

'How did that feel?' asks Emlyn.

'It felt brilliant! To fertility!'

We swig from our water bottles.

'It's not too far to Winchester now. Not really.'

'I hope not, or we'll miss the gig.'

'Has that ever happened before?'

'Never. But there's always a first time.'

'Could Laura manage a solo set by herself if it came down to it?'

'I doubt she'd really want to. I mean she'd only have her tambourine.'

It's 8 p.m. and at last we reach the outskirts of Winchester. The band are due onstage in half an hour and everybody, except for Alex who is still some distance behind, is getting excited. Despite the fatigue of a twenty-five-mile hike, rock 'n' roll anticipation visibly courses through their tie-dyed, patchouli-infused veins. I find it contagious, and can't help but whoop along. We cross the M3 footbridge over Twyford Down.

'Good evening, Winchester!' shouts Matt over the roaring traffic.

'Winchester, are you ready to rock?'* echoes Emlyn.

There is air-guitaring. Fist pumps. The pace quickens; eyes sparkle. We arrive at the bottom of the High Street, and two young women smoking cigarettes sitting on a bench outside the chip shop stare at us.

'Groupies!' whispers Emlyn.

---

* A line I never thought I'd have to write ever again.

Five minutes later we are standing, dazed in a pool of streetlight, outside O'Neill's public house.

'We made it!' says Matt, instigating a clumsy group hug.

After a slight tussle with the two bouncers, we march triumphantly inside. It's a big pub, and kind of empty. Laura is sitting alone at a table towards the back. She waves. Her table is next to a small raised stage area. Emlyn plonks his backpack and bass down.

'What do you think you're doing?' comes a voice.

Emlyn turns around. He says, 'Pardon?'

'Get that shit off there,' says a young, angry-looking man in a fitted black corduroy jacket. 'What are you effing playing at?'

'But we're playing,' says Matt. 'We're playing here, tonight, *we're the band*. Hi, it's nice to meet you.'

'No, you are effing not,' says the man in the corduroy jacket. '*We* are playing here tonight, mate. Look the poster. There. See? *Alias*. That's us. Playing here. Tonight. Not you. See your name anywhere? No. So get your crap off my stage. Right now.'

Somewhat taken aback, Matt and the boys just stand there looking at one another, puzzled. Bravely, I look at the floor.

'But . . .'

'But nothing, mate. You'd better just eff off.'

There's obviously been a mix-up along the line somewhere, but this in-your-face aggression is freaking everybody out. Well, it's freaking the hippies and me out. Matt and corduroy jacket go over to speak to the manageress. The manageress says yes, there are two bands playing tonight, and that Nimomashtic are going on first, with Alias headlining after – what's the problem? Corduroy jacket shouts that nobody told them it was two bands! This is an outrage! She tells him she tried to contact Alias but they didn't leave a contact number or email address, so she couldn't. And anyway, is it really such a big deal? There's no one here anyway; and there are just two bands on tonight – often there are three or four.

Matt tries to explain the greater, environmental, positivist concept behind Nimomashtic, but corduroy jacket waves him away. He flatly turns down Matt's pleas to let them use their microphones or amps or PA (the venue doesn't have one of their own).

'Absolutely no way,' says corduroy jacket.

'But we were told we could use the other band's mics,' protests Matt. 'We've walked all the way from Brighton, and we're carrying all our stuff, and we can't carry a whole PA system too. Please. We beg you. This isn't our fault. Have a heart.'

'Too bad,' says corduroy jacket. 'I don't give a shit. You can't use any of our stuff. You just can't. In fact you can eff right off.'

Bands on multiple bills always share stuff. That's just what you do. This is yer basic rock 'n' roll solidarity. Alias have got this all the wrong way around. If I hadn't been so angry, I would have pitied them.

The rest of Alias arrive. They are just as bad – aggressive and aloof and wholly unyielding. Matt and the boys and Laura retire to the corner of the pub to gather their thoughts and eat their first proper meal of the day. Basic priorities. They are exhausted, disorientated and bewildered. Not only that, but another heated debate regarding Laura's role in proceedings spontaneously erupts. I make myself scarce. Matt then goes over to plead with the rest of Alias to allow them to use just a few microphones, not even any amps but, again, they tell him to eff the eff off, you effing hippy C–.*

People arrive – friends that I'd exhorted to attend. Nimomashtic still don't know whether or not they'll get to play. Alias have a lot of gear: massive drumkit, Marshall stacks, the works. Still no punters though, amusingly. They haul all their kit self-importantly through the pub, bumping into people and huffing as they go. They all look like forty-something *Blind Date* contestants – clearly less a bona fide low-slung rock 'n' roll outfit, more a delusional troupe of weekenders. I ask corduroy where Alias hail from.

'*Dorset*,' he snaps.

After threatening to punch Matt, Emlyn and Spanish Alex, Alias's guitarist† then threatens to punch Laura too. This is the last straw

---

* Sorry, mother.

† This guy makes corduroy jacket look like Nigel Havers.

for the venue manageress, and she asks Alias to leave. Their attitude changes immediately – suddenly they're all meek and repentant. Corduroy jacket sidles over to where Matt's sitting devouring a plate of chips and says they'll let them play four songs, but they still can't use any of their gear. By this point, I'm all up for a full-on punk rock riot, as are a number of my friends when they learn exactly what's been going down. Matt however – a gentleman and frankly far too much of a hippy – thanks him profusely. The Nimomashtic dudes clearly just want to let their music do the talking. How grown-up. How well-adjusted. How *naïve*.

Five minutes before showtime, Matt, the manageress and I have one final, last-ditch attempt at persuading Alias to let the hippies use their backline. Cornered by our three-line whip, their singer finally, reluctantly concedes. Nimomashtic snatch up their instruments (Alex the *cajon*, which also serves as his stool as he plays it) and hurry to the stage, where after thirty seconds' preparation, they begin. Matt, messiah hat firmly in place, begins – without a trace of irony – by thanking Alias for their kindness. There is booing. The audience of roughly twenty-five people are fully aware of the dynamic, and are on the hippies' side before they've even played a note. The atmosphere is thick with tension; this is like the Stones at Altamont, man, with Alias as the brown acid. Alias stand glowering at the bar, clutching pints of lager, chins jutted.

While Matt is introducing the band, Alias's guitarist stamps over to ('his' side of) the stage and pushes Alex off the *cajon*, picking it up and throwing it off the stage. Then he pushes over Laura's microphone stand, shoving her off-balance as a result.

Matt freezes and the place goes silent. Nobody knows what to do next. Fortunately there aren't any Hell's Angels wielding pool cues. Instead, two Aliases come over and have to restrain their guitarist forcibly: 'Leave it, she's not worth it,' etc. Nimomashtic are utterly non-confrontational, despite my suggestions that they should really start to behave otherwise. Laura and Alex are visibly shocked. Alex goes to fetch the *cajon*; sits tentatively back down. Laura stares aghast at the guitarist with wide, terrified eyes. He lurches at them again, but is held back by his bandmates. The man is clearly a psychopath. None of this is very funny any more. Nobody's sure where things go from here.

'Erm,' Matt says into the microphone. 'We're Nimomashtic. What's going on?'

Emlyn suggests they just get on with it; and so they do. They play a pop-folk tune, called 'The Charlatan and the Crow', and it's great – sinewed and breezy and effortless and organic-sounding, and Matt, behatted, is a good frontman. He owns the stage; owns the whole room and he knows it. There's no 'revenge' in Matt's performance – just a plain-speaking righteousness. Joy even. His hours of meditation* have clearly paid off. The song ends and they receive a fantastic ovation. Everybody looks over at Alias at the bar, snarling. They play a few more songs. People clap along; sing; ride the vibe. Corduroy jacket goes over and tells Matt to make their next song their last, or else. Matt thanks everybody, including Alias, again. They exit as the evening's modest heroes. People come over and congratulate them.

Alias strut onstage and play earnest, stilted cover versions of Oasis, Stiltskin, Dandy Warhols and Kaiser Chiefs songs. There is slow-clapping between the numbers. Booing. Nimomashtic politely applaud, however, because they're nice guys.

'Matt, I know now what I want to do for my pledge,' I shout over the angry guitarist's portly, worthless, xeroxed-in Flying V-isms.

'Fantastic!' he replies. 'Are you going to come with us up Ben Nevis?'

'No, I'm going to go over and punch the guitarist in Alias.'

Matt smiles sadly and shakes his head. 'That's not what we mean by a pledge. Your pledge has to involve doing something positive to combat climate change. Punching that idiot might feel good at the time, but Mother Earth is not going to reap much of a reward, is she?'

'I suppose she isn't.'

* And bongs.

'Also he'll probably kick your head in,' interjects Emlyn. 'Personally, I think we should just try to forget all about Alias, and move on.'

'You guys are just *too nice*.'

They smile. I buy them Guinness. We all drink Guinness, and then hobble back to my house. They sleep on the floor in my spare room; Matt on the sofa. Tomorrow they're off to play a gig in Southampton, twelve miles down the Itchen Way in a community centre, and I miss them already. I'm seriously considering joining them going up Ben Nevis with the patio heater. Because little ripples make waves. Little ripples make waves. Little ripples make waves. Little ripples make waves. Little ripples make waves. Little ripples make waves. Little ripples make waves. Little ripples make waves. Little ripples make waves. Little ripples make waves, brothers and sisters.

This ain't fatuous. Recycle. Take public transport. All that stuff. Cuz if we all do, then in the end, others will have to as well, even India and China. So walk your talk. You really don't have to walk all that far. Because little ripples ...

Peace. To Alias. Even I forgive you, for Christ's sake.*

Hello, sudden complete hippies anonymous?

---

* Yes, I know I still haven't come up with a pledge yet. Hopefully a non-violent one will occur to me soon.

Step Eleven

Independent Custody Visitor
Mongo Police Station,
Mongo

I'd like to inform y'all that I'm signed up for another sodding year of this Independent Custody Visiting lark*. While you're sitting in your comfy chair enjoying this book immensely and planning to buy multiple copies for friends and family for Christmas, go on, please spare a fleeting thought for me still hard at work†out there in exciting towns such as Aldershot, in the cells with my clipboard, a colleague and a mildly resentful attitude. Why not drive down here and get arrested and we can hang out?** I'll have to black out everything you say, but hey, it'd be fun! Funner. And I'll make sure you get a drink. Hot chocolate or whatever you like. Hot chocolate.

Anyway, today's visit is in Mongo, again. I arrive in plenty of time and greet friendly, retired Jill outside the police station front doors.†† We are well received by the duty sergeant. There is one detainee in the custody suite; we visit the detainee and, for the first time, I lead the conversation. It goes OK – I am not attacked. We inspect the rest of the cells; fill out our paperwork; and then, just as we're about to leave, Jill asks the duty sergeant, 'Is there anything

---

* Although in actual fact I resigned two months later. The Police Authority in question requested I 'fess up to this in the text. In fact they said: 'I am also disappointed that in a book entitled "How to be a Better Person" you state that you have signed up for another year of custody visiting when this was not the case.' This is, quite literally, a fair cop.

† Or perhaps not, as the case might actually be.

** Hey look, we can still hang out, right?

†† Jill tells me that when she retired, she did three things: learned how to drive a rally car, travelled across Asia on the Trans-Siberian Railway, and became an Independent Custody Visitor. Fantastic!

else you'd like to mention while we're here?'

'Actually, yes,' he replies. 'It's about the food we have to serve to the detainees. It's just not good enough, I'm afraid. In order to reach the official recommended daily calorific intake, you'd have to eat ten of these ready-meals. Their nutritional content is risible. OK, often people are in and out of here in a matter of hours, but then sometimes we get people in here for three days at a time. And in these cases, three of these "meals" just isn't enough. We should be able to give them chocolate, or let their friends or family bring food in for them. These people aren't animals. Have you ever tasted these things?'

'These police station ready-meals? No,' I say. 'I tend to go to the supermarket, you know.'

'I've tasted them,' says Jill. 'Actually I am working my way through the whole range.'

'You are?'

'Yes. It's rather an exercise in empathy.'

'They're not very nice, are they?' says the sarge.

'No, they certainly are not. Although the lamb hotpot was almost acceptable. You can just about tell that's meat. Unlike the lasagne. The lasagne was unspeakable.'

'Christ, don't mention the lasagne.' The duty sergeant turns to me. 'Would you like to try some?'

'The detainees' ready-meals? Are you serious?'

'Yeah, why not? See what they have to put up with. You can take a couple away with you if you like.'

'Well. I hadn't really, erm. OK then. Why not! If you don't mind.'

One of his colleagues nips off to the kitchen and returns with two small blue and white cardboard boxes.

'All out of lasagne, I'm afraid,' he says, handing them over. 'You've got one "Beans and Potato Wedges" and one "All Day Breakfast". That's the most popular one.'

'And arguably the most revolting,' says the sarge.

'I'll second that,' says Jill.

'Thank you so much. For these.'

I put them in my bag and drive home, not looking forward to lunch all that much.

Detainees' Ready-Meals Taste Test
My kitchen, Winchester

Gleaming chrome surfaces.
Aesthetically positioned bowl of oranges.
Teeth-whitener.

Let us begin with 'All Day Breakfast'. A quick scroll down the ingredients list reveals the primary ingredient to be water; or rather *aqua*. The sausages contain 11 per cent meat (the remaining 89 per cent is made up of water, rusk, seasoning, preservative and antioxidant). I pierce the plastic lid, place the meal in my microwave and cook it on full power for three minutes. The microwave pings. I peel back the plastic lid and let the contents, which look remarkably like a Mark Rothko painting – one of his very brown ones – 'stand'. Inside the plastic container are two small sausages, a few cubes of potato and a steaming grey/brown suspension of 'baked beans'. It smells like the Appleby House midsummer pig bin. It smells 'of despair'.

I slice off and spear a mouthful of sausage, and attempt to chew it. I fail, as the sausage has the texture of dead jellyfish. It flops about miserably in my mouth until I eventually summon forth the courage to swallow it. Down it slips, like hot snot. It tastes what one might call 'fatty, savoury'. There is a slightly metallic, slightly plasticky, stark processed aftertaste. The grey beans taste the same but feature additional peculiarly adhesive qualities in the finish. The potatoes are mealy and acidic. How much of this do I have to actually eat?* I'm one of those people who likes aeroplane food, by the way, and looks forward to it and everything, and would ask for seconds if I ever had the guts.

Marks out of ten for the 'All Day Breakfast': 0.5. Half a point for the fact that if you were genuinely starving to death, this cardboard

---

* All in, I managed four mouthfuls.

box of food might just about save your life. The box, I mean, not the food. The box is significantly better for you; also you could write your farewell note on the back of it. And yes, manufacturers,* you can use that quote in your marketing, go ahead.

For our second course, we have the 'Beans and Potato Wedges'. The primary ingredient is also fashionable *aqua*. In fact, the 'Beans and Potato Wedges' turn out to be the 'All Day Breakfast' only minus the jellysnot bangers. In its favour, 'Beans and Potato Wedges' has a best before date of January 2009.

I heat the box in my microwave. It pings. I let it stand.

Marks out of ten: 0.25. And you can find this recipe on Ceefax, page 666.

Moral of the story: remain law-abiding.

Roll credits; over The Bill *theme tune.*

Mild coshing.

Step Back in Time
Winchester Marathon, Winchester 1986
Number of countries participating in Bob Geldof's 1986
Sport Aid charitable event: 78
Estimated number of participants, worldwide: 20+ million

In 1986 my father ran a half-marathon, also in the Winchester environs. He and his friend, the blind broadcaster Peter White, pushed a disabled friend thirteen miles in his wheelchair. They made quite an impression, especially since my father secreted a half-bottle of whisky in the back of the wheelchair, to which all three helped themselves as and when necessary, which was every time they were overtaken (in fraternal consolation). The overtakers were apparently offered a slug too, but mostly they declined, my father told me. I always loved that 'mostly'. My father also smoked Silk Cut cigarettes as he ran. And he ran in a bright blue woollen track suit. He was incredibly thin, and it was with this 'runner's physique' that he used to justify the modest amount of training he had done in

* Westlers. Since 1960.

preparation for the race. In a way things have changed.

The Great Clarendon Way, full, half- and relay marathon
My house, Winchester
Winning time (half-marathon), 2006: 1.20.29
Person who came in last's time (half-marathon), 2006: 3.39.38

Steve, Paul and his friend Nick, who's running this too, all stayed over at my house last night. We went to a restaurant and stuffed ourselves with Nepalese carbohydrates (it was Saturday night – everywhere else was booked out). At lunchtime I ate three extra large portions of spicy tomato and tuna pasta,* with added pasta, as a result of which my stomach became visibly distended and I felt sick all afternoon.

'Is this definitely the right thing to do before a race? Completely stuff oneself with carbohydrate edibles? Aren't I just loading myself up with extra weight to have to carry around the course?'

None of the lads could reply as their mouths were jammed full of Nepalese noodles. They shrugged a little. There wasn't much pre-race dinner banter either, as it was soft drinks all around. What a memorable, bacchanalian feast this was. We walked back to my place amid the usual small-town weekend English chaos† and then everybody slept incredibly badly.

Race day! *Runner's World* recommends porridge, and so it's porridge and plenty of water for four. As we sit around my dining room table digging into all this porridge and water, Paul, a lifelong obsessive fan of high-pitched prog bores Rush, painstakingly attempts to draw their Starman logo in his porridge** with the golden syrup he had forced me to buy.

'I have to have golden syrup on my porridge,' he had said.

And so, wanting to be a good host, I got some.

'And where are the bananas I asked for?'

'I forgot the bananas.'

'This is useless.'

---

* Another recipe available on Ceefax page 666.
† Winchester Litter Pickers will deal with this.
** Paul is 38.

'No, thank *you*.'

'I just can't get this Starman logo right with this golden syrup.'

'Good.'

'Nor can I,' says Steve.[*]

'*Good.*'

Reuben[†] eats his porridge, regarding the three strangers with brooding distrust. Then, afterwards as we stretch, Reuben frowns and delivers a few well-placed heckles before being taken upstairs for his own safety and a nappy change.

Downstairs, running gear is donned; GPS watches are strapped on; trainers are laced and re-laced; I pull on my swimming trunks and tie back my hair. My swollen tummy pokes out through my red T-shirt. I suppose this is my fuel tank. My family and I then engage in emotional farewells and a small regurgitation of porridge before we four men pile into a taxi and head off to the start point at the village hall of the small village of Broughton, halfway to Salisbury. We note what a particularly long car ride it is. We also note that it's pouring with rain.

'Are you sure it's this far?' we nag the taxi driver. 'Are you sure you haven't made some sort of huge detour, slash, mistake?'

The taxi driver merely chortles, and ploughs on through the downpour.

Inside the village hall it's like election day: trestle tables staffed by smiling pensioners sitting in front of endless sheets of paper full of names. We queue to collect our numbers and a handful of safety pins with which to affix them to our tops. First, though, we must write our next of kin's contact details in a space on the back of our numbers. Also 'fess up to any medical problems plus the medication we might be taking to counter them, and details of allergies.[**] Credit card details too, as down payment for any ambulance fees that may be incurred. In the meantime, there is much loo-dashing; I am beginning to fear that I have overhydrated.

[*] Steve is also 38.

[†] 15 months.

[**] Running.

'How many cups of tea did you drink this morning?' asks Paul.
'Two.'

'That's two too many! Tea is a diuretic – you'll be pissing like a horse all day.'

'Oh, well, that kind of explains it.'

Because this has been a little horse-like. So much so that I have felt myself becoming steadily *de*hydrated. Thus I drink even more water and then five minutes later have to pee it all out again. Altogether I pee five times in the village hall gents' before the start of the race. The Rotary Club ex-colonel chap regulating access to the lavs begins to eye me with great suspicion, but then to be fair he's eyeing everyone with great suspicion. His fingers twitch at an imaginary blunderbuss.

In between urinations, I stand with the others out in the drizzle doing yet more stretching and waiting for the race to begin. I am worried about my hip. Steve is worried about his foot. Paul is worried about an old scar on his leg. Nick's not worried about anything, as he is Australian. Around us, our fellow competitors enact their own pre-race rituals: downing jelly babies and energy drinks, firing up mp3-players and strapping them to biceps, triceps, bananas.

'I'd kill for a banana,' says Paul.

'Well, maybe you should have brought a few of your own,' I snap.

It's the tension, you see? It has this effect on all of us. We discuss our race strategies: Paul and Nick plan to accelerate through the field from the off, while Steve and I have decided to bide our time from slightly further back.

An unfashionable man emerges from the village hall carrying a megaphone and gives us the five-minute warning. We file around to the road in front of the hall to ready ourselves for the start; it's packed with runners of all shapes and sizes and ages. The atmosphere is one of benevolent bewilderment. Nervous laughter. Darting eyes. The scent of Deep Heat and old shoes and new shoes. Rain continues to fall. This is all so unreal. The last thing in the world I feel like doing now is running. This is a fascinating anthropological study, not a *race*. Also, I really need to go to the toilet again.

'I really need to go to the toilet again,' I mutter to Steve.

'You can always do a Paula Radcliffe,' he says.

'What, you mean win the race? Are you mad?'

'No, I mean just pull down your swimming trunks and do a shit in the middle of the road.'

I panic. Whisper frantically, 'How did you know these were swimming trunks? I never told you they were swimming trunks. Is it really obvious that they're swimming trunks?'

'Really obvious.'

'Oh no! Everyone knows I'm wearing swimming trunks! How humiliating!'

Somewhere up ahead, the starting gun fires, and a weak cheer goes up. We continue to stand there. Nick says that he hopes this wasted standing time will be taken off his finishing time at the end. After a few minutes, the crowd around us begins to move forward at walking pace. Nick and Paul attempt to push through the pack.

'Ouch,' says a pensioner standing in front of them. They shove through regardless.

'Goodbye!' I call. 'See you at the end!'

'You never know what will happen,' says Paul before disappearing into the pack.

I turn to Steve. 'What did he mean by that?'

Steve and I allow ourselves to drift with the ebb. Soon everybody is jogging along, and we are being overtaken by eighty-year-olds wearing those angular tinted sunglasses. Jimmy Savile, you have so much to answer for.

As we shuffle through the leafy outskirts of Broughton being passed by yet more plump, elderly and female fellow runners, villagers and their families stand at the roadside and cheer us all on. I feel intensely self-conscious, and can't meet any of their eyes; instead I pull tragic Princess Diana expressions and stare at the ground blushing. Finally out of the village, we are running along a flat country road flanked by high hedges.

'So how are you feeling so far?' I ask Steve.

'Fine.'

'Yeah, me too. This is really great! Except that I need to go to the toilet.'

It's then that I notice a low-pitched yet distinct rumbling sound immediately behind us. I glance back to see the front of an ambulance, trundling discreetly along at our heels – clearly the race support vehicle.

'Steve, whatever you do, don't look back, man.'

He looks back.

'Ah, shit.'

'Does this mean what I think it means?'

'Yes.'

We are in last place already.

'Never mind,' I urge. 'We've counted them all out, and we'll count them all back in again. I mean reel them all back in again. One-by-octogenarian-one.'

'Damn right.'

So there's no point in accelerating really. Keep things steady. Avoid getting run over by the ambulance.

All marathons are *contractually obliged* to have within their ranks[*] a small squad of squaddies all running in full camouflage fatigues with full-to-burst backpacks. Backpacks filled with polystyrene, I'll wager. Our own event's squadron comes into sight fifty yards ahead of us: there are six of them, wearing berets. Their sergeant major is shouting at his men; we can hear him from all the way back here. Quick march! Left, right, left right! You 'orrible shower, and so on. Steve and I gain on them; in fact we're passing quite a few people now since there's a little uphill, thus a little backmarker flagging. As our pace is already so slow, steady rather, we don't 'do' flagging: we are the Levellers.[†] Unfortunately everybody we've just levelled now passes us again down the other side of the hill – squaddies included.

[*] Ranks!

[†] Only with less straw in our clothes.

'Bastards,' says Steve, nice and quietly, as they all elbow past.

And this back-and-forth continues for a number of miles. We overtake the squaddies and then a few minutes later they overtake us again. It's getting a bit niggly, a bit personal, especially since the rutted paths are becoming narrower.

'OK, let's just overtake them and stay ahead this time, yeah?'

'You mean up the pace?'

'Yeah.'

'But I don't know how to!'

Yet we do — we surge past into clearer water — a steep, claggy field. We climb the crest and accelerate and then never see the squaddies again. Perhaps they were just a mirage; perhaps they're always a mirage — running ghosts. Wouldn't that be nice?★

We come to another village. Many of its inhabitants are also out at the roadside to encourage us. Their children jump up and down in wellington boots.

'Hooray!'

'Well done!'

'Chin up!'

'You're doing brilliantly, keep going!'

'Come on you two, pick it up. It's not a stroll in the park!'

'What did she just say?'

'That was outrageous.'

'*What* did that woman just say?'

'She shouted at us to "pick it up". Can you believe it?'

'That's what I thought she said. Is that allowed?'

'It's an outrage.' Steve cranes his neck around. 'Hey, you! Piss off!'

We continue to run through the village. It's still raining. Ahead we spot a heavily whiskered old man in a Barbour jacket, holding up a cardboard Union Jack. He earnestly shakes it.

'Jolly good!' he calls.

'Here we go,' mutters Steve.

★ Conflicts legal in the eyes of the United Nations excepted.

'*Deutschland über alles*,' I call back.

We come to our first Drinks Station. I am excited. The whole Drinks Station ritual is something I've admired on the television for many years. And here I am, about to enact my own very own variation thereupon! Over at the side of the road is a table full of plastic cups manned by kindly villagers hurriedly filling them with water. Four or five more stand anxiously, pressing sloshing cups into runners' outstretched hands. I reach out excitedly. An overflowing cup is thrust forth. I grab at it. Miss. It falls to the ground. I have now run beyond the Drinks Station. Thirsty and rather heartbroken, I notice that Steve, still running alongside, is not only sipping calmly from a full cup, but also has a fistful of jelly babies in his other hand.

'Mmm, delicious,' he says.

'Where did you get them from?'

'There was a little girl with a big jar of them. Didn't you get any?'

'No, I was too busy . . . I don't know!'

Steve drains his cup and then tosses it dramatically aside, the part of the ritual that I'd been *particularly* looking forward to; it's not often you can litter willy-nilly with a clear conscience like that, not unless you've eaten an apple in a wood. Thus I am fuelled by bitterness for the next half-mile. *Nice day for it.*

Five miles in now, and I am pleased to report that my body is experiencing no problems other than that *I seriously need to go to the toilet now.*

'If that's all you're worrying about, then you're in good shape,' says Steve.

'Nnnggg.'

We are starting to reel other runners in now, in earnest. Well, one or two of the older women, at least. In earnest.

'Coming through!' we holler, as we elbow the crones into a bush. We are then elbowed into copses of our own, as the full-length marathon runners begin to pass us: forty-, fifty- and sixty-somethings in seventies-style '[Town Name*] Harriers' vests who all run

* Andover; Crawley; Horsham; Tring; Guildford; Basingstoke; Ringwood; Waterlooville...

like a cross between Richard III and Tommy Cooper; their bodies resemble hunched old pistons. Gnarled scuttlers – running outside themselves – ghoulish twisted faces like Hieronymus Bosch's weird flying fish demons.*

'Coming through!' they wheeze, in taut Lycra and utility belts. This can't be good for them, can it? They should be back home in their bungalows gumming at Werthers, not out here panting like this in the rain. Help the aged, don't encourage them.

Another Drinks Station appears ahead. I note they have a selection of either water or orange squash.

'Which are you going to have?' I ask Steve. 'Water or squash?'

'Water.'

'Not squash?'

'Yeah, maybe squash.'

'Not water?'

'Maybe water.'

'I'm going for squash.'

'Not water?'

'I don't know now. Aaaarrrgghhhh!'

'Aaaaarrrrrggghhh!'

In these hellish procrastinations, we almost ran straight past it.

Have you ever tried to drink a cup of water while running? You can't actually get any of it down your throat. You can get plenty down your chin, chest, fuel tank and legs, but precious little where you actually require it. I manage a few swallows; unfortunately mostly swallows of air. I burp. Hic. Burp. Hic. Most importantly, however, I then throw my empty cup triumphantly down among the others festooned upon the muddy path, and the magnificent post-toss euphoria† lasts for a good quarter-mile. Although it's not really *so* much of a 'good' quarter-mile, as the miles don't feel quite so good any more, they're starting to feel a little more 'bad', 'painful' and 'I'm not so sure about this now'.

* Late. Night. *Review.*

† Not *that* kind of post-toss euphoria.

'These hills are starting to get to me,' grunts Steve.

I grunt back. Just a grunt. Our fellow competitors aren't running up the hills now – they're walking. Unlike us. *Chariots of Fire* and that. The tortoise. Further metaphors.

'We're reeling them in again, look.'

'Nnnggg.'

But the bastards always overtake us again on the downhill. Perhaps we ought to be utilizing gravity a little more in these sections. I wish I knew what *Runner's World* had to say on the matter. They ought to have representatives dotted along the course.

I decided against running to music in the end. When Steve said he'd be running with me, I decided not to bother, since running alongside somebody else turns it from a solitary, introspective endurance test into a bona fide social situation. It's much better. When you're alone, your every tingle, twinge and niggle assumes terrifying, biblical proportions. YOU ARE FALLING APART; IN FACT YOUR LIMBS ARE ALL ABOUT TO SNAP LIKE MATCHSTICKS AND THEN YOU WILL *FALL DOWN DEAD*, bellows Brian Blessed at every minor ache and pain. But when there's someone beside you, you can't micro-obsess over your body's failings; instead you have somehow to attempt to maintain a conversation. And, believe me, that's not easy – at least not one that makes any sense.

Today I have discovered that trying to hold any kind of conversation while running – even a super-banal one about the weather or whatever – is a bit like trying to stay standing when you've got one foot off the ground with your eyes shut. It sounds easy, but it's not. Your brain just doesn't function properly. It's like you're operating at high altitude or something; or drunk.* Whatever you open your mouth to say, a slurred, lysergic version comes out instead. For example, I try to say to Steve: 'I wish I hadn't drunk that water back there; I can feel it all lurching about in my stomach.'

But what I actually say is: 'I wish I . . . haddruck tha'waaaar there;

---

* A wheelchair, a wheelchair, my kingdom for a wheelchair.

I feel sortff. I feel sort of, lursh, swill in, you know, my stomach, lur-shing all waaar, do you know? Djew know, yeah? Yeah? Steve?' And then I pant some. Do a big spit. Steve maintains a dignified silence. I notice that much of the spit has gone down my front, like translu-cent go-faster stripes.

There is a small sweat stain on the front of my T-shirt. I am quite inordinately proud of it. *Look!* I want to shout at all the spectators. *Sweat!* Sweat and spit! *I am an animal.*

I am the Tortoise.

Eight miles. Nine. I am amazed at how relatively straightforward this has been so far. All the training is really paying off. I had some-how expected the actual race to contain hidden traps – additional extra-confounding hazards of mysterious Machiavellian nature. But actually it's way simpler – you rise to it. One is buoyed by the event, by the people, by the strung-out multicoloured trail of struggling fellow competitors. The empathy. The agony. The sights and the sounds. The spectacular Hampshire countryside. The bridges over rivers. The mud. The breathing. The pigeonsong. The *life*. The whole beautiful Zen of it. And the huge wobbly female backsides that one must continually negotiate one's way around.

I turn to Steve to make a non-sexist comment about all these fat arses. We are running through a wood. There is no reply to my quite witty comment.

'Sorry, was that sexist?'

Silence.

'Sorry, perhaps that was somewhat sexist after all.'

Silence.

'Was it not sexist enough, maybe?'

Silence.

'Steve?'

But he's not there. I check in front; behind; above. He's nowhere to be seen.

'Steve!'

Could he have exploded? I give it five minutes, slow down a

little. Still no sign. I can only imagine his foot gave way beneath him – this was his big pre-race worry. Who knows? I run on, in confusion. Alone. Askew. Left to its own mawkish devices, my attention glazes gradually inwards, and soon my left knee starts to hurt more than a twinge. Ditto right knee. When the going gets tough, the tough get going, but what are the rest of us supposed to do? I begin to weep silently. Oh, what the hell – loudly as well. *What would my father have done?* None of my fellow competitors appears to have any Silk Cut-shaped bulges in their shorts and they all seem sober, so God only knows. Taken a turn in the wheelchair?

Respite arrives in the form of another Drinks Station. At this one they have three choices: water, orange squash or Vimto. Vimto! I snatch at a cup of Vimto and pour it all down my front, obliterating my small yet profound sweat stain. Also I have forgotten all those 'loneliness of the long-distance runner' gags. And Vimto isn't as nice as you remember it. This is a guess as none went in my mouth.

I run on, alone and in serious pain now, and sort of hallucinating. The field has thinned out. I am no longer running smoothly – I'm moving in jerks and spasms and my bladder is screaming at me. I briefly wake up to myself and plunge into some bushes off to the left of the forest track and pee for a good minute and a half. It's heavenly; I grunt like a hog. Then I amble back on to the course and have to confront the dreadful prospect of having to start running all over again – one of the most difficult things I've ever had to do. Standing still like this is ecstatic bliss; even just walking feels delightful; running, though: deep technicolour blooms of muscular agony. The body is refusing. You gotta force yourself. Only however many miles it is to the finish. How many now? What did the last mile counter say? I can't remember. Three to go, I think. It is dawning on me that long-distance running can be a genuinely psychedelic experience: a bad trip, basically.

With less than two miles left to go, I suddenly remember the small plastic bag of jelly babies in my back pocket. Paul had divvied these up earlier, with strict instructions: 'Only eat them when you've got absolutely zero energy left, when you feel like you can't go any further. They'll give you an important energy boost, and might help you make it to the end.'

I'd forgotten all about them. I rip open the bag and shove a handful into my slobbering mouth and have a kind of 'head orgasm': sensations of blissful sweet delirium shoot through my unsteady consciousness. They are so wonderful that I can't stop – the rest go in too – my mouth becomes seriously gummed up. This is, no bullshit, the greatest meal I have ever eaten. Jelly baby tears roll down my cheeks; jelly baby spittle spins down my chin. For three or four minutes I am completely unaware that I am running. It's just like heaven. Then, sugar rush abruptly over, I crash back down to earth. My right knee has got so bad that I actually gasp with pain at every stride. I begin seriously not to enjoy myself. My face is screwed up in a hot ball of pain, like fresh out of a, um, fresh out of a *hot wok*. Have you ever seen a giraffe being born? Well, that's what I look like right at this minute. Drenched in giraffterbirth. Not a pretty sight. Or smell. Or much else. Father?

You've got to search for the hero inside yourself, son.

But that wasn't released until after you had died, Papa.

OK, calling all the heroes then.

But I don't know their number.

Falling back on a risible 'dream sequence' in an attempt to make your noticeably disabled-person-free race more interesting is truly lowest common denominator stuff, son. Adopted son, I ought to add.

That's a low one, especially since you're dead and supposed to be an inspiration right at this moment, instead of heckling me like this.

You did ask for my input. And to be fair, if I were alive, I would be heckling you.

I should have known better.

Better the devil you know, eh?

You don't have to pay to use song titles, Father, do you?

No, son, just lyrics. Bollocks to Survivor. Bollocks to all of them except for, what have you written here? Black Sabbath. What's a Black Sabbath?

Step Eleven

We *had* this discussion. I miss you, Papa.
I miss you too, son. What's a Black Sabbath?

One mile to go. We're on the outskirts of Winchester – I vaguely recognize it. The landscape is slurry. Agonizing stumbles now – barely running at all, but there's nothing to lose. Everything hurts – it might as well hurt a little more. Death or glory. Accelerate!

Whoa now. Decelerate. Not that much. Not that way either – that's a tree. Thanks, steward. Yes, I am OK, thanks for asking. Oh, you're imaginary! I did wonder why you were eight feet tall and purple.

There is some time missing from this next bit. Everything is blank. Anything might have happened. Nothing actually did, but it might have.

A vortex (with advertisements).

Suddenly I can hear cheering! Can't see where it's coming from, though. Maybe it's another hallucination. I clump on, as best I can, still overtaking one or two people – fellow shambling zombie deadbeats. I hear one of the yellow-bibbed (real) stewards calling something about two hundred something. Two hundred what? I am confused and everything is spangled.

'Two hundred yards to go!' is what he's saying. 'You're nearly there now. Keep going!'

Can this be true? I lurch through a hole in a hedge into a bright school playing field full of people. A long funnel for runners with cheering spectators on either side. A man yammering into a megaphone, that familiar tone. Newborn giraffe idiot Princess Diana grin. Lumber. Towards the funnel, over, towards the funnel, run down the funnel. No, the funnel! I drunkenly peruse the audience, faces blur, but then I spot Faye waving excitedly over to the right. She's holding Reuben! Reuben! I can't believe it! I run into the back of somebody.

'Hey!'
'Sorry.'
Into the funnel.

'You can stop running now.'

'Oh, but.'

All right.

Stand and sway.

Be counted.

Well done.

Stagger; scratch head.

Erm.

So.

Errrrm.

Hello, it's my mother. What's she doing here? She gives me a big hug.

I am 341st.

It took two hours, thirty-two minutes and fifty-four seconds.

Not fast.

But better than nothing, ladies and gentlemen.

Better than nothing.

Step Twelve

Southampton and Winchester Visitors Group,
Southampton Library Café
10 a.m.

My new client is called Benjamin. He is from a non-specific,* war-torn African nation. Benjamin grew up in a remote village. He didn't go to school; instead his father taught him Islamic studies at home. When he was still a young teenager, rebel soldiers stormed through Benjamin's village, setting houses on fire and seizing all the young men. Benjamin was thus taken away and forcibly conscripted into the militia, never to set eyes on his parents, sister or younger brother again. Five years ago he escaped from the militia, managing to flee to the United Kingdom, where he claimed asylum at Heathrow's Terminal Three.

Over here he met and fell in love with a girl from his own country, with whom he had a daughter. His partner's claim for asylum was subsequently accepted and she was granted Right to Remain; but Benjamin wasn't. After five years in the UK without either work or social security, Benjamin now faces forced repatriation to his still unstable country of origin, where he faces an unknown, though quite possibly incredibly dangerous future. If this happens, he will lose his family all over again. He turned to the SWVG in despair. He is an extremely damaged young man.

I buy him a cup of coffee and we sit at a table by the window, looking out over the fountain in front of the library.

'So, Benjamin. What can I do to help you? Do you have a solicitor?'

Benjamin looks down into his cup, takes a deep breath and begins to talk.

* His case is extremely sensitive, thus I think it's best to keep him as anonymous as possible.

Walk Your Talk
2007 Tour Update

I couldn't just let them walk off into the sunset of the unknown. So here's a snapshot of what went down over the remainder of Nimomashtic's Walk Your Talk Tour 2007, starting from the morning they left my house in Winchester:

Good gig in the community centre in *Southampton*.

Collective psychosis in the *New Forest*.

Gig falls through in *Christchurch*.

Gig falls through in *Poole*.

Laura leaves the band on the approach to *Weymouth*, but rejoins the next day just in time for a . . .

Good gig on the outskirts of *Weymouth*.

Good acoustic gig in *Lyme Regis*.

Laura threatens to leave the band once more, but then a . . .

Good gig in *Otterdon Mill* . . .

. . . means that Laura is in a better mood come the next morning, and decides to continue for the time being.

I text Emlyn, suggesting that he give Laura a slap . . .

. . . to which Emlyn replies that she's just had a few days off, and seems to be behaving, at least for now.

Good gig on the outskirts of *Exeter* (with Laura).

Laura finally throws in the towel and leaves the band.

Introspective free camping on *Dartmoor*.

Great gig in *Tavistock* (as a three-piece), with celebrities in the audience, apparently.

Let down by yet another promoter in *Plymouth*.

Good gig in *Liskeard* followed by free-camping on *Bodmin Moor*.

Final, triumphant gig in *Bodmin*.*

---

* Or rather, as Matt's Tour Blog puts it: 'Our final gig was not the busiest in the world, as the man with his dog at the bar would testify, but we had fun jamming our way through the tunes on a togetherness which you could only get from walking 300 miles. It was that togetherness which saw us laugh, sing, cry, moan, groan, dance, joke and essentially walk our talk. My final thought rests with the seeds we planted, not the apple or the wildflowers but the ones we hopefully

Step Twelve

Nimomashtic take the train back home to *Brighton*.

Laura rejoins the band.

God gave rock and roll to you. God gave rock and roll to you.
God gave rock and rooooooll, to everyone.*

Southampton and Winchester Visitors Group,
Portsmouth Library Café
Lunchtime

Appo's OK but has started to have to sign the immigrants' register
at his local police station every week.

'Why?' I ask.

'Because!' he says, and laughs. 'I don't know. I do what I am told.'

'But I mean, after five years in this country, why suddenly now?'

'This was one of the questions I was going to ask you.'

Recently, despite much humanitarian protest, the government
began to send people back to the Democratic Republic of the
Congo on a regular basis. A major airline the Home Office had
chartered regularly to deport failed asylum seekers has even refused
to allow the government to use its planes any more.

'We will not be operating any further flights of this nature,' said
its chief executive, somewhat heroically. 'We are not neutral on the
issue and have sympathy for all dispossessed persons in the world,
hence our stance.'

'I think you'll be safe, Appo. Your appeal is ongoing, at least.
You've just got to hang on in there and hope for the best, I'm
afraid,' I said, somewhat less heroically.

'And, Seb, I have heard rumours of a new amnesty for people
who have been here for over five years. Have you heard about this
amnesty?'

'Another one.'

'Yes, another!'

sowed in others' minds. If only one of those seeds grows, then that would be a
success, and of course there is no way of judging that, so the best thing to do is
to just keep on walking...' Amen, brother.

* Except Alias.

'It's not going to happen.'

We laugh.

Uneasily.

And Appo walks back to his apartment, to wait a little longer.

The Great Clarendon Way, full, half- and relay marathon
My house, Winchester, a few days later

Nick came 125th.

Paul came 245th.

Steve hobbled in 362nd (it was his foot).

I managed to raise: £597.44 for Wells for India and £260 for the Southampton and Winchester Visitors Group.

I couldn't walk for two days.

Thank heavens, then, for the Royal Wave.

Nice guys finish last. Or at least towards the back.

Pledge Coda

I have finally come up with a pledge: to keep on running half-marathons,* raising (or at least attempting to raise) £1,000 for every organization that has welcomed me into their schism-ridden bosom throughout the duration of this book. All told, that adds up to round about £12,000, depending on whether or not I run† for those ungrateful bastards at Marwell Zoological Park, plus whether I just give Messiah Matt a grand or what, plus whether it's actually possible to raise money for the, erm, ███████ Constabulary. Let's hope not. But all this will take at least six half-marathons,** which I promise you I will run.†† So I hope this pledge is OK. Feel free to come and run*** with me. Don't forget to bring your Bruckner and your Agitation Free: the first album not the – albeit equally seminal – second, self-titled one. Here endeth my pledge.

---

* Sadly, I have subsequently taken medical advice about my dodgy knees, and been advised that it's a Very Bad Idea Indeed to try to continue running long-distances. My knees simply aren't up to it. So I'm going to do thirty-mile sponsored walks instead.
† Walk.
** Thirty-mile sponsored walks.
†† Walk.
*** Walk. Sorry for all the footnotey digressions in the Pledge here. I thought it best to be honest about it.

Conclusion

So, phew, am I a Better Person now then or what?

I think so. I *hope* so.

I used to be uptight about time and money and money and time and my priorities thereabouts. And I mean, although I think I've always been a *nice* person, I realize now that giving up one's time and energy to help other people can give you something extra: a new vista upon one's place in the scheme of things. A little objectified wisdom – cosmological breathing space, maybe. I am definitely more at ease with myself. It's hard to explain; harder still to measure. But this has all freed up my greater sense of social responsibility, which previously I'd been somewhat studiously avoiding. Not on purpose particularly, but that's the way modern life tends to set you up: in your own little bubble. And you can close yourself off against what in actual fact can be very small, very subtle and extremely enjoyable gestures. A little bit of time can go quite a long way. As far as you're prepared to let it take you.

Also the realization that, for example, bussing a bunch of old people you don't know around some village in the middle of nowhere can be an almost inspirationally enriching experience. It sounds stupid, I'm sure, but I have learned – and am still learning – that giving really is receiving. That Wilfred Grenfell quote: 'Real joy comes not from ease or riches or from the praise of men, but from doing something worthwhile' is actually true! And I feel like I've opened this great big scary door to quasi-enlightenment ever so slightly, and that doing this stuff I've been doing over these last few years is actually just the start. I've got to carry on, else it'll all be rendered meaningless. Or rather *I* will be rendered meaningless. I mean why stop? Volunteering is really no big deal, no terrible sacrifice. *It's easy.* You soon forget that big, looming no-money thing; that's mostly irrelevant; in fact it feels fantastic to get beyond it – like breaking through clouds into blue sky. Volunteering puts you somewhere new – in a different place; it offers fresh perspectives. And this can only ever be a good thing; a *necessary* thing. It has been for me, at least, and I hope that it will continue to be so. (For example, I plan to remain an SWVG visitor for many years to come; indeed I've recently been 'promoted' to their Money Allocation Group and become another visitor's back-up.)

We can all spare a little time. Our lives aren't that busy; we just like to create the illusion that they are, because the flipside – perceived boredom – is so unacceptable these days. We prefer to drown ourselves out. People are afraid of their inner silence. Of detecting the hole in their soul.* And then having the courage to address it. We all know we have one; or at least most people do. So the question arises: am I going to attempt vaguely to address this hole, or am I going to ignore it for ever? Can the white noise chitter-chatter of my life drown out my intrinsic benevolent humanity? The answer? No!

Another important, perhaps subliminal thing helping my goodwill bubble along has simply been having a baby. Parenthood can be likened to losing a layer of skin: you become (alarmingly) more sensitized to the world around you, resulting in a distinctly more tender-hearted worldview. One becomes radically 'feminized' which, as we all know deep down, means being warmer, more empathetic and benevolent towards other folk. Thus another tip for becoming a better person would certainly be: *have a baby*.† You will be nicer. And you'll have a baby too!** So you will also be much poorer; yet richer where it counts. Be your own hero – it's cheaper than a cinema ticket. Yes, even I have started to feel nauseous now. I apologize.

And as for proving Margaret Thatcher†† wrong, well, by spending two years looking out for somebody other than number one for a change, I have made a small but positive difference to a few people's lives. And that's proof enough for me. There *is* such a thing as society, you just need to get your arse out there and *manifest* it.

---

* Abba B-side.
† Or a sex change.
** Or a nice pair of breasts.
†† And Geoffrey Howe.

The End

Yes, it's the End.

   Although of course it isn't – this is just the beginning.
   Go and do some volunteering, you lazy people.
   Go on! *You*'ll start feel better about *your* selves, I guarantee it.
   Or rather my publisher guarantees it.
   Cue: *The Very Best of Vangelis*.
   Mild coshing.
   To fade.

Exit

The best portion of a good man's life is his little, nameless, unremembered acts of kindness and of love.

William Wordsworth

Thank You

Neil and Ali Taylor; Small, Pete and Mel; Owen Oakeshott; Sarah Castleton, Toby Mundy, Daniel Scott, Bunmi Oke, Frances Owen and all at Atlantic Books; Morag Lyall; Christian 'The Goatfucker' Misje; Appo, Marie and Joy; David and Anne Vinnell; Christine Knight; Anna and Ian at WHR; Winchester Litter Pickers; the Winchester Volunteer Centre; sad Rush fans Turf and Snaggers (Paul and Steve); rhinos everywhere; Tania and Julia at Wells for India; the Gadhlulas; Ropley Station staff; Park Ranger Zed; Steve Webster rock vocalist; Brian and Christine Hayward; all staff at Oxfam in Kensington; Fran at Age Concern in Acton; all marine mammals; the Bahs; the astronaut Buzz Aldrin; Johnny Evans and family (for Appo's bike); THE VOICE OF BRIAN BLESSED; Matt Kemp and the Nimomashtic dudes; John Cooper for the music; Joan and Helen at the ▇▇▇ Police Authority; my fellow ICVs; everyone at Appleby House; the late and legendary Ron Purse; Bob and Rosemary Nimmo; Pauly Fop Twat Erdpresser; Lord Rodders of Troubridgeshire; the Raggs; the Dunns; J and D; JD; beer; wine; meths; Knut Ellingsen.

Also thanks to: Glenn Collins.

Extra special thanks to: Faye and Reuben: gah!

Organizational Contact Details

Oxfam
Oxfam Supporter Relations, Oxfam House, John Smith
Drive, Cowley, Oxford OX4 2JY
0870 333 2444

Age Concern
Astral House, 1268 London Road, London SW16 4ER
0800 00 99 66

Winchester Litter Pickers
4 Bereweeke Close, Winchester SO22 6AR
01962 620 300

Marwell Zoological Park
Colden Common, Winchester SO21 1JH
01962 777407

Winchester Hospital Radio
Royal Hampshire County Hospital (Mailpoint 66), Romsey
Road, Winchester SO22 5DG
01962 824343

The Mid Hants Railway
The Railway Station, Alresford, Hampshire SO24 9JG
01962 733810

The Southampton and Winchester Visitors Group
PO Box 1615, Southampton SO17 3WF
05601 791621

Independent Custody Visiting Association
PO Box 1053, Colne BB9 4BL

Wells for India
The Winchester Volunteer Centre, 68 St George's Street,
Winchester SO23 8AH
01962 848043

Walk Your Talk
Matt Kemp
01273 261100

Last Exit

We have met the enemy, and he is us.
                                    Walt Kelly